MAKING AN IMPACT ON POLICING AND CRIME

Making an Impact on Policing and Crime: Psychological Research, Policy and Practice applies a range of case studies and examples of psychological research by international, leading researchers to tackle real-world issues within the field of crime and policing.

Making an Impact on Policing and Crime documents the application of cutting-edge research to real-world policing and explains how psychologists' insights have been adapted and developed to offer effective solutions across the criminal justice system. The experts featured in this collection cover a range of psychological topics surrounding the field, including the prevention and reduction of sexual offending and reoffending, the use of CCTV and 'super-recognisers', forensic questioning of vulnerable witnesses, the accuracy of nonverbal and verbal lie detection interview techniques, psychological 'drivers' of political violence, theoretical models of police–community relations, and the social and political significance of urban 'riots'.

This collection is a vital resource for practitioners in policing fields and the court system and professionals working with offenders, as well as students and researchers in related disciplines.

Clifford Stott is currently a Professor of Social Psychology at Keele University and founder and Director of the Keele Policing Academic Collaboration (KPAC). His interdisciplinary research expertise focuses on issues of social identity, procedural justice, human rights and group level dynamics as these relate to crowds, riots, hooliganism and policing.

Ben Bradford is Professor of Global City Policing at University College London (UCL). He is also Director of the Institute for Global City Policing, which is funded by UCL, the Metropolitan Police Service and the Mayor's Office for Policing and Crime to conduct policing research in London. His research focuses on police–community relations, with a particular emphasis on procedural justice theory and questions of trust, legitimacy, cooperation and compliance.

Matthew Radburn is currently a Post-Doctoral Research Fellow at Keele University working on a range of policing-related projects as part of the academic team within the Keele Policing Academic Collaboration (KPAC). This includes the ESRC funded project 'From coercion to consent: social identity, legitimacy, and a process model of police procedural justice (CONSIL)'.

Leanne Savigar-Shaw is a Lecturer in Policing at Staffordshire University. She is currently involved in ethnographic research concerning police–public interaction, procedural justice and fairness within policing. Her research interests also include road safety, driver education and, in particular, mobile phone use by drivers.

"This is a really important and impressive collection of the best of recent psychological research applied to crime and policing. The benchmark of using the Research Evaluation Framework has focused the book on high quality research with demonstrated impact which makes this collection both relevant and compelling for both students and practitioners."

—*Dr Peter Neyroud, former Chief Constable of Thames Valley Police, CEO of the National Policing Improvement Agency, University of Cambridge, UK*

"Across the world, police and criminal justice systems are wrestling with demanding issues of sexual offending, facial recognition, terrorism, rehabilitation, peaceful order maintenance, securing the truth and legitimacy. For those inside or outside those systems who want to make a difference, this collection of ideas and research, supported by promising or more convincing evidence of real impact, is a great starting point."

—*Sir Denis O'Connor, HM Chief Inspector of Constabulary 2009–12, Institute of Criminology Cambridge, UK*

Routledge Psychological Impacts
Series Editor: Graham Davey

Routledge Psychological Impacts is a series of books illustrating how psychological research can make meaningful contributions to social policy. Each book in the series covers a specific topic, showcasing a range of research projects that have either made a direct impact on policy, or brought about a wider awareness of the issues.

Chapters in the books describe the context of specific research projects, discuss the methodological and practical challenges faced by the researchers, and describe how the results are interpreted and communicated before outlining the impact and legacy of the research. Within each chapter, contributors discuss what lessons they learnt in the process, as well as offering advice to the research community about engaging with policy issues.

With the understanding of human behaviour as one of the main purposes of psychological science, psychological research has a great deal to contribute when it comes to finding solutions for our important social problems. This series aims to describe how psychologists are making a difference.

Making an Impact on School Bullying
Interventions and Recommendations
Edited by Peter K. Smith

Making an Impact on Mental Health and Illness
The Applications of Psychological Research
Edited by James N. Kirby and Paul Gilbert

Making an Impact on Policing and Crime
Psychological Research, Policy and Practice
Edited by Clifford Stott, Ben Bradford, Matthew Radburn and Leanne Savigar-Shaw

For more information about this series, please visit: www.routledge.com/Routledge-Pschological-Impacts/book-series/IMPACTS

MAKING AN IMPACT ON POLICING AND CRIME

Psychological Research, Policy and Practice

Edited by Clifford Stott, Ben Bradford, Matthew Radburn and Leanne Savigar-Shaw

Routledge
Taylor & Francis Group
LONDON AND NEW YORK

First published 2021
by Routledge
2 Park Square, Milton Park, Abingdon, Oxon OX14 4RN

and by Routledge
52 Vanderbilt Avenue, New York, NY 10017

Routledge is an imprint of the Taylor & Francis Group, an informa business

British Library Cataloguing-in-Publication Data
A catalogue record for this book is available from the British Library

Library of Congress Cataloging-in-Publication Data
Names: Stott, Clifford John T., editor. | Bradford, Ben, editor. | Radburn, Matthew, 1990- editor. | Savigar-Shaw, Leanne, editor.
Title: Making an impact on policing and crime: pyschological research, policy, and practice/edited by Clifford Stott, Ben Bradford, Matthew Radburn and Leanne Savigar-Shaw.
Description: Abingdon, Oxon; New York, NY: Routledge, 2021. | Includes bibliographical references and index. |
Identifiers: LCCN 2020020064 (print) | LCCN 2020020065 (ebook) | ISBN 9780815353560 (hbk) | ISBN 9780815353577 (pbk) | ISBN 9780429326592 (ebk)
Subjects: LCSH: Criminology. | Police. | Police-community relations. | Crime prevention. | Criminal justice, Administration of.
Classification: LCC HV6025 .M3135 2021 (print) | LCC HV6025 (ebook) | DDC 363.2/3019–dc23
LC record available at https://lccn.loc.gov/2020020064
LC ebook record available at https://lccn.loc.gov/2020020065

ISBN: 978-0-8153-5356-0 (hbk)
ISBN: 978-0-8153-5357-7 (pbk)
ISBN: 978-0-429-32659-2 (ebk)

Typeset in Bembo
by Deanta Global Publishing Services, Chennai, India

CONTENTS

ILLUSTRATIONS

Table

Boxes

CONTRIBUTORS

Samantha J. Andrews is an Assistant Professor in Developmental Psychology at Keele University and Associate Editor of Applied Cognitive Psychology. She conducts research into the reliability of children's testimony and forensic interviewing best practices. She regularly serves as an Expert Witness in criminal proceedings, providing evidence on the quality of investigative interviews.

Nicholas Blagden is an Associate Professor in Forensic Psychology and Chartered Psychologist. He is Head of the Sexual Offences Crime and Misconduct Research Unit at Nottingham Trent University. He has worked and researched within the Criminal Justice System and HM Prison Service for nearly 15 years. He started his career as a paralegal before moving to Nottinghamshire probation service. He has trained police officers and worked in prison settings.

Ben Bradford is Professor of Global City Policing at University College London (UCL). He is also Director of the Institute for Global City Policing, which is funded by UCL, the Metropolitan Police Service and the Mayor's Office for Policing and Crime to conduct policing research in London. His research focuses on police–community relations, with a particular emphasis on procedural justice theory and questions of trust, legitimacy, cooperation and compliance.

Josh P. Davis is a Consultant Psychologist and a Reader in Applied Psychology at the University of Greenwich. His research focuses on super-recognisers, eyewitness identification, facial composite systems (e.g., EFIT6), facial comparison evidence and jury decision-making. He relaxes by writing and playing music in his band: 'JD and the Longfellows'.

Neil Ferguson is Professor of Political Psychology at Liverpool Hope University and recently served as a Visiting Research Fellow to the Changing Character of War Programme at Pembroke College, Oxford. His research has focused on political conflict and its psychological implications since he studied towards his PhD at the University of Ulster.

Ronald Fisher is currently a Professor of Psychology at Florida International University. Ron co-developed the Cognitive Interview technique (with Ed Geiselman) to enhance witness recall, and has conducted training programmes for several investigative agencies, including the FBI, US and UK police, and other organisations (e.g., NASA).

Megan Hermolle is a second-year PhD student at Keele University. She is currently conducting quantitative and qualitative research into the extent and impact of rape myths in the United Kingdom, beginning with the general population and continuing with police ABE interviews with rape complainants.

Ching-Yu S. Huang is a Lecturer (Assistant Professor) in Developmental Psychology at Keele University. Her research examines the effects of sociocultural factors, such as immigration, on children's access to justice. She serves on several advisory panels for governmental and non-governmental organisations internationally to improve policy regarding investigative interviews.

Sarah J. Krähenbühl is course leader for Forensic Psychology at Staffordshire University. She conducts both quantitative and qualitative research into the facilitation of children's engagement in legal processes through improving investigative practices. Until recently Sarah has worked as an Expert Witness, evaluating the quality of investigative interviews with children in criminal proceedings.

Rosie Meek is a Professor of Psychology in the Department of Law and Criminology at Royal Holloway University of London. Her research explores prisoner healthcare, education and rehabilitation, with a particular focus on voluntary and community organisations, and the role of physical activity and sport in our prisons.

Matthew Radburn is currently a Post-Doctoral Research Fellow at Keele University working on a range of policing-related projects as part of the academic team within the Keele Policing Academic Collaboration (KPAC). This includes the ESRC funded project 'From coercion to consent: social identity, legitimacy, and a process model of police procedural justice (CONSIL)'.

Leanne Savigar-Shaw is a Lecturer in Policing at Staffordshire University. She is currently involved in ethnographic research concerning police–public interaction, procedural justice and fairness within policing. Her research interests also include road safety, driver education and, in particular, mobile phone use by drivers.

Clifford Stott is currently a Professor of Social Psychology at Keele University and founder and Director of the Keele Policing Academic Collaboration (KPAC). His interdisciplinary research expertise focuses on issues of social identity, procedural justice, human rights and group level dynamics as these relate to crowds, riots, hooliganism and policing.

Aldert Vrij is a Professor of Applied Social Psychology at the University of Portsmouth. His research expertise is verbal and nonverbal deception and lie detection. He has more than 500 publications. In 2016 he received the International Investigative Interviewing Research Group (iiiRG) Lifetime Achievement Award in recognition of his significant contribution to investigative interviewing.

Belinda Winder is a Professor in Forensic Psychology. She is Research Director of the Centre for Crime, Offending, Prevention & Engagement (COPE) at Nottingham Trent University, and part of the Sexual Offences, Crime and Misconduct Research Unit (SOCAMRU). The main focus of her work is applied research in the area of sexual offending and sexual crime, but she also has a deep interest in working with people with lived experience, desistance research and research that contributes to facilitating those with convictions to lead a purposeful life post conviction.

SERIES FOREWORD

Routledge Psychological Impacts is a series of books illustrating how psychological research can make meaningful contributions to social policy. Each book in the series covers a specific topic, showcasing a range of research projects that have either made a direct impact on policy or brought about a wider awareness of the issues.

Chapters in the books describe the context of specific research projects, discuss the methodological and practical challenges faced by researchers and describe how the results are interpreted and communicated before outlining the impact and legacy of the research. Within each chapter, contributors discuss what lessons they learnt in the process, as well as offering advice to the research community about engaging with policy issues.

In this volume on the impact of psychological research on policing and crime, editors Clifford Stott, Ben Bradford, Matthew Radburn and Leanne Savigar-Shaw have drawn together an exciting and timely spread of contributions on topics such as prevention, detection, investigation, prosecution and imprisonment, and covering controversial issues such as terrorism, child abuse, sexual offending and mass facial recognition.

Each contributor describes first-hand accounts of how their cutting-edge psychological research has impacted on the real-world of crime and policing and helped to develop the policies and practices of professionals in these areas. These chapters discuss in detail how distinct disciplinary areas within psychology have achieved these impacts – regularly as a result of interdisciplinary collaborations between psychologists and researchers from other disciplines such as criminology and penology. In many cases, these impacts were only achieved as a result of the career-long journeys required to foster collaborative relationships and successfully translate psychological knowledge into evidence-based practice and policy.

Graham Davey

PREFACE

Over the last decade the term 'impact' has firmly embedded itself as a term of reference within the lexicon of academic research. Arguably the key catalyst for its emergence as a strategic research concept was the inclusion of 'Impact Case Studies' (ICS) in the UK's Research Evaluation Framework in 2014, constituting 20% of each unit's overall score. As a direct consequence, every Higher Education Institution (HEI) in the UK that planned to enter the REF had to develop a series of ICSs outlining how the research work they had produced provided some measurable benefit to communities and organisations outside of academia. This was a sea-change for the research agenda in HEIs, who now needed to give serious focus to and actively promote the external relevance of their research or risk suffering catastrophic declines in their measurable research performance and therefore capacity to obtain government funding for research.

At its most benign, the so-called 'impact agenda' was an attempt to empower what academic research should ultimately always be about: addressing itself to issues in the world that matter. Nonetheless it is impossible to ignore the fact that the advent of 'impact' is a culmination of a process of measuring academic performance in the UK that first appeared under the government of Margaret Thatcher in the 1980s. Arguably, the motivation behind the introduction of this process of research evaluation was to justify the massive expenditure that the UK government contributes to universities by way of the 'block grant'. From Government perspectives it became necessary to develop ways of measuring the positive impacts this investment was having in order to defend it in a context of public funding cuts. Over various iterations this process evolved into the Research Assessment Exercise in 2008 (RAE, 2008) that began to use 'Measures of Esteem' as a vehicle to acknowledge the status of academic research among communities outside the 'ivory towers' of academia. The metric of performance initially related almost entirely to academic publications and research environments, but as part of the next step in the growing dominance of the assessment exercise – the Research Evaluation Framework – the language of 'impact' was given structural form.

There can be little doubt that universities across the UK adapted to and performed very well within the new 'impact agenda' in the 2014 assessment. Indeed, some reflected on an almost 'ceiling effect' with institutions across the sector scoring at the top end of the performance distribution. So much so that for the following REF, in 2021, planned Impact Case Studies took on even greater significance. First, they constitute 25% of the REF return for every submitting Unit of Assessment. Second, the number of Impact Case Studies relates directly to the number of academic staff that can be included and every Unit of Assessment has to deliver at least two ICS in order to return at all. This has had a very powerful effect requiring all universities to take the development of impact very seriously and to resource it accordingly. As a consequence, those academics whose work is impactful – at least in the ways envisaged in the REF – and/or who aspire for it to be so, have begun to find a more sympathetic context within which to develop and operate.

Nonetheless, the agenda has its downsides. For many, there still remains a fundamental tension between doing research that is highly relevant to, and suited for publication in, academic journals and at the same time working to overcome the theory–practice divide. There remains an objective tension between these goals in some disciplines and fields. As with any way of evaluating, the criteria of measurement can also become all-defining. Rather than acting as some neutral means through which we understand the positive contribution academic research makes to society, there is a danger that impact case studies become an end in and of themselves. This can feed into a strategic research agenda where specific areas of impact become the focus and others, perceived to be 'less valuable', experience neglect for no other reason than they are not being taken forward as formal Impact Case Studies for a REF return. There also remains the thorny issue of the tension between intellectual capital and property. Even in the current context impact can often be reliant on ambitious and motivated individual academic staff going 'above and beyond' what is required in their university employment contracts. Yet, any impact they achieve remains firmly rooted into their host institution and is not transferrable with them should they move on to another institution, unlike their academic publications, which can be counted twice.

Bearing these positive and negative issues in mind we nevertheless felt that the new Routledge series on 'psychological impacts' was an ideal opportunity to draw together in a single volume a series of examples of world-class researchers who have made impacts with their work in the fields of crime and policing. The criminal justice system is a particularly salient arena for this endeavour. Over the past decade or so policing, in particular, has opened up significantly in terms of a willingness to collaborate with and take on board the work of academics, both in the UK and internationally. It is no coincidence that of the eight chapters presented in this book, six concern policing (broadly defined). Police organisations have provided fertile ground for the impact agenda described earlier. Yet, as some of those chapters reveal, this is a partial and ongoing process. Barriers to impact remain, perhaps particularly at the level of full integration, into day-to-day practice, of ideas developed in the academy. Such words of caution provide a useful counterpoint to the boosterism often found in university accounts of research impact.

Our primary approach to selecting what to include this book was to explore all the ICSs returned for the 2014 REF and identify those with a policing and crime focus. We then approached these authors and invited them to provide a chapter on their work and how it had, and was continuing to have, impacts. Notably, almost everyone we contacted agreed to contribute a chapter. As a result, we have drawn together a broad array of contributions focused on prevention, detection, investigation, prosecution and imprisonment. The chapters focus on some highly controversial topics such as terrorism, child abuse, sexual offending and mass facial recognition.

The chapters draw out the wide range of ways in which distinct disciplinary areas of psychology are achieving real world impact. Indeed, some of the contributions are from academics who sit more firmly within Criminology or Penology, reflecting the way psychological theory and psychologists focused on impact are working across often artificial disciplinary boundaries. But whatever the topic and perspective, several of the chapters have taken somewhat of an autobiographical and first-person turn. Indeed, it was often impossible to write about the journey to impact without reflecting on the career-long journeys that are often required to navigate the complex, often personal relationships, that underpin translating psychological knowledge into practice in policy areas that are often very political and politicised.

In Chapter 1, Belinda Winder and Nicholas Blagden describe the work of the Sexual Offences, Crime and Misconduct Research Unit (SOCAMRU) that is jointly led by the two authors. They present a series of research programmes concerning the prevention and reduction of sexual offending and reoffending, describing various challenges encountered throughout the research process and how they were overcome. The authors highlight the impact their research has had upon the evidence base surrounding anti-libidinal medication, UK policy concerning core sex offender treatment programmes and the use of treatment programmes within the UK and beyond.

In Chapter 2, Josh P. Davis draws on over ten years of research and practical application relating to CCTV and 'super-recognisers' (i.e., people who possess exceptional facial recognition skills) within policing, security and other business contexts. Dr Davis charts the innovations of London's Metropolitan Police Service (MPS). Underpinned by his research, and in the wake of the 2011 riots, the MPS established the world's first full-time 'Super-Recogniser' Unit at New Scotland Yard which led to international police, media and museum interest, as well as inspiring authors of fiction. Dr Davis explores the potential research economic and cultural impacts of this body of psychological research, enterprise and consultancy work as well as its international reach.

Chapter 3 focuses upon forensic questioning, with Ching-Yu Huang and colleagues presenting a number of research-informed guidelines considered best practice within the field of forensic questioning of vulnerable witnesses, such as children who have suffered abuse. Despite the guidance of such principles, the authors point out various challenges that are faced in ensuring research evidence informs best-practice guidelines and policy. They highlight a general issue of translation, as some research findings are not systematically being incorporated into best-practice guidance, before focusing upon more specific challenges pertaining to forensic questioning. The chapter ends with a discussion of the lessons learnt, ongoing obstacles and what is still to be achieved to enhance best practice within the area. The authors conclude that an open dialogue between various stakeholders is required to support those engaging with the legal system.

In Chapter 4, Aldert Vrij and Ronald Fisher chart the progress of collaborations between academics and practitioners in relation to improving the accuracy of nonverbal and verbal lie detection interview techniques. They demonstrate that theory-informed interview protocols obtain an accuracy rate of 70–75% in terms of being able to classify 'truth-tellers' from liars. They then discuss the important challenges that they have encountered in attempting to transfer this research knowledge into practice, including developing an evidence and theory-based lie detection training package.

In Chapter 5, Neil Ferguson documents his research which has focused on studying psychological 'drivers' of political violence. In particular, his work has focused on the 'arc of terrorism' and why people initially engage in 'terrorist activity', sustain and develop their involvement in paramilitary groups and how and why people disengage from paramilitary organisations and consequently how they psychologically 'transition' into 'mainstream' community life. Prof Ferguson then summarises some of the key weaknesses in the terrorism studies literature before going on to explain some of the important ethical and moral dilemmas involved in researching political violence. The benefits and opportunities of stakeholder engagements, including opportunities to shape policyholder and governmental thinking on the aetiology of politically motivated violence are then discussed. Chapter 5 ends with an exploration of how there can be better collaboration between academics and practitioners, whilst also describing some cautionary tales for the potential issues that new researchers in this domain may face.

In Chapter 6 we return to the context of prisons where Rosie Meek considers the rehabilitative potential of sport and physical activity. Drawing on her own experience of working on behalf of the Ministry of Justice (MoJ) in the United Kingdom, she shows how her highly influential and groundbreaking work has shaped government policy and practice. In particular, Chapter 6 details the 12 key recommendations derived from Prof Meek's review submitted to the MoJ titled '"A Sporting Chance": An independent review of sport and physical activity in youth and adult prisons'. Prof Meek then goes on to focus specifically on four different research-based recommendations: 1) the need for a physical activity strategy for women and girls, 2) the staffing and resource of physical activity in prisons, 3) using sport to resolve conflict and, far more controversially, 4) the use of martial arts and boxing-related programmes in custodial settings. Chapter 6 concludes with a reflection on the policy and practice developments that have occurred since the publication of her review.

In Chapter 7, Ben Bradford, a criminologist based at UCL, explores the impact of Procedural Justice Theory (PJT) which is a model of police–community relations that is grounded in concepts of fairness. He explains that, according to PJT, policing that is open, honest, transparent, neutral and unbiased generates public trust, legitimacy, cooperation and compliance, and that the theory presents a normatively and ethically desirable model of policing that is based on consent rather than coercion. Chapter 7 explores the impact that academic work on procedural justice and related issues has had on policing in the UK. Equally, though, it considers some of the barriers to impact, particularly in relation to resistance among police organisations and officers and the difficulties of translating 'good ideas' into practice.

In Chapter 8, Clifford Stott begins by emphasising the social and political significance of urban 'riots'. He then highlights that there is often a disconnect between government responses to 'riots' and the relevant academic crowd research and theory. Thus, a key question in this chapter is: How can we advance the relationship between theory and practice in this important domain of public policy? Chapter 8 aims to answer this question by first providing an overview of the developments of crowd theory in psychology. Following this, Prof Stott then highlights the significant impact of this theory and research in terms of shaping national (UK) and international policies and practices with regards to policing crowds. Chapter 8 concludes with a discussion of the lessons learnt from this journey of applying theory into police practice, specifically relating these challenges to the broader 'impact' agenda within academia in the UK.

Our ambition in drawing these chapters and researchers together was to develop an edited book that would give each author the opportunity to talk first-hand about their world-leading research in ways that can engage psychologists, criminologists and others looking to make their own research more impactful, as well as to describe to professionals in the field of crime and policing how psychology can, and is, making meaningful contributions to the development of policy and practice in this important domain of inquiry.

1

PREVENTING AND REDUCING SEXUAL ABUSE

Belinda Winder and Nicholas Blagden

Dedication

This chapter is dedicated to Ruth Mann, a Chartered Forensic Psychologist, previous Head of Evidence for HMPPS, and a wonderful human being. Ruth is an inspiration to us all – her kindness, intelligence, thoughtfulness and passion humble us, and we are, and will always be, indebted to her. Go well, Ruth.

Introduction

This chapter focuses on the prevention and reduction of sexual offending and reoffending. It details work conducted by the Sexual Offences, Crime and Misconduct Research Unit (SOCAMRU). SOCAMRU was set up by the first author in 2007 and is now jointly led by the two authors. The purpose of SOCAMRU was to build upon the collaborative relationship between ongoing research within the Psychology department at Nottingham Trent University (NTU) and Her Majesty's Prison Whatton (HMP Whatton). Whatton is one of the largest prisons in Europe for prisoners with sexual convictions, housing approximately 840 individuals. HMP Whatton is a specialist institution with a large Programmes and Psychology department which provides almost two thirds of all specialist treatment to people serving custodial sentences for sexual offences in the UK (K. Hocken, personal communication, March 24, 2020). Its ethos is therapeutic, respectful and progressive, with research utilised to drive forward changes and rehabilitative initiatives. The prison houses predominantly adult males, with a small population of transgender prisoners.

SOCAMRU's primary aim is to conduct and facilitate applied forensic research in the area of sexual crime. The unit sits at the juxtaposition between the domain of prison, police and criminal justice practitioners and that of academia. Researchers in the unit, including ourselves, spend lengthy periods of time in prisons housing people with sexual convictions. Working alongside the governors, senior management teams, psychologists, programme facilitators and prison staff, as well as spending considerable amounts of time with the prisoners themselves, allows us to conduct research that is consonant with prisons, prisoners and prison life. As part of our work within the unit, the authors of this chapter have a monthly service user group at Whatton prison where we meet with six to eight prisoners and discuss research ideas with them. We listen to what prisoners and prison staff say is important to them, and we link this with the literature on understanding prevention and reduction of sexual abuse. We also work regularly in several other prisons throughout the UK, including HMP Stafford, HMP Grendon, and HMP Whitemoor (Fens unit). All this is done with the primary aim to conduct research that makes a significant contribution to our understanding of sexual crime and people who commit such offences. In SOCAMRU, we utilise a range of methodologies, including qualitative, mixed methods and quantitative methods; we maintain a strong service user approach and focus in order to ensure the research is authentic, useful, and robust, bringing together theories and practice. Our work stretches more broadly than this, however. We have moral and social objectives, and envision part of SOCAMRU's work as existing to challenge the culture, politics and rationale for excluding ex-prisoners, particularly those with sexual convictions, from reintegrating positively and purposefully back into society.

Perhaps because of this social objective, and as one of the consequences of our strong service user focus, a small group of us co-founded a charity, the Safer Living Foundation (SLF). The Safer Living Foundation (www.saferlivingfoundation.org) was founded 13 February 2014 as a joint venture between HMP Whatton and Nottingham Trent University, and is supported by the likes of the National Probation Service (East Midlands) and Nottinghamshire Police. As a charitable incorporated organisation that adopts a multi-agency approach with a strong research component, the Safer Living Foundation is focused on reducing offending, particularly sexual offending through rehabilitative and preventative initiatives. The charitable objectives of the Safer Living Foundation are:

- To promote the protection of people from, and the prevention of, sexual crime
- To promote the rehabilitation of persons who have committed or who are likely to commit sexual offences against others

SOCAMRU works with the Safer Living Foundation charity to conduct work, and to research and evaluate this work, in order to create and evidence a demonstrable impact in reducing and preventing sexual crime.

Context of the research

There are approximately 13,400 people in UK prisons with sexual convictions, which is around 19% of the overall UK prison population (MoJ, 2018). This is an increase from the early 1990s when 10% of the prison population comprised people with a sexual conviction (MoJ, 2016). The number of people with sexual convictions in society is growing and this increase is not restricted to the prison population. Approximately 55,000 members of the UK general public have previously been convicted of a sexual offence and are now living in the community, albeit under the conditions set out by the Sex Offenders' Register (SOR; i.e. who committed a sexual offence post the UK's Sex Offenders Act, 1997). There is a further unknown number of people living in the community who committed a sexual offence before 1997 and who therefore were not required to be on the Register. In summary, this means that around 1 in 950 people in the UK currently have a sexual conviction.

The number of people charged and convicted with a sexual offence and the number of people serving custodial sentences for a sexual offence is increasing (ONS, 2019). There are several explanations for this. Public attitudes to reporting sexual offending have changed given some high-profile cases over the last five years and the rise of valuable social campaigns and movements such as #metoo. Consequently, people are now more likely to report sexual crimes. The number of possible imprisonable sexual offences has increased (CPS, 2017), prison sentences are longer (ONS, 2019) and the proportion of people prosecuted and serving sentences for non-recent sexual offences has grown (ONS, 2018).

Most individuals who serve a custodial sentence for a sexual offence are released back into the community. Post-release, approximately 90% of these individuals will live out their lives offence-free. Thus, recidivism rates for sexual crimes are around 10% (Mews, Di Bella & Purver, 2017). Each year, prisons housing residents with sexual convictions release individuals into the community. For example, HMP Whatton alone released around 40 men into its local area (Nottinghamshire) last year; other prisons throughout the UK will also be releasing prisoners into each area. Consequently, there are hundreds of individuals with sexual convictions released into each county in the UK each year.

Research has shown that individuals with sexual convictions are most likely to reoffend in the first few years following release, and the likelihood of reoffending reduces the longer the individuals remain offence free in the community (Hanson et al., 2018). Research also suggests that the risk of sexual reoffending is increased when people are socially and emotionally isolated; however, having a sexual offence creates emotional and social isolation. The empirical evidence points to the need to assist individuals with sexual convictions in reintegrating back into society and there is currently a large gap in service provision for this group (Blagden & Winder, 2019; Kitson-Boyce et al., 2018a).

Outline of projects

The research outlined in this chapter focuses on reducing sexual offending and reoffending. Our starting position has invariably been practical issues that have been highlighted by Her Majesty's Prison and Probation Service and/or the current evidence base on what works with individuals who commit sexual offences. We have also listened carefully, and at length, to prisoners in formal and informal research settings including our regular service user group, prison staff, and psychologists and healthcare workers in order to understand what undermines the treatment, management and rehabilitation of people who have committed sexual offences.

We will consider three separate research programmes. All have utilised mixed methods to understand a particular challenge in managing, treating and preventing sexual abuse. Our first research project is focused on ongoing evaluation of medication to manage problematic sexual arousal in individuals convicted of sexual crime. The question was whether the medication was effective in reducing problematic sexual arousal (and there were a number of related questions regarding the attitudes and experiences of prisoners being offered the medication, the interaction of medication with psychological treatment programmes, and the role of medication in reducing risk of sexual harm both in the prison and, importantly, in the community). The second project we outline focuses on individuals who maintain their innocence apropos their sexual convictions ('deniers'); this group were highlighted as a problem within the prison system. The question there was 'what do we do with deniers?' Finally, the chapter sets out research and evaluation of Circles of Support and Accountability (Circles/CoSA), a project delivered by organisations such as the Safer Living Foundation charity and researched and evaluated by the authors. Circles are a post-release intervention for high-risk and very high-risk individuals who have committed a sexual offence. The work outlined comprises research findings from the first prison-based Circles, together with data from the national evaluation of community-based Circles which is led by the two authors.

Project 1: Medication to manage problematic sexual arousal

Problematic sexual arousal has been cited as one of the most important factors for sexual reoffending (Hanson & Morton-Bourgon, 2005). The term 'problematic sexual arousal' (PSA) is represented by a number of different terms including: sexual preoccupation, sexual compulsivity, nymphomania, excessive non-paraphilic behaviours (Garcia & Thibaut, 2010), hypersexuality (Kafka, 2010), sexual addiction and excessive sexual desire disorder (Fong, 2006), obsession with sex and sexual appetite. A common feature among these, and the key elements of problematic sexual arousal, is the presence of intense sexual thoughts and/or the behavioural element in which individuals engage in excessive sexual behaviours. Problematic sexual arousal can also be related to sexual deviance, that is, an attraction to children or non-consenting adults. The presence of problematic sexual arousal is a serious health as well as a criminal justice concern. It is linked to adverse outcomes in relation to the wellbeing of individuals. This includes effects on psychological and emotional wellbeing with multiple psychiatric comorbidities associated with problematic sexual arousal (Khan et al., 2015). Problematic sexual arousal has been found to be the most strongly present treatment need for people who have offended sexually (Hocken, 2014) and is recognised as a crucial risk factor for, and significant predictor of, sexual recidivism (Mann, Hanson & Thornton, 2010). Despite this, it is the only risk factor that is not directly addressed by current UK sexual offending treatment programmes. Whilst the National Offender Management Service's Healthy Sexual Functioning Programme (HSP) does address deviant arousal (arousal to children and other types of non-consenting sex, including non-consensual sex with adults) and promote healthy sexual functioning (HMPPS, 2016), it does not actively help men struggling with sexual preoccupation, a fundamental aspect of problematic sexual arousal. Post-conviction, problematic sexual arousal also impedes treatment progress for those convicted of sexual offences, affecting the ability of individuals to focus on treatment programmes (Winder et al., 2018), with problematic sexual arousal a key factor for treatment ineffectiveness (Grubin, 2018).

Research conducted by SOCAMRU has evaluated the effectiveness and role of anti-libidinal medication in reducing problematic sexual arousal and demonstrated the positive impact of prescribing anti-libidinal medication on the management, treatment and wellbeing of people convicted of sexual offences (Winder, Lievesley & Elliot, 2014; Winder et al., 2015; Winder, 2016; Winder et al., 2018; Winder, 2019b). These findings have been influential nationally and internationally, driving forward prevention work in the community as medication could become an important treatment option for some people *before* they commit a first offence.

While inability to manage problematic sexual arousal is a primary risk factor for sexual reoffending, its route of action and underpinnings are not clearly understood. Problematic sexual arousal can be classified in three ways: (i) as a clinically diagnosed paraphilia, (ii) as excessive thinking about sex (sexual preoccupation or hypersexual cognition) and (iii) as excessive impersonal sexual behaviours, or hypersexual behaviour (see Winder et al., 2019). In each of these instances, psychological treatment programmes have struggled to 'treat' problematic sexual arousal. Indeed, the majority of psychological treatment programmes do not aim to treat problematic sexual arousal, with the only exception being the Healthy Sexual Functioning programme (Winder et al., 2018). Yet, the challenge remains that problematic sexual arousal in one of these above forms is recognised in research as a crucial risk factor for and significant predictor of sexual recidivism (Hanson & Morton-Bourgon, 2004; Hanson et al., 2007; Beech, Fisher & Ward, 2005; Hanson & Harris, 2000; Mann, Hanson & Thornton, 2010). Although the potential of pharmacological treatment for problematic sexual arousal had previously been recognised as a potentially valuable addition to current psychological interventions for individuals with sexual convictions in the UK (Guay, 2009; Home Office,

2007; Turner, Basdekis-Jozsa, & Briken, 2012), prior to the SOCAMRU research, this claim had yet to be evaluated empirically. Additionally, according to our research, individuals with problematic sexual arousal reported difficulties responding to current psychological programmes designed to address other dynamic risk needs relating to their offending because they were unable to distract themselves from sexual preoccupation and compulsive sexual behaviour (Lievesley et al., 2014; Winder et al., 2015). As a result, pharmacological treatment, in the form of anti-libidinal medication was recognised by the research team to have the potential both to reduce the key dynamic risk factor for sexual reoffending and also reduce sexual preoccupation and compulsive sexual behaviour to such an extent that psychological interventions could be more effective.

Context

In 2007, Her Majesty's Prison and Probation Service (HMPPS) facilitated a pilot trial at Whatton prison to offer medication to manage problematic sexual arousal for people convicted of sexual offences. Three types of medication were offered to individuals with problematic sexual arousal housed at HMP Whatton: Anti-androgens (AAs; Cyproterone Acetate; CPA), gonadotropin-releasing hormone agonists (GnRH; Triptorelin) and Selective Serotonin Reuptake Inhibitors (SSRIs; fluoxetine/paroxetine). Winder and colleagues were initially asked to conduct an evaluation of the medication, which, at the time, had been used sporadically by a handful of psychiatrists working within UK prisons.

Challenges

This research programme was subject to numerous challenges from the outset. These included acquiring funding to conduct the research, gaining ethical approval from various stakeholders, working with various partners to conduct and disseminate the research, navigating the political climate that exists within the criminal justice system, coping with the government and media interest in this area, and remaining aware of the vulnerability of the participants and the sensitivity of the subject matter. The following section outlines some of these challenges and how we dealt with them.

The request for the research and the evaluation came from the governing Governor of HMP Whatton, where the medication to manage problematic sexual arousal was being piloted. Whatton prison (and its

Governor, Lynn Saunders OBE) has a reputation for being progressive, humane, evidence-based and seeking practical outputs from research. One of the initial barriers to the evaluation was funding. Since the idea for the pilot had come from the Governor and consultant psychiatrist there, there was little or no funding to underpin the evaluation. Nevertheless, it was important to the Governor, psychiatrist and lead psychologist there that this programme to offer medication to prisoners should go ahead. We agreed, and the evaluation was initially funded through a mutual agreement between Whatton prison and Nottingham Trent University which determined that the research would be funded via costs in kind. After 12 months, some additional funding was received from Nottinghamshire Offender Healthcare, and then via the Offender Personality Disorder pathway (as at Autumn 2019).

Training, experience and awareness of the working prison environment are crucial to successfully conducting research in prisons. Where the project also overlaps with the healthcare department in a prison, and where there are three stakeholders involved (university, prison and the health service), matters become even more complex. Practical challenges included working out the process through which we could conduct the evaluation, appropriate information sharing and data management protocols, and the storage and maintenance of a non-anonymised database. The research team were concerned about ensuring there was informed consent from participants (with a vulnerable population), and this became even more pronounced when the preliminary data highlighted that almost 40% of the referrals for medication were borderline or mildly intellectually disabled. This meant a continuing review of the documentation used, and of the process for administration of the scales. The research team also needed to reassess the reliability of the scales for mildly and intellectually disabled participants and consider how to improve the process for conducting the assessments (e.g. we printed colourful, pictorial response sheets for all the measures to aid participants' understanding of response options).

We also conducted research on the views and experiences of probation staff and therapists (see Elliott et al., 2018) and subsequently wrote a report for the Independent Monitoring Board (for individuals sitting on the Parole Boards) as we became aware that the Parole Boards were sometimes 'seeing' prisoners on anti-libidinal medication as being more risky than other prisoners, since they needed 'drugs' to control themselves. We also needed to ensure that prisoners were not scared off from taking the medication and that prisoners did not feel under pressure to participate in the university-led evaluation. The research team considered carefully how recruitment of the participants to the research was handled. Prisoners could either be referred by staff members (with the individual's consent), or they could self-refer to the service. Once a referral was made, a member of the service (either the consultant psychiatrist or associated psychologist) would meet with the prisoner to assess their suitability for anti-libidinal medication. Within this meeting, the clinician would inform the prisoner about the research and what it entailed, emphasising the voluntary nature of the research, and how taking part (or choosing not to) would not impact their access to medication. The clinician would provide the prisoner with a consent form for the use of medication, whereby there is a tick box that individuals could tick if they are happy to participate in the research. If a prisoner consented to being contacted for the purposes of research, the clinician would contact the research team and pass on the details of the prisoner. A member of the research team would then arrange a separate appointment with the potential participant. At this meeting, they would explain the research in greater depth (verbally and written via information sheet and consent form), further emphasising the voluntary nature of the research, and how participating (or not) would not impact on their access to anti-libidinal medication.

Despite the aforementioned consent collected from the clinician, the participant could choose at this point not to participate in the research. Equally, if the prisoner chose to participate in the research, individual consent was gathered for each study and each time the participant completed psychometrics. Three sets of ethical approvals were required (university, prison and probation service, and NHS), with each stakeholder having a different focus when assessing the research project. There was less understanding of each other's processes and systems than one might envisage; consequently, ironing out difficulties and misunderstandings took time and patience. Given the dynamic nature of ethical reflections, there have been – to date – over 15 amendments to the original ethics applications, in order to ensure that the research integrity and the experience of participants were underpinned by ethical best practice. Conducting research in prisons is a time and labour-intensive role that requires ongoing thought and a dynamic ethical process, with a willingness to adjust protocols as findings (such as further information about the characteristics of the participant sample) dictate. It is of course also important to protect the integrity of the data and research design. This is an ongoing and careful balancing act.

Maintaining communication between the two departments we were working between (healthcare, where the medication was administered and Programmes/Psychology, who 'owned' the treatment programmes that are delivered at HMP Whatton) was important. Misunderstandings of who was responsible for what, and who owned the medication project, were also an issue. This division between healthcare and Psychology was echoed in larger forums with discussions between the NHS and HMPPS. There was disagreement as to whether problematic sexual arousal was a healthcare (wellbeing) issue or a forensic one (reducing sexual reoffending). As the use of medication expanded to other prisons, the evaluation has found additional challenges, with each NHS region requiring regional permissions (so many more ethical submissions to complete on research that was underway) and in accessing data from the other prison sites spread throughout the UK. Additional challenges arose where, in one instance, a Government Minister had apparently expressed an opinion that if this medication worked so well then it should be mandatory for all individuals who committed sexual offences. The research team were called upon to submit a written report (via HMPPS) detailing reasons as to why this would not be appropriate (B. Winder, personal communication, 2018). This report, and the reasons contained therein, were incorporated into the Ministerial Briefing submitted to the then Minister of Justice, David Gauke MP. The report outlined a range of issues. Three examples are: first, since the majority of people with sexual convictions have lower levels of sexual compulsivity than would benefit from the medication, giving everyone medication would not help (approximately 5–8% of people convicted of sexual offences have a sufficiently high level of sexual preoccupation to benefit clinically from the medication). Second, giving people medication would potentially be seen as a 'cure', and other important treatment and rehabilitative approaches would be neglected. Third, medication in the UK is always voluntary unless there are exceptional circumstances as set out in the Mental Capacity Act 2005 or the Mental Health Act 1983, such as being sectioned; if the medication was made mandatory, this would require a significant change in the law and in medical practice, the ramifications of which could be widespread.

The research programme

Having navigated these complexities, Winder and colleagues decided upon a mixed-method longitudinal evaluation, which included studies to evaluate the effectiveness of the use of pharmacological treatment to reduce problematic sexual arousal. All participants were recruited voluntarily, with an emphasis on ensuring that participants understood this was the case for each and every part of the research, evaluation and clinical service. The research programme also included a series of qualitative studies to better understand the experiences, thoughts and understanding of the treatment of individuals with sexual convictions with anti-libidinal medication. Qualitative research included studies with: (i) psychological treatment programme facilitators (ii) probation staff who managed and supervised people with sexual convictions in the community and (iii) interviews with prisoners who had been prescribed the medication. Quantitative studies included research examining putative differences in clinical and psychometric measures pre and post medication. Additionally, studies investigated the characteristics of those referred for medication (approximately 10% of the prison population), studies of those who were referred but not suitable for medication, and research exploring the underpinnings of problematic sexual arousal as a phenomenon in itself.

Research findings, impact and legacy

The quantitative research (Winder, Lievesley & Elliot, 2014; Winder et al., 2018) demonstrated that both SSRIs and anti-androgens significantly reduce problematic sexual arousal in people with sexual convictions. Even after three months, prisoners taking either type of medication showed statistically and clinically significant reductions in comparison to an unmatched control group. The control group comprised prisoners in the same prison who were not taking medication, but who had consented to participate in the research. They were recruited on arrival to HMP Whatton (the latter is not typically the first prison for people post-sentencing, so the control participants were not 'new' prisoners), and completed the baseline psychometrics as part of a screening battery (see Winder et al., submitted, for more information). The research examining the effectiveness of SSRIs is particularly important since these medications are currently 'off label' (that is, not licensed for use in the community as an anti-libidinal medication). Thus, prior to our research there was little evidence to show effectiveness as an anti-libidinal, despite reduction in libido being one of the stated side effects of taking SSRIs. Indeed, the NICE 2015 Guidelines cite Winder, Lievesley and Elliot (2014) as one of just three studies providing evidence for the potential effectiveness of SSRIs to treat hypersexuality.

In turn, the research and evaluation findings (communicated through reports to the Prison and Probation Service, HMS Whatton and NHS England) provided the evidence for the creation of a new treatment pathway for people convicted of sexual offences. The research and evaluation provided an evidence-informed basis for the use of anti-libidinal medication, together with evidence for the need for this treatment focus. Thus, after presentation of the findings and wider dissemination amongst the forensic and forensic healthcare paths, it was agreed that the medication offered a valuable adjunct to the psychological treatment already offered. Therefore, the medication programme (and accompanying research and evaluation) were rolled out nationally two years ago, and medication is now available in eight prisons housing people with sexual convictions in the UK. The research programme is shortly to be broadened out into the community so that the research team (together with the head of research of the Offender Personality Disorder pathway, HMPPS) are following up how people are managing on the medication once in the community. The research will be looking at whether ex-prisoners are still taking the medication or not and examine their wellbeing and risk. HMPPS and NHS England are working together to help ensure that individuals with a sexual conviction who have left prison can still access medication to manage their problematic sexual arousal in the community.

The qualitative research findings highlighted prisoner perspectives around taking the medication, a group who are considered vital in the research and evaluation of treatment interventions (NICE, 2011). Expectations and fears about taking the medication, and reasons for agreeing to do so, were highlighted by prisoner participants. These data fed into the referral process and the publicising of the availability of the medication (this, in turn, led to more self-referrals from prisoners). Research findings from the studies with treatment facilitators and probation staff highlighted the need for more training, education and awareness around the medication. The findings led to the development of a training course for prison staff and therapists (since both groups could make an initial referral for prisoners). This course helped prison officers, probation staff and therapists make appropriate referrals and also helped them to deal with individuals in their care who were taking medication to manage problematic sexual arousal. Dissemination of the findings through prison newsletter and full staff briefings also led to a request for the publication of the findings in the Independent Monitoring Board magazine (Winder, Lievesley & Elliott, 2014). This also resulted in changes to Parole Board Guidance to help the Parole Board understand more about the medication. The research findings have also been used by the Californian penitentiaries when they considered offering anti-libidinal medication to their prisoners with sexual convictions (this required a change to their current legislation). In June 2019, the Justice Health Research Program in Sydney, Australia requested ongoing support and guidance in setting up their own programme and evaluation of the medication. The research team has worked with a group of international experts to create consistency and encourage good practice world-wide, disseminated through a publication drawing together practice in UK, US, Canada, Russia and the Czech Republic (see Winder et al., 2019).

Future directions

As a consequence of the research findings, it is intended that the medication can be offered to people who have not offended. Indeed, the medication (together with clinical care offered by the prescribing medic) may be one of the best tools to underpin prevention of sexual abuse. Expansion into the community is thus hopefully a first step in promoting the availability of the medication to individuals who are struggling with sexual urges but who have not yet committed an offence. The Safer Living Foundation charity hopes to be able to offer medication in the future as part of their prevention programme, The Aurora Project (http://saferlivingfoundation.org/what-we-do/adult-projects/aurora-project/).

The importance of medication as one of the pathways to reducing sexual offending and reoffending is being recognised worldwide. As part of this ongoing international drive to set out best practice, the publication of more robust research (with matched controls or a randomised controlled trial) is an important next step. We need to look at the levels of evidence required to be able to offer SSRIs in the community to help people struggling with problematic sexual arousal. Our research on understanding the underpinnings of sexual preoccupation is indicating a strong trauma component (see Hamilton et al., 2020) but much more research needs to be done in this area. We need to recognise the extent to which problematic sexual arousal, in the form of paedophilia, is accepted as an unchangeable sexual orientation and treated as a mental health issue, since it causes stress and anxiety to the 1–5% of the general population who have an enduring sexual attraction to prepubescent children (Seto, 2019). We also need to accept that many of these people will not commit a sexual offence, but that they may still find their sexual arousal problematic to live with.

Initial challenges around funding (and then ensuing debates as to whether the funding should be a criminal justice or a health issue) are ongoing. Is treating people with problematic sexual arousal a medical (wellbeing) issue or a forensic (offending / reoffending) one? Some of the problems here are that community psychiatrists and general practitioners have shown a marked reluctance to offer medication to treat problematic sexual arousal. We have heard comments such as 'why waste money on sex offenders'? and these are echoed through almost all strands of our work. The answer rests not only on human decency and respect, but also on the importance of prevention. If we reduce sexual abuse, then all these evidence-driven initiatives are worthwhile. Sometimes the lack of enthusiasm for prescribing medication to manage problematic sexual arousal rests on a lack of confidence. Disseminating our research findings to GPs, urologists and community psychiatrists helps to address this (see Winder et al., 2015; Winder et al., 2016; Winder, 2017; Winder et al., 2018; Winder, 2019a).

It is nevertheless important to remind ourselves of the data set out at the start of this chapter around sexual offending. There are currently around 13,500 people in prison in England and Wales serving a sentence for a sexual offence; this equates to almost one fifth of the entire prison population (MoJ, 2019). This number has grown significantly since the early 1990s when 10% of the prison population comprised individuals with a sexual conviction (MoJ, 2016). In the last 12 months, the UK police recorded over 150,000 sexual offences (ONS, 2019) and it is estimated that there are more than 50,000 people under investigation at any one time. That demonstrates that current approaches to preventing sexual crime are simply not working. Whilst societal concern is focused on the moral panic around those convicted of sexual offences, the reality is that only one in ten of these will reoffend (Mews et al., 2017). While it is important that we reduce this figure, it highlights the issue that remains, which is around the prevention of first-time offences. Almost 80% of sexual offences are committed by someone without a previous sexual conviction, and there is a crucial need for prevention to take centre stage in the reduction of sexual offending. Our research has highlighted the need to let those who have committed sexual offences reintegrate into society, to access the medication which is often denied them in the community by general practitioners who have been reported as being more likely to call the police than offer a tailored medical service (Winder, Hocken & Allen, 2017), and moreover to allow those individuals who are concerned they may offend to access support before they commit a first offence. The work of the Safer Living

Foundation charity (of which we are both co-founders and trustees) has resulted in a project to do just this – The Aurora Project (see http://saferlivingfoundation.org/what-we-do/adult-projects/aurora-project/), in addition to a project designed to improve the resources and support available to those who have already offended (Corbett Centre project: see http://saferlivingfoundation.org/what-we-do/the-corbett-centre-for-prisoner-reintegration-2/). The public reaction to individuals convicted of a sexual offence has been dominated by panic and disgust; we have ourselves received death threats just for working on the projects outlined in this chapter. This demonstrates how difficult this arena is for many people to navigate emotionally. Conversely, we have also received many supportive communications from some members of the general public, including survivors and victims of sexual abuse who recognise the need for more work in this arena.

Committing a sexual offence is most typically seen as the result of an illness; medication as a 'cure' makes sense to people. However, where people have heard that the medication 'works' for some people who have committed a sexual offence, it is subsequently seen as a panacea for 'curing' all 'sex offenders'. Ministers, the media and even the Parole Board may wonder why not everyone is given medication. Research showing the utility of medication may make it all sound too easy; people might think it should be mandatory. We would challenge such misinterpretations. Our findings indicate merely that it is an important tool in helping reduce problematic sexual arousal among specific 'high risk' populations. We next need to establish if this has a direct effect on reducing sexual recidivism – a more complex and long-term task.

Project 2: Treating and managing men with sexual convictions maintaining their innocence

In the UK, around 52% of all people convicted of sexual offences previously refused treatment, with denial regarded as one of the major contributing factors to this predicament (Mann et al., 2013; OBPU, 2002). It has been reported that roughly two-thirds of those imprisoned for sexual offences continue to deny that they have committed an offence following conviction (Hood et al., 2002; Haywood & Grossman, 1994; Marshall, 1994; Kennedy & Grubin, 1992). This has implications both for the criminal justice system and wider society. First, serious sexual assaults have a long-term deleterious impact on victims and society (Briere et al., 2008), making effective services which attempt to reduce victimisation and re-victimisation imperative. Second, denial often excluded people with sexual convictions from treatment programmes, such as the former Sex Offender Treatment Programme (SOTP), meaning that untreated deniers may have had outstanding criminogenic needs post-release. One of the first goals of over 90% of treatment programmes in the UK, North America and Canada is to help people convicted of a sexual offence to accept responsibility for their offence(s) (McGrath et al., 2009). Thus, access to treatment comes with stipulations – the acceptance (albeit partially) of responsibility by the individuals for their actions is a prerequisite for admittance on to a treatment programme (Marshall et al., 2001). Thus, categorical deniers, even if they were inclined to do so, were (in most jurisdictions) not permitted to participate on SOTPs. Third, because individuals in total denial are not able to participate in treatment programmes, they will typically serve longer sentences as they cannot demonstrate that they have addressed their offending behaviour, which has implications for progression and parole (see e.g. Hood et al., 2002).

The study of denial in people with sexual convictions has suffered from conceptual and definitional difficulties, which has contributed to a fragmented and insufficient knowledge of the phenomenon (Cooper, 2005; Ware, Marshall, & Marshall, 2015). Denial was previously conceptualised as a dichotomous construct (one is either 'in denial' or not); however, evidence suggests that it is more appropriately considered as a multidimensional concept (Jung, 2004; Carich & Calder, 2003). Denial has typically been understood not as a binary construct or categorical variable but instead as a continuum (see Barbaree, 1991; Gibbons, DeVolder, & Casey, 2003; Levenson, 2011; Marshall, Anderson, & Fernandez, 1999; Schneider & Wright, 2004). For instance, Levenson (2011, p. 361) argued that denial exists on a 'continuum of distorted cognitions' which includes minimising impact of sexual assault on victims, externalising blame, or low acknowledgment of their sexual behaviour problem and its impact. However, there is little evidence that denial exists on a continuum and this has led to conceptual ambiguity which has conflated denial with terms such as cognitive distortions, excuses and justifications (Ware & Blagden, 2016; Ware & Mann, 2012). Whilst the majority of men with sexual convictions appear to make excuses for their sexual crimes through omitting or underplaying certain aspects or their consequences, a small number will categorically deny responsibility. However, because of the reactions they evoke from risk assessors, i.e. 'They feel risky', many approaches to treatment focus too heavily on admission and confession (Blagden et al., 2013; Northey, 1999).

Despite the appeal of the idea that maintained categorical denial increases risk of recidivism, there is almost no evidence for this (Mann, Hanson & Thornton, 2010). Large-scale meta-analyses have found no consistent relationship between denial and reoffending in men with sexual convictions (Hanson & Bussiere, 1998; Hanson & Morton-Bourgon, 2004). Harkins et al. (2015) found that denial of responsibility was not significantly associated with sexual or violent recidivism. However, lower levels of sexual recidivism were found for those who denied responsibility for their offence, independent of static risk. This challenges the notion that high amounts of denial make individuals more risky. While forensic and clinical settings may view denial as something that needs to be tackled or challenged, denial in people with sexual convictions could be seen as unsurprising given the vociferous public denigration that men with sexual convictions face, more than with any other type of offence. As Worrall (1997, p. 125) states 'the sex offender has been constructed as irredeemable. It is no longer his [sic] crimes that are unacceptable; he himself is unacceptable as a member of the community. He is forever non-reintegratable'.

To construe denial as wholly maladaptive is not a tenable position, as it fails to account for the ubiquity of the phenomenon in human beings (Rogers, 1951; Saxe, 1991). Everyone 'does' denial on a regular basis to avoid potentially awkward situations. Denial operates in everyday settings through social interaction, and in highly adversarial settings where the costs of disclosure come with internal and external ramifications (see Sewell & Salekin, 1997; Rogers, 1988; Rogers & Dickey, 1991). Clinicians need to be mindful of this and the benefits of denial. As Yalom contended, 'Never take away anything [from the client] unless you have something better to offer. Beware of stripping a patient who can't bear the chill of reality' (Rogers & Dickey, 1991, p. 154). Indeed, denial should not be considered symptomatic of a mental disorder (Lazarus, 1983). Paradoxically, research suggests that honest self-appraisals are linked to depressive disorders (Lazarus, 1983; Seligman et al., 1979). As Cohen (2001, p. 56) argues 'mental health, it turns out, depends not on being in touch with reality, but on illusion, self-deception and denial'. Later studies have suggested that denial may be a way of doing identity management (Blagden et al., 2014). Denial and identity transformation are shaped by and through social interactions (Presser & Kurth, 2009); therefore, it is necessary to consider the relational properties of denial in forensic contexts and the latitude denial allows for doing identity management and deviance disavowal. In Blagden et al.'s (2014) study all deniers rejected the label 'sex offender' and actively distanced themselves from such a label. However, this is likely an adaptive strategy as it allows the individual to resist internalising a problem category that may impair one's ability to achieve self-respect and affiliation with mainstream society. Similarly, Hulley (2016) and Winder et al. (2014) found neutralisations appeared to assist desistance narratives from sexual offending by allowing for the negotiation of stigma and rejection of the 'sex offender' label, thus providing for the development of a non-offending, prosocial identity.

Our programme of research argues for a more sophisticated conceptualisation of denial, one that does not view deniers as untreatable, but instead as an issue that requires greater creativity and flexibility on the part of academics and clinicians. Our approach also advocates a move away from seeing denial as a marker of poor progress/insight, and instead consider denial as clinically relevant, with deniers' accounts a form of identity management. The research studies focus on understanding prisoners' transition through denial to admittance, the sense-making and construing of deniers, and staff perspectives on the treatment and management of denial. Understanding such positions is vital for informing the process of how to work with deniers and help to make treatment and management in custody more successful.

Context

This project arose in response to a request from the senior psychologist at HMP Whatton to help the prison work better with those in denial. In 2007, the level of people denying they had committed a sexual offence at HMP Whatton was approaching 25%. For the reasons set out above, this level was causing concern since those in denial were felt to be disruptive to the treatment ethos at HMP Whatton. Further, the lack of help and support that could be given to people denying their offences was worrying for the Psychology team, who were keen to help these individuals reduce the risk they were judged to pose.

Challenges

One of the key challenges here was working within a prison with people who had been convicted of an offence, but who were maintaining their innocence, and working within a climate whereby denial was actively seen as 'risky' and something to be challenged. It would be foolish not to acknowledge that miscarriages of justice do occur and that lives are ruined through such injustices (see www.innocenceproject.org/). However, it should also be recognised that these cases are rare. What is far more common is the desire to deny that which we do not wish to be true, or that for which we do not wish to take responsibility. Individuals maintaining their innocence can be a difficult population to work with from both a practitioner and a researcher perspective. When conducting qualitative research in particular, we are asking people to tell their story (Waldram, 2007). If the story is a difficult one for us to hear, that is our issue, not the participant's. Giving people maintaining their innocence a voice brought with it moral and ethical challenges and maintaining a perspective that listened to, and interpreted, a person's 'truth', rather than necessarily 'the truth' as we understood it, was emotionally exhausting and ethically challenging at times.

The research programme

There had been no sustained qualitative investigation on denial in men with sexual convictions and so Blagden et al. (2011, 2013, 2014) elected to conduct a series of qualitative studies, using a combination of interpretative phenomenological analysis and repertory grids. Blagden et al. researched prisoners who had previously denied their offences, prisoners who were currently maintaining their innocence, treatment facilitators of the treatment programmes for people with sexual convictions, and prison staff. The underlying question that this research sought to illuminate was 'why do a substantial proportion of people with sexual convictions continue to deny their actions, despite their conviction?' More specifically, the research sought to answer a plethora of related questions, namely: (i) What is meant by denial in terms of people with sexual convictions and their crimes? (ii) What do treatment staff feel is important when working with deniers, what challenges do they pose, and do you feel denial is risky? (iii) How do 'deniers' account for their convictions and what do such positions achieve? (iv) How and why do those denying transition to accepting responsibility? (v) Should this group be allowed to participate in treatment?

The crux of our position was an idiographic phenomenological study of denial in men with sexual convictions. Our position did not see participants' verbalisations as truths; rather, they tell us about the 'meaning' or intentionality of human experience (Churchill, 2000). As Carr (cited in Churchill, 2000, p. 47) contends, 'narratives will reveal themselves to be not distortions of, denials of, or escapes from reality, but extensions and configurations of its primary features.' Thus, this approach asks critical questions, such as 'what is the participant trying to achieve?' and 'is something leaking out' of his narrative that gives an insight into his worldview? (Smith & Osborne (2008, p. 53). Thus, our position became one of 'making sense' of denial and understanding the participants' constructions of their world. This position was complemented by the use of repertory grids. Repertory grids allow for the assessment of personal constructs and allow an understanding of the individual's worldview. The position is highly idiographic and can allow a unique insight into the way an individual construes aspects of his or her world (Houston, 1998). In essence, repertory grids are a technique for studying personal and interpersonal systems of meaning (Neimeyer, 2004). One of the primary aims of using repertory grids is to make underlying patterns of an individual's thinking more apparent and this has clear benefits for research and clinical/forensic practice (Leach et al., 2001). There has been a limited amount of personal construct work applied within forensic settings, which is surprising given that such an approach can aid in identifying, exploring and formulating issues relevant to an individual's offending behaviour and idiosyncratic beliefs (Horley, 2008; Houston, 1998; Mason, 2003). The repertory grids allowed for an understanding of the participants' personal constructs, their construing and how they viewed themselves in relation to others in their world.

Research findings, impact and legacy

The research on denial by Blagden (Blagden et al., 2011; Blagden et al., 2013; Blagden et al., 2014) highlighted the need to rethink the notion that acceptance of responsibility was, or should be, a core organising principle of treatment. Blagden inputted into the process of redesigning sex offender treatment programmes in England and Wales and his research was used extensively as part of the evidence base for the new programmes. Consequently, the core sex offender treatment programme was redefined, taking into account our position that denial is a form of sense-making and should not matter to the treatment process. Our research argued that 'admittance' of offending does not equate to personal reform and that distancing self from the label 'sex offender' is inherently positive. The research findings, particularly through the repertory grid interview and analysis, allowed – for the first time – people who were denying their offences to access treatment. This programme of research changed UK policy and led to the creation and rollout of a new treatment programme, Horizon, across the entire UK prison estate. Over the next few years, data will be available on the difference this has made in terms of sexual reoffending. This is timely as recent evaluation of the previous treatment programmes (Mews et al., 2017) indicated they were not working.

HMPPS have acknowledged that they took considerable account of Blagden's research findings and have stated that it was his research into denial that convinced them to change the policy we have had for the last 20 years to exclude 'deniers' from treatment programmes (Ruth Mann, HMPPS, personal communication, 2014). Deniers are now accepted on to treatment and the model of treatment has shifted away from being a disclosure-based initiative. This means that 30–35% of men with sexual convictions are eligible for the treatment they need, which may mean fewer future victims. Blagden's work is referenced in the theory manual for the new Kaizen and Horizon treatment programmes. Importantly, HMPPS have recognised that they need to train their staff to have a greater understanding of the relationship between denial and stigma, and to have greater insight into their own emotional reactions to denial. Blagden has delivered several key training events on denial in people with sexual convictions including to their professional practice forum, which includes all HMPPS treatment managers in the Prison and Probation Service. Summaries of his research and the key points from the research were also disseminated to all treatment staff in Prison and Probation.

Future directions

The impact our research has had on traditional sex offender treatment programmes has been significant. However, the challenge remains of ensuring this research can have international reach and significance. This research and its findings have led to collaborations with Correctional Services Australia and in February 2018 Blagden visited Correctional Services New South Wales and the group director Dr Jayson Ware, who is responsible for all programmes and staff training in the New South Wales area. Blagden delivered training to staff, and Ware and Blagden agreed a programme of research studying the difference between deniers and admitters and their trajectories through the criminal justice system. This collaboration has already yielded a peer-reviewed publication. In Ware, Blagden and Harper

(2018), we found that deniers differed to admitters in a number of ways and, crucially, deniers endorsed more shame. This fed back into Blagden's work on denial being a form of identity management and shame reduction (see e.g. Blagden et al., 2014). Given that still over 90% of treatment programmes in Australia have 'accepting responsibility' as a treatment target and force admission, there is much work to be done internationally on the focus on denial.

Project 3: Safer Living Foundation and Circles of Support

There are very few initiatives available to help people with sexual convictions reintegrate into society. Currently, the main such initiative is Circles of Support and Accountability (abbreviated to Circles or CoSA). Circles were initially developed in Ontario, Canada, as a community-based programme designed to assist in the reintegration of individuals (termed the 'core member' of the Circle) who have a high or very high risk of sexual recidivism (Wilson, 2018). Circles emerged within a broader sociopolitical climate where legislators and criminal justice officials alike were keen to determine the most appropriate and successful means of protecting communities from the risk posed by individuals who have committed a sexual offence (Petrunik, Murphy & Fedoroff, 2008). Since its origin in the 1990s, Circles has emerged as the key initiative in the successful reintegration of individuals with sexual convictions into the community. Prison and community Circles are comprised of a group of three to five trained volunteers, who are mentored and supervised by the project coordinator. Circles provide social, emotional and practical support for high-risk individuals. They aim to assist with community reintegration, as men with sexual convictions face many barriers (employment, licence conditions, loss of family and other relationships) which can lead to lifestyle insecurity and may elevate a core member's risk.

The evidence base for Circles is emerging and evaluations are promising as an intervention that reduces risk and protects the community. Research has found that being a core member of Circles resulted in a reduction in sexual recidivism when compared to individuals who were not in a Circle (5% sexual recidivism in the Circles group vs. 16.7% sexual recidivism in the comparison group) (Wilson et al., 2005). Furthermore, recent research has shown that Circles can significantly reduce sexual recidivism, lowering the risk of rearrest for a new sexual offence by 88% and reducing general recidivism by 57% (Duwe, 2018).

Context

The Safer Living Foundation (SLF) is a charitable organisation with the objective to promote the protection of people from, and the prevention of, sexual crime and to promote the rehabilitation of persons who have committed or who are likely to commit sexual offences against others. It is a collaborative venture between members of Nottingham Trent University and HMP Whatton, with input from Nottinghamshire Probation and Nottinghamshire Police. The charity developed due to the close working relationships between SOCAMRU and HMP Whatton, and through collective concerns about the lack of support many men from prison had post-release. This led to the Safer Living Foundation charity being established. This organisation operates from bases at Nottingham Trent University and HMP Whatton; the charity aims to reintegrate and rehabilitate men with sexual convictions, helping them lead productive offence-free lives and preventing further victimisation. Both Winder and Blagden are trustees and co-founders. Five years on, the SLF is an established and multi-award-winning charity; it was awarded the Third Sector Charity of the Year in 2019.

In 2014, the SLF commenced a novel form of Circles: prison-based Circles. The charity was at the time the only organisation worldwide to deliver this type of Circle. In this format, the Circle commences *before* an individual is released into the community. This is important since reoffending is more likely to occur within the first six months post-release (Hanson et al., 2018). Building a supportive Circle around individuals before they leave prison, so that they have established support to help them through the often difficult and hostile transition into the community, was an important adaptation to the standard model of Circles of Support and Accountability. This novel brand of Circles has subsequently been adopted by other charities throughout the UK.

Winder, Blagden and other members of SOCAMRU have been conducting the research and evaluation of all projects carried out by the SLF charity. This includes research and evaluation of prison, young people's and community Circles. Kitson-Boyce et al.'s (2018b) study on prison Circles in the UK focused on individuals' transitions from prison to the community. The study concluded that the prison-model Circles may be best placed to support core members in their progression towards desistance, over the transitional period of release from prison. They postulated that the model reduced anxiety in core members and helped with reintegration. Winder and Blagden have also been responsible for research and evaluation of 188 Big Lottery-funded Community Circles on behalf of Circles UK (the accrediting body for organisations wishing to deliver Circles in the UK). This national evaluation has meant receiving data from eight other organisations in the UK, together with data collated centrally by Circles UK. Our evaluations of community Circles have found that they reduced dynamic risk and increased wellbeing.

Challenges

This research has faced a number of difficulties. First, working with non-academic organisations can be a challenge in itself. Time and care are required to build up relationships and smooth the research process. Even where there are excellent relationships with another organisation (in this case, we are both co-founders and trustees of the Safer Living Foundation) there are still challenges in ensuring the people collating the data (Circles coordinators who work for the charity) understand the importance of data collection, and the timing of data collection. Further, many organisations who work on the front line have little, if any, money to fund evaluations. In part this is because they prioritise actually running projects, and they would not be delivering these projects if they did not believe in them. Spending money to evaluate what they are doing therefore seems perhaps a waste of valuable resources. There are also ongoing discussions about which measures are important to use, the terminology used to denote a Circle that results in a rearrest for a core member, and challenges with funding (the National Probation Service announced it would cease funding Circles in 2019), meaning even greater challenges to funding. There are also challenges for the SLF charity in funding projects, given the population we seek to rehabilitate. We are often seen as an unpopular choice by funders. However, we have been fortunate to receive substantial funding from charitable trusts. Yet much of the funding is from short-term (12-month) grants. This means that we need to constantly apply for further funds. Running a charity alongside our day jobs presents its own challenges, despite the incredible support we get from the management of the School of Social Sciences and of the Nottingham Trent University executive.

Research findings, impact and legacy

The Safer Living Foundation and Circles research evaluations are mixed-method research design. The importance of both qualitative and quantitative research in this area has been promulgated by researchers such as Clarke, Brown and Völlm (2017) who stated that whilst good quality evaluations of recidivism are important, they do not capture the full extent of the impact participating in a Circle can have. This has led to a demand for qualitative studies with the core members and the volunteers taking part in Circles (Wilson, Bates & Völlm, 2010; Bates et al., 2014).

The outputs from this research are changing policy and practice nationally and internationally. Alongside this research is evaluation and research on the world's first prison-based adaptation of the standard model of Circles. Research and evaluations around Circles have been published in leading international journals. Circles UK have changed their policy in light of the research, and the research has provided recommendations/guidance for other prison-models. Other organisations are beginning to adopt this alternative model. In terms of our legacy, the collaboration between Nottingham Trent University and HMP Whatton through the SLF charity is yielding tangible and impactful results. So far, the SLF has worked with over 80 high-risk individuals across all projects and we have had zero sexual reoffences. Through our work, our service users have reported higher levels of wellbeing and reduced social isolation which assists with helping them lead positive offence-free lives. Social isolation is one of the biggest risk factors for further offending. Our evaluations demonstrate that scores for dynamic risk of reoffending of the people we work with reduce as they are supported and monitored with our interventions. Over time, the people supported through our programme are assessed to be at a significantly lower risk of reoffending than other people convicted of sexual offences. Finally, our volunteers have committed more than 4,000 hours to our projects. Not only do they provide real evidence to our service users that 'normal' members of the general public are willing to see them as human beings, but the volunteers also create a ripple effect in which their attitudes to people with sexual convictions, which is steeped in first-hand experience, diffuses out to their family and friends. Society begins to see people with sexual convictions as human beings who have done monstrous things, rather than monsters per se.

Conclusions

For most people, someone who commits a sexual crime is an uncontrollable monster who can henceforward never be trusted to live an offence-free life. Committing a sexual offence gives you membership of a homogenous group of 'sex offenders', linked in the public eye with the most heinous and terrible examples of a sexual crime that the media have presented to the general public. Committing a sexual offence is evidence for an incurable, even untreatable, disease. Yet this picture belies the truth: that the majority of people who commit a sexual offence and are brought to account for it by the courts, will not commit another one. There are circumstances and factors that mean people are more likely to commit a further offence (even an initial offence), and equally there are circumstances and factors that make it less likely for people to commit a sexual (re)offence. This chapter explored three research programmes that have changed policy and practice in managing, treating and rehabilitating people with sexual convictions in the UK and beyond, reducing and preventing sexual abuse.

This is a field we are passionate about. We understand the appalling damage of sexual harm and we see that damage as impacting on victims, victims' families and friends, but also on the perpetrators' families and friends, and indeed the perpetrators themselves. We are aware that many perpetrators were themselves victims. We are not apologists for people committing sexual offences, but we recognise that the emotional and moral panic around sexual offending is unhelpful both for society and for the prevention of offending and reoffending.

The work is difficult: there are numerous practical and emotional challenges. It is time-intensive, difficult to get funded and can be corrosive to those working in it. It requires a good team spirit, the ability to empathise but also to switch off, a non-judgemental attitude, a sense of humour, some courage and a lot of hard work. It has changed our television-viewing habits (thank goodness for 'Grand Designs' and 'Masterchef Australia'), as we need to switch off from the world we have been researching in. So why do we do it? The answer is partly that it is about doing research that we feel is meaningful and makes a difference, that helps people lead good lives, but there is also underpinning this a psychological curiosity about why human beings should commit such harmful acts. It has been said that it is a measure of a society how they treat the most unloved. We feel that for humanity to make evolutionary progress as a species, we need to take along with us, in an integrated fashion, all individuals, and that everyone should be treated with decency and respect as both an expression of humanity but also simply because this will be far more likely to encourage desistance and lead to a safer society for all.

Acknowledgements

We would like to thank and acknowledge all the participants in these research projects, together with prison and probation staff, and other gatekeepers who helped facilitate these research programmes. We would also like to thank Alice Stringer, Emily Grenville and Jackie Hamilton for their help in tidying up the text and the reference sections. Any remaining errors are our own responsibility.

References

Barbaree, H. E. (1991). Denial and minimization among sex offenders: Assessment and treatment outcome. *Forum on Corrections Research, 3*(4), 30–33.

Bates, A., Williams, D., Wilson, C., & Wilson, R. J. (2014). Circles south east: The first 10 years 2002–2012. *International Journal of Offender Therapy and Comparative Criminology, 58*(7), 861–885.

Beech, A., Fisher, D., & Ward, T. (2005). Sexual murderers' implicit theories. *Journal of Interpersonal Violence, 20*(11), 1366–1389.

Blagden, N., & Winder, B. (2019). Helping to rehabilitate sex offenders is controversial–but it can prevent more abuse. *The Conversation*. Retrieved from https://theconversation.com/helping-to-rehabilitate-sex-offenders-is-controversial-but-it-can-prevent-more-abuse-111861.

Blagden, N., Winder, B., Gregson, M., & Thorne, K. (2013). Working with denial in convicted sexual offenders A qualitative analysis of treatment professionals' views and experiences and their implications for practice. *International Journal of Offender Therapy and Comparative Criminology, 57*(3), 332–356.

Blagden, N., Winder, B., Gregson, M., & Thorne, K. (2014). Making sense of denial in sexual offenders: A qualitative phenomenological and repertory grid analysis. *Journal of Interpersonal Violence, 29*(9), 1698–1731.

Blagden, N., Winder, B., Thorne, K., & Gregson, M. (2011). "No-one in the world would ever wanna speak to me again": An interpretative phenomenological analysis into convicted sexual offenders' accounts and experiences of maintaining and leaving denial. *Psychology, Crime and Law, 17*(7), 563–585.

Briere, J., Kaltman, S., & Green, B. L. (2008). Accumulated childhood trauma and symptom complexity. *Journal of Traumatic Stress: Official Publication of the International Society for Traumatic Stress Studies*, 21(2), 223–226.

Carich, M. S., & Calder, M. C. (2003). *Contemporary treatment of adult male sex offenders*. CT, USA: Crown House Publishing Company.

Churchill, S. (2000). "Seeing through" self-deception in narrative reports: Finding psychological truth in problematic data. *Journal of Phenomenological Psychology, 31*(1), 44–62.

Clarke, M., Brown, S., & Völlm, B. (2017). Circles of support and accountability for sex offenders: A systematic review of outcomes. *Sexual Abuse, 29*(5), 446–478.

Cohen, S. (2001). *The states of denial*. London: Routledge.
Cooper, S. (2005). Understanding, treating, and managing sex offenders who deny their offence. *Journal of Sexual Aggression, 11*(1), 85–94.
Crown Prosecution Service. (2017). Violence against women and girls crime report, 2015–16. Retrieved from https://www.cps.gov.uk/cps/news/cps-report-shows-more-offenders-are-being-successfully-prosecuted-sexual-crimes-ever.
Duwe, G. (2018). *Minnesota Circles of Support and Accountability (MnCoSA) at 50: Updated results from a randomized controlled trial* (Research Report). St. Paul, MN: Department of Corrections. Retrieved from https://mn.gov/doc/assets/2018%20MnCOSA%20 Outcome%20Evaluation_tcm1089-326700.pdf.
Elliott, H., Winder, B., Manby, E., Edwards, H., & Lievesley, R. (2018). "I kind of find that out by accident": Probation staff experiences of pharmacological treatment for sexual preoccupation and hypersexuality. *Journal of Forensic Practice, 20*(1), 20–31.
Fong, T. W. (2006). Understanding and managing compulsive sexual behaviours. *Psychiatry (Edgmont), 3*(11), 51.
Garcia, F. D., & Thibaut, F. (2010). Sexual addictions. *The American Journal of Drug and Alcohol Abuse, 36*(5), 254–260.
Gibbons, P., de Volder, J., & Casey, P. (2003). Patterns of denial in sex offenders: A replication study. *Journal of the American Academy of Psychiatry and the Law Online, 31*(3), 336–344.
Grubin, D. (2018). The pharmacological treatment of sex offenders. In A. R. Beech, A. J. Carter, R. E. Mann & P. Rotshtein (Eds.), *The Wiley Blackwell handbook of forensic neuroscience* (pp. 703–723). Oxford: Wiley.
Guay, D. R. P. (2009). Drug treatment of paraphilic and nonparaphilic sexual disorders. *Clinical Therapeutics, 31*(1), 1–31.
Hamilton, J., Winder, B., Blagden, N., Pandya-Wood, J., & Hocken, K. (2020). *Exploring the relationships between personality disorder, sexual preoccupation, and adverse childhood experiences among individuals who have previously sexually offended* (Doctoral Thesis). Nottingham Trent University, Nottingham, England.
Hanson, R. K., & Bussiere, M. T. (1998). Predicting relapse: A meta-analysis of sexual offender recidivism studies. *Journal of Consulting and Clinical Psychology, 66*(2), 348.
Hanson, R. K., & Harris, A. J. R. (2000). Where should we intervene? Dynamic predictors of sexual offense recidivism. *Criminal Justice and Behavior, 27*(1), 6–35.
Hanson, R. K., Harris, A. J. R., Letourneau, E., Helmus, L. M., & Thornton, D. (2018). Reductions in risk based on time offense-free in the community: Once a sexual offender, not always a sexual offender. *Psychology, Public Policy, and Law, 24*(1), 48–63.
Hanson, R. K., Harris, A. J. R., Scott, T. L., & Helmus, L. (2007). *Assessing the risk of sexual offenders on community supervision: The dynamic supervision project* (Vol. 5, No. 6). Ottawa, Ontario: Public Safety Canada. Retrieved from https://www

.punlicsafety.gc.ca/cnt/rsrcs/pblctns/ssssng-rsk-sxl-ffndrs/sssng-rsk-sxl-ffndrs-eng.pdf.

Hanson, R. K., & Morton-Bourgon, K. E. (2004). *Predictors of sexual recidivism: An updated meta-analysis*. Ottawa: Public Works and Government Services Canada. Retrieved from https://www.publicsafety.gc.ca/cnt/rsrcs/pblctns/2004-02-prdctrs-sxl-rcdvsm-pdtd/index-en.aspx.

Hanson, R. K., & Morton-Bourgon, K. E. (2005). The characteristics of persistent sexual offenders: A meta-analysis of recidivism studies. *Journal of Consulting and Clinical Psychology, 73*(6), 1154–1163.

Harkins, L., Howard, P., Barnett, G., Wakeling, H., & Miles, C. (2015). Relationships between denial, risk, and recidivism in sexual offenders. *Archives of Sexual Behavior, 44*(1), 157–166.

Haywood, T. W., & Grossman, L. S. (1994). Denial of deviant sexual arousal and psychopathology in child molesters. *Behavior Therapy, 25*(2), 327–340.

HMPPS. (2016). Offender behaviour programmes (OBPs). Retrieved from https://webarchive.nationalarchives.gov.uk/20130206061717/https://www.justice.gov.uk/offenders/before-after-release/obp.

Hocken, K. (2014). *How effectively does the Structured Assessment for Risk and Need (SARN) assess risk in men with Intellectual Disability who have committed a sexual offence* (Unpublished PhD Thesis). Nottingham, UK: Nottingham Trent University.

Home Office. (2007). *Review of the protection of children from sex offenders*. London: Home Office. Retrieved from https://dera.ioe.ac.uk/8671/2/A9R2808.pdf.

Hood, R., Shute, S., Feilzer, M., & Wilcox, A. (2002). Sex offenders emerging from long-term imprisonment. A study of their long-term reconviction rates and of parole board members' judgements of their risk. *British Journal of Criminology, 42*(2), 371–394.

Horley, J. (2008). *Sexual offenders: Personal construct theory and deviant sexual behaviour*. London: Routledge.

Houston, J. (1998). *Making sense with offenders: Personal constructs, therapy and change*. Chichester: John Wiley & Sons Ltd.

Hulley, J. L. (2016). While this does not in any way excuse my conduct...the role of treatment and neutralizations in desistance from sexual offending. *International Journal of Offender Therapy and Comparative Criminology, 60*(15), 1776–1790.

Jung, S. (2004). *Assessing denial among sex offenders* (Unpublished Doctoral Dissertation). University of Victoria, British Columbia, Canada.

Kafka, M. P. (2010). Hypersexual disorder: A proposed diagnosis for DSM-V. *Archives of Sexual Behavior, 39*(2), 377–400.

Kennedy, H. G., & Grubin, D. H. (1992). Patterns of denial in sex offenders. *Psychological Medicine, 22*(1), 191–196.

Khan, O., Ferriter, M., Huband, N., Powney, M. J., Dennis, J. A., & Duggan, C. (2015). Pharmacological interventions for those who have sexually offended or are at risk of offending. *Cochrane Database of Systematic Reviews*. doi:10.1002/14651858.CD007989.

Kitson-Boyce, R., Blagden, N., Winder, B., & Dillon, G. (2018a). A prison-model of CoSA: The potential to offer "through the gate" support and accountability. *Journal of Sexual Aggression*, *24*(3), 294–310.

Kitson-Boyce, R., Blagden, N., Winder, B., & Dillon, G. (2018b). "This time it's different" Preparing for release through a prison-model of CoSA: A phenomenological and repertory grid analysis. *Sexual Abuse*, *31*(8), 886–907.

Lazarus, R. S. (1983). Costs and benefits of denial. In S. Breznitz (Ed.), *The denial of stress* (pp. 1–30). New York, NY: International Universities.

Leach, C., Freshwater, K., Aldridge, J., & Sunderland, J. (2001). Analysis of repertory grids in clinical practice. *British Journal of Clinical Psychology*, *40*(3), 225–248.

Levenson, J. S. (2011). "But I didn't do it!" Ethical treatment of sex offenders in denial. *Sexual Abuse*, *23*(3), 346–364.

Lievesley, R., Elliott, H. J., Winder, B., & Norman, C. (2014). Understanding service users' and therapists' experiences of pharmacological treatment for sexual preoccupation and/or hypersexuality in incarcerated sex offenders. *The Journal of Forensic Psychiatry and Psychology*, *25*(3), 262–287.

Mann, R. E., Hanson, R. K., & Thornton, D. (2010). Assessing risk for sexual recidivism: Some proposals on the nature of psychologically meaningful risk factors. *Sexual Abuse*, *22*(2), 191–217.

Mann, R. E., Webster, S. D., Wakeling, H. C., & Keylock, H. (2013). Why do sexual offenders refuse treatment? *Journal of Sexual Aggression*, *19*(2), 191–206.

Marshall, W. L. (1994). Treatment effects on denial and minimisation in incarcerated sex offenders. *Behaviour Research and Therapy*, *32*(5), 559–564.

Marshall, W. L., Anderson, D., & Fernandez, Y. (1999). *Cognitive behavioural treatment of sexual offenders*. Chichester: J. Wiley.

Marshall, W. L., Thornton, D., Marshall, L. E., Fernandez, Y. M., & Mann, R. (2001). Treatment of sexual offenders who are in categorical denial: A pilot project. *Sexual Abuse: A Journal of Research and Treatment*, *13*(3), 205–215.

Mason, J. (2003). The use of the repertory grid as an aid to assessment and formulation in a sex offender with a learning disability. *British Journal of Forensic Practice*, *10*(4), 37–44.

McGrath, R. J., Cumming, G. F., Burchard, B. L., Zeoli, S., & Ellerby, L. (2009). *Current practices and emerging trends in sexual abuser management*. Brandon, VT: Safer Society Press.

Mental Capacity Act. (2005). Retrieved from https://www.legislation.gov.uk/ukpga/2005/9/contents.

Mental Health Act. (1983). Retrieved from http://www.legislation.gov.uk/ukpga/1983/20/contents.

Mews, A., Di Bella, L., & Purver, M. (2017). *Impact evaluation of the prison-based Core sex offender treatment programme*. Ministry of Justice Analytical Series. Retrieved from https://assets.publishing.service.gov.uk/government/uploads/system/uploads/attachment_data/file/623876/sotp-report-web-.pdf.

Ministry of Justice (MoJ). (2016). *Story of the prison population: 1993–2016 England and Wales*. Retrieved July 15, 2019, from https://assets.publishing.service.gov.uk/government/uploads/system/uploads/attachment_data/file/541667/prison-population-story-1993-2016.pdf.

Ministry of Justice (MoJ). (2018). *Offender management statistics bulletin, England and Wales*. Retrieved August 12, 2020, from https://www.gov.uk/government/collections/offender-management-statistics-quarterly.

Ministry of Justice (MoJ). (2019). *Offender management statistics bulletin, England and Wales*. Retrieved July 15, 2019, from https://assets.publishing.service.gov.uk/government/uploads/system/uploads/attachment_data/file/775078/offender-management-quarterly-q3-2018.pdf.

National Institute for Care and Health Excellence. (2011). *Service user experience in adult mental health: Improving the experience of care for people using adult NHS mental health services* (Clinical Guidance CG136). Retrieved from https://www.nice.org.uk/guidance/cg136.

Neimeyer, R. A. (2004). Repertory grid methods. Retrieved from www.pcp-net.org/encyclopaedia/repgrid-methods.html.

Northey, W. (1999). The politics of denial: A post-modern critique. *The Sex Offender: Theoretical Advances, Treating Special Populations and Legal Developments, 3*, 32–31.

OBPU. (2002). *National deniers strategy*. London: HM Prison Service.

Office for National Statistics (ONS). (2018). *Sexual offences in England and Wales: Year ending March 2017*. Retrieved from https://www.ons.gov.uk/peoplepopulationandcommunity/crimeandjustice/articles/sexualoffencesinenglandandwales/yearendingmarch2017.

Office for National Statistics (ONS). (2019). *Crime in England and Wales: Year ending September 2018*. Retrieved from https://www.ons.gov.uk/peoplepopulationandcommunity/crimeandjustice/bulletins/crimeinenglandandwales/yearendingseptember2018.

Petrunik, M., Murphy, L., & Fedoroff, J. P. (2008). American and Canadian approaches to sex offenders: A study of the politics of dangerousness. *Federal Sentencing Reporter, 21*(2), 111–123.

Presser, L., & Kurth, S. (2009). 'I got a quick tongue': Negotiating ex-convict identity in mixed company. In B. Veysey, J. Christian & D. J. Martinez (Eds.), *How offenders transform their lives* (pp. 72–86). Cullompton, UK: Willan Publishing.

Rogers, C. R. (1951). *Client-centered therapy: Its current practice, implications and theory*. Boston, MA: Houghton Mifflin.

Rogers, R. (1988). *Clinical assessment of malingering and deception*. New York, NY: Guilford.

Rogers, R., & Dickey, R. (1991). Denial and minimization among sex offenders. *Annals of Sex Research, 4*(1), 49–63.

Saxe, L. (1991). Lying: Thoughts of an applied social psychologist. *American Psychologist, 46*(4), 409–415.

Schneider, S., & Wright, R. (2004). Understanding denial in sexual offenders: A review of cognitive and motivational processes to avoid responsibility. *Trauma, Violence and Abuse, 5*(1), 3–20.

Seligman, M. E., Abramson, L. Y., Semmel, A., & Von Baeyer, C. (1979). Depressive attributional style. *Journal of Abnormal Psychology, 88*(3), 242–247.

Seto, M. C. (2019). The motivation-facilitation model of sexual offending. *Sexual Abuse, 31*(1), 3–24.

Sewell, K. W., & Salekin, R. T. (1997). Understanding and detecting dissimulation in sex offenders. In R. Rogers (Ed.), *Clinical assessment of malingering and deception* (2nd ed., pp. 328–350). New York, NY: Guilford.

Sex offenders Act. (1997). (Commencement) Order, 1997, Chapter 51, article 2.

Smith, J. A., & Osborn, M. (2008). Interpretative phenomenological analysis. In J. A. Smith (Ed.), *Qualitative psychology: A practical guide to research methods* (2nd ed., pp. 53–80). Thousand Oaks, CA: SAGE.

Turner, D., Basdekis-Jozsa, R., & Briken, P. (2012, September). Prescription of testosterone-lowering medications in sex offender treatment in German forensic-psychiatric institutions. *International Association for the Treatment of Sexual Offenders. Talk presented at, 2012 International Association for the Treatment of Sexual Offenders conference*, Berlin, Germany.

Waldram, J. B. (2007). Everybody has a story: Listening to imprisoned sexual offenders. *Qualitative Health Research, 17*(7), 963–970.

Ware, J., & Blagden, N. (2016). Responding to categorical denial, refusal, and treatment drop-out. In *The Wiley handbook on the theories, assessment and treatment of sexual offending* (pp. 1559–1574), Chichester: John Wiley & sons.

Ware, J., Blagden, N., & Harper, C. (2018). Are categorical deniers different? Understanding demographic, personality, and psychological differences between denying and admitting individuals with sexual convictions. *Deviant Behavior, 41*(4), 399–412.

Ware, J., & Mann, R. E. (2012). How should "acceptance of responsibility" be addressed in sexual offending treatment programs? *Aggression and Violent Behavior, 17*(4), 279–288.

Ware, J., Marshall, W. L., & Marshall, L. E. (2015). Categorical denial in convicted sex offenders: The concept, its meaning, and its implication for risk and treatment. *Aggression and Violent Behavior, 25*, 215–226.

Wilson, C. (2018). A history of the development of circles of support and accountability. In H. Elliot, K. Hocken, R. Lievesley, N. Blagdon, B. Winder, & P. Banyard (Eds.), *Sexual crime and circles of support and accountability* (pp. 1–23). Cham, Switzerland: Palgrave Macmillan.

Wilson, C., Bates, A., & Völlm, B. (2010). Circles of support and accountability: An innovative approach to manage high risk sex offenders in the community. *Open Criminology Journal, 3*(1), 48–57.

Wilson, R. J., Picheca, J. E., & Prinzo, M. (2005). *Circles of support and accountability: An evaluation of the pilot project in South-Central Ontario* (p. 1). Ottawa, Ontario: Correctional Service of Canada.

Winder, B. (2016). The management of hypersexuality. *Trends in Urology and Men's Health*, 7(5), 9–12.

Winder, B. (2017, September). The management of hypersexuality in men and women. *British Association for Sexual Health & HIV.* Invited workshop at Keele University, UK.

Winder, B. (2019a, March). Hypersexuality and relationships. *Keynote Paper at 20th International European Association of Urology Nurses (EAUN) and the Australian and New Zealand Urological Nurses Society (ANZUNS) Conference*, Barcelona, Spain.

Winder, B. (2019b). The next steps in managing people who are high risk, with personality disorder and who have committed a sexual offence post-release. *Personality Disorder Conference 'Innovations in practice - 2020 and beyond'. Keynote presentation.* Forums and Events, St Albans, London.

Winder, B., Elliott, H., Blagden, N., & Lievesley, R. (2016, September). *A mixed method, national, evaluation of 188 Community Circles of Support and Accountability (CoSA).* Munster, Germany: European Society of Criminology.

Winder, B., Fedoroff, J. P., Grubin, D., Klapilová, K., Kamenskov, M., Tucker, D., & Vvedensky, G. E. (2019). The pharmacologic treatment of problematic sexual interests, paraphilic disorders, and sexual preoccupation in adult men who have committed a sexual offence. *International Review of Psychiatry, 31*(2), 1–10.

Winder, B., Hocken, K., & Allen, E. (2017, November). *The safer living foundation and the SLF prevention project. Keynote presentation at crime in mind, second forensic psychiatry research seminar: Interventions for sex offenders post-SOTP.* Nottingham, UK: Institute of Mental Health.

Winder, B., Lievesley, R., & Elliott, H. (2014). *Evaluation of the use of pharmacological medications with convicted sexual offenders experiencing high levels of sexual preoccupation.* Summary briefing to the Independent Monitoring Board, Her Majesty's Prison Service, July 2014. Nottingham: Sexual Offences, Crime and Misconduct Research Unit.

Winder, B., Lievesley, R., Elliottt, H., Hocken, K., Faulkner, J., Norman, C., & Kaul, A. (2018). Evaluation of the use of pharmacological treatment with prisoners experiencing high levels of hypersexual disorder. *Journal of Forensic Psychiatry and Psychology, 29*(1), 53–71.

Winder, B., Lievesley, R., Elliott, H., Norman, C., Hocken, K., & Payne, N. (2015, March). Evaluation of the use of anti-libidinal medication with convicted sex offenders with high levels of sexual preoccupation. *Presentation at a Conference entitled 'Sex Offender Treatment: A Case Study Approach to Issues and Interventions'.* University of Birmingham.

Worrall, A. (1997). *Punishment in the community: The future of criminal justice.* London: Longman.

2

CCTV AND THE SUPER-RECOGNISERS

Josh P. Davis

Context: CCTV management and suspect identification in the twenty-first century

CCTV is 'an utter fiasco' and 'not fit for purpose' were 2008 headlines quoting the head of the London Metropolitan Police Service's ('the MET') CCTV management unit (Bowcott, 2008). At least £4–5 billion of public and private funds (Norris, McCahill, & Wood, 2004) had been invested in 4.1–5.9 million cameras in the UK (British Security Industry Association, n.d.). With 90% public approval rates (Gill et al., 2003), CCTV was marketed as a crime deterrent (McCahill & Norris, 2003). However, research revealed only minor crime reduction effects (e.g. see Gill et al., 2005 for a review), and simply displaced some to nearby locations (e.g., Ditton & Short, 1998). London is one of the most surveilled cities in the world, and yet the MET revealed only 3% of crimes were solved by CCTV; 1 per 1,000 cameras per annum (BBC News, 2009). Not surprisingly, criminals viewed systems as unmonitored and no threat to their activities (Gill & Loveday, 2003).

The massive investment had been directed at bespoke CCTV equipment employing technologically diverse standards. Far less was spent on staff, and the police struggled with footage collection, forensic processing and best image selection and distribution, for officer, public and court viewing (Bowcott, 2008). Indeed, the MET shooting of the innocent Brazilian Jean Charles de Menezes in 2005, mistaken for a terrorist, was partly due to poor-quality CCTV image distribution to surveillance teams, when better images were available (Davis & Valentine, 2015; H.M.

Coroner, 2009). Between the negative headlines, the MET announced plans to professionalise CCTV management. This included the creation of a 'Caught on Camera' website to display London's wanted suspect images, with the aim that they would be identified by police or public familiar with those depicted.

Empirical experiments reveal robust familiar face recognition of even poor-quality photos (e.g., Bruce, Henderson, Newman, & Burton, 2001; Burton, Wilson, Cowan, & Bruce, 1999), suggesting that making images available to those most likely to recognise them should enhance suspect identification rates (hereafter 'idents'). However, most suspects are unknown to most police, and even in optimum conditions, unfamiliar face identification is often unreliable (e.g., Bruce, Henderson, Greenwood, Hancock, Burton, & Miller, 1999; Burton et al., 1999; Davis & Valentine, 2009; for a review see Davis & Valentine, 2015). In terms of individual differences in face recognition, research prior to 2009 had focused on those at the lower end of the spectrum, who struggle to recognise photos of family members due to brain damage (acquired prosopagnosia) (e.g., Rossion, Caldara, Seghier, et al., 2003), genetics (Wilmer, Germine, Chabris, et al., 2010), or from birth and with no known trauma (developmental prosopagnosia) (e.g., Kennerknecht, Grueter, Welling, Wentzek, Horst, Edwards, & Grueter, 2006). Overall, the generally negative appraisals of visual image identification suggested that even if police CCTV management systems were improved, increased ident rates might not be guaranteed.

At the same time as the MET planned these changes, research by Russell, Duchaine, and Nakayama (2009) in the USA was gaining traction. This described four participants self-reporting exceptional face recognition ability, and who provided anecdotes such as:

> 'It doesn't matter how many years pass, if I've seen your face before I will be able to recall it. It happens only with faces'; or 'I've learned to stop surprising people with bizarre comments like, "Hey, weren't you at that so-and-so concert last fall. … I recognize you." Before that, I'd occasionally make people uncomfortable'
>
> *(p. 253).*

After scoring near maximum on empirical tests of face recognition ability, the authors labelled them 'super-recognisers'. Once 'Caught on Camera' was established, the MET also realised that despite a workforce of 48,000, a substantial proportion of idents were being made by a small cohort of about 25 police (Davis, Lander, & Jansari, 2013). Many of these police completed face recognition tests first administered by my team in April 2011 (Davis, Lander, Evans, & Jansari, 2016). Some performed at the level of Russell et al.'s (2009) super-recognisers. Supported by additional case evidence, many of their idents, even of briefly encountered suspects not seen for a number of years, led to convictions. Descriptions were redolent of Russell et al.'s (2009) super-recognisers' anecdotes:

> One spotted and arrested a robber walking along a busy high street, 18 months after last viewing him in a poor-quality video of an armed robbery. Another arrested a suspect eight months after viewing an E-FIT facial composite. A third recognised a distinctive scar, last seen 10 years previously.
>
> *(Davis et al., 2013, p. 727)*

Our unfunded research programme was however interrupted by the August 2011 London riots, which resulted in five deaths and £300 million damage. Police ($n \approx 100$) we most wanted to test identified multiple often-disguised rioters from over 200,000 hours of mainly poor-quality CCTV footage captured at night, from above head height (Dodd, 2011). Twenty of the police tested in April 2011 identified 600 rioters. One identified 190 (Manzoor, 2016). In total, approximately 4,000 rioters were identified by humans and prosecuted; a stark contrast to the single rioter identified by a face recognition algorithm.

As the riots investigation closed in 2013, the MET announced plans to create a suspect image database to exploit future technological advances, and a system for distributing new suspect images to those most likely to identify them – the super-recognisers. For this, police with superior abilities in each London borough were given time to view some of the MET's approximately 500 new suspect images per week, particularly those matching their specialist local or crime-type knowledge. My research team were asked to facilitate a search for more MET super-recognisers. As will be described, this led to substantial ident rate increases, positive media scrutiny and public engagement in research following the establishment of a full-time New Scotland Yard Proactive Super-Recogniser Unit. Other worldwide police forces and businesses subsequently asked my team for help in creating similar super-recogniser teams.

Underpinning research: identification from CCTV and other visual images

For decades, research has demonstrated human memory malleability (i.e., from delay, stress, interference). It is therefore unsurprising that eyewitness identification errors can lead to wrongful convictions (e.g., Garrett, 2011; Munsterberg, 1908). Indeed, misidentifications contributed to almost three-quarters of the first 360 US DNA exoneration cases (Innocence Project, n.d.). Despite promising reforms to procedures, about 25% of witnesses identify innocent foils from UK and US police line-ups, a clear demonstration of memory fallibility (Behrman & Richards, 2005; Horry, Memon, Wright, & Milne, 2012; for a review see Clark, Moreland, & Rush, 2015). Empirical research reflects concerns (for an edited volume see Valentine & Davis, 2015). Valentine, Davis, Memon, and Roberts (2012: Experiment 3) demonstrated that 35.9% of 125 participants misidentified an 'innocent suspect' present in person in a show-up procedure as someone seen arguing with a lecturer 15 minutes previously. Most (85%) repeated their identification when viewing the same person in video line-ups between a day and a month later. Errors were higher with the actual target presented in a target-present show-up, in that 54.4% of 92 participants incorrectly reported that the person standing in front of them was not the same as the person initiating the attention-drawing argument.

The investment in CCTV was seen as a panacea. With no time pressures or stress, police could directly compare footage with suspect photos. Policy-makers reasoned that in London, with blanket coverage, a trawl of CCTV from crime scene localities should generate good-quality identifiable images. Nevertheless, most of the extant research showed that whereas familiar face recognition is normally reliable, unfamiliar face identification is error-prone (e.g., Davis & Valentine, 2015). With high-quality close-up images, and no demands on memory, simultaneous face matching designs reveal high rates of false-positive (mistakenly believing two images of two different people are of the same person), and false-negative (believing two images of the same person are of different people) errors (e.g., Burton, White, & McNeil, 2010; Henderson, Bruce, & Burton, 2001). Even when matching photos with targets present in person errors are high (Kemp, Towell, & Pike, 1997). In an experiment at London's Science Museum, Davis and Valentine (2009: Experiment 2) found 44% of visitors failed to correctly match a good-quality CCTV video with the depicted actor standing by the monitor screen. Errors (33%) were almost as high when a different actor was depicted in the video. Subsequent research has revealed that as a group, highly experienced passport officers who make multiple daily face matching decisions, perform no better than those with no experience (e.g., White, Kemp, Jenkins, Matheson, & Burton, 2014), although there is substantial within-group variability.

Forensic facial comparison techniques used by expert witnesses to attribute identity in crime scene images and undisputed images of defendants were also subjected to negative scrutiny (e.g., Davis, Valentine, & Davis, 2010; Moreton & Morley, 2011; for reviews see Davis, Valentine, & Wilkinson, 2012; Edmond, Davis, & Valentine, 2015), perhaps not surprisingly as different experts using virtually identical techniques have offered opposing opinions of identity in court (e.g., *R v Clarke*, 1995). The research literature was therefore justifiably negative in its assessment of the reliability of unfamiliar face identification from CCTV, as such errors in police investigations might lead to innocent individuals being suspected of crimes. However, almost all relevant research had ignored within-group variability (Young & Noyes, 2019), perhaps treating high-scoring outliers as anomalies.

In the first super-recogniser research, Russell et al. (2009) employed the 'Cambridge Face Memory Test: Extended', a standardised short-term six-person face learning and recognition test, since employed in most subsequent super-recogniser research; a 'Before They Were Famous Test', in which participants identify photos of celebrities when young; and the 'Cambridge Face Perception Test', a test with no memory demands. The authors described the super-recognisers' performances as 'about as good at face recognition and perception as developmental prosopagnosics are bad' (p. 252). Later research (Bate et al., 2018; Russell, Chatterjee, & Nakayama, 2012; Tardif et al., 2019) suggested that rather than possessing qualitatively different cognitive or neurological mechanisms, super-recognisers and developmental prosopagnosics inhabit opposite ends of a quantitative population-wide spectrum of face recognition ability (although see Belanova, Davis, & Thompson, 2018; Bobak, Bennetts, Parris, Jansari, & Bate, 2016; Bobak, Parris, Gregory, Bennetts, & Bate, 2017; Russell et al., 2009, for evidence of qualitatively different face processing strategies). Based on statistical conventions, in which scores more than two standard deviations outside the mean are designated outliers, this suggests prevalence of super-recognisers and developmental prosopagnosics at about 2% in the population (see Kennerknecht, Ho, & Wong, 2008). This standard has been an arbitrary threshold in most subsequent research. When my research team started testing police in 2011, this suggested there might be 480 to 960 super-recognisers in the MET alone (1–2% of 30,000 officers and 18,000 civilian staff).

To be eligible for our first MET super-recogniser research in 2011, police had made at least 15 idents within 12 months from 'Caught on Camera'. My team employed tests designed to match possible drivers of success (Davis et al., 2016). First, to replicate poor-quality CCTV idents of suspects not seen for years, a 'Famous Face Recognition Test' (Lander, Bruce, & Hill, 2001) required recognition of 30 images of celebrities taken 12 years previously whose subsequent media profile had varied. Another ten trials depicted non-celebrities. Images were rendered harder-to-identify by degrading using thresholding. Second, in an 'Unfamiliar Face Recognition Array Test' (adapted from Bruce et al., 1999), participants viewed 40 male faces, each immediately followed by a ten-person target-present or target-absent array. Participants selected a face or rejected the array. Third, in an 'Unfamiliar Face Recognition Test' (old/new)', participants viewed ten male and ten female photos, depicted from the waist up. In a 40-face test phase, with no warnings, only internal facial features were displayed. Participants responded 'old' (20 faces) or 'new' (20 faces). Fourth, in the 'Glasgow Face Matching Test' (Burton et al., 2010), participants viewed 40 pairs of unfamiliar faces and decided whether each was 'matched' (20) or 'mismatched' (20).

Most police (*n* = 36) and participants, who at a London Science Museum event had attained Russell et al.'s (2009) super-recognition criteria on the 'Cambridge Face Memory Test: Extended (n = 10)', individually outperformed age-, gender-, and ethnicity-matched controls (*n* = 143), some significantly. Effects were found with correct identifications (hits), and correct rejections (CRs) of non-targets. There were no differences between super-recogniser groups and police group. There was, however, large score variability within police groups and within super-recogniser groups, although some low performances were easily explained (i.e., brief face learning times, unexpected context changes, unfamiliarity with celebrities, police fatigue after night shifts). Importantly, many of the lowest performing police claimed that their 15 idents had been of highly familiar suspects, with often the same suspect, or groups of suspects, identified more than once, a task not requiring exceptional ability. If these police had been excluded from analyses, effect sizes would have been far larger.

Supporting models suggesting face processing is driven by face-specific neural pathways (Gobbini & Haxby, 2007; Haxby, Hoffman, & Gobbini, 2000), no reliable between-group differences were found in an additional object (flowers) recognition test (see also Bobak, Bennetts, et al., 2016). Importantly, a few super-recognisers and police producing outstanding face memory scores were relatively poor at simultaneous face matching (see also Davis et al., 2020; Bobak, Bennetts, et al., 2016; Bobak, Dowsett, & Bate, 2016). Assuming experimenter error, we asked one super-recogniser (based on face memory tests) from the Science Museum sample to retake the 'Glasgow Face Matching Test'. His second score, below the control mean, was worse. These findings, since replicated, suggest dissociations. Some are exceptional at face memory *and* matching. Others possess superior face memory only. Later research has also found evidence for 'super-matchers', working in specialist forensic facial comparison roles whose skills may not transfer to memory tasks (e.g., White, Dunn, Schmid, & Kemp, 2015). These results match analogous findings with prosopagnosics, suggesting heterogeneous neurological and cognitive mechanisms (Bate, Haslam, Jansari, & Hodgson, 2009; De Haan, Young, & Newcombe, 1987, 1991). For policing deployment, it was clear that super-recognisers should possess superior unfamiliar face memory *and* matching ability.

Parts of the MET data were presented at a wind-down conference at New Scotland Yard for Operation Withern – the London Riots investigation (Security News Desk, 2013). As our data provided evidence that many (but not all) police who were making large numbers of idents possessed empirically tested exceptional abilities (Davis et al., 2016), the MET started describing them as super-recognisers. At the same event, the MET announced methods to capitalise on their skills, and a search for unidentified super-recognisers. Critically in terms of research impact and legacy, in December 2013, our pilot battery of multi-ethnic face recognition and matching tests was uploaded to the MET intranet. This was for an unpublished undergraduate project supervised by me (Maigut, 2014). The aim had been to test IT system utility, rather than to accurately measure ability. We were pleasantly surprised when nearly 1,500 police voluntarily started the test battery, with many leaving contact details to be invited to contribute to future research. This was fortuitous. In August 2014, we were asked by senior MET management for a list of the highest pilot test scorers (after gaining participant consent) as they wished to deploy these officers in operations that might draw on their skills. A few were eventually seconded to the MET's Super-Recognition Unit (see later).

Our pilot tests were uploaded to the MET system following an award of over €8,500,000 from European Commission research funds (Large Scale Information Exploitation of Forensic Data (LASIE), 2014). The LASIE project started in May 2014, when the MET and the University of Greenwich joined an 18-partner consortium from 10 countries. LASIE aimed to improve police digital evidence use, with a focus on CCTV footage search. My team's role was to develop super-recognition tests, to promote the concept, and for this particular grant-type, to commercially exploit intellectual property rights. For this, we compiled photos and videos of over 500 multi-ethnic volunteers as well as footage of actors in London tourist sites. Details of a 'Spotting the Face in a Crowd Test' (Davis, Treml, Forrest, & Jansari, 2018; Durova, Dimou, Litos, Daras, & Davis, 2017), and a 'Long-Term Face Memory Test' (Bretfelean & Davis, 2017; Davis et al., 2020) have been disseminated (see Davis, 2019).

The 'Spotting the Face in a Crowd Test' (Davis et al., 2018) was designed to match CCTV review operations requiring vigilance and attention to detail, skills unlikely to be possessed by all super-recognisers given its face-specific characteristics. Video clips depicted actors walking through crowded scenes. Participants had to spot the actors, identify clips empty of targets, and avoid bystanders. Participants were police from the MET super-recogniser unit (n = 7), police from the MET super-recogniser pool of front-line officers regularly viewing unidentified suspect images (n = 46), police applicants to super-recogniser roles (n = 46) and controls (n = 152). In the previous 30 months, the unit (n = 7) and established pool members (n = 46) had made a total of 3,740 idents; one had made 481. Overall, effect sizes were small, partly a consequence of low target-actor numbers and statistical power. However, the test was primarily designed to exclude police unsuitable for these roles. Some police achieving 'Cambridge Face Memory Test: Extended' (Russell et al., 2009) super-recogniser range scores performed relatively poorly – due to the test drawing on non-face processing demands. Others were exceptional on both tests. The MET Super-Recogniser Unit team outperformed other groups. They made more correct target identifications, mainly with higher confidence, and fewer false alarms of bystanders, mainly with lower confidence, demonstrating good confidence–accuracy calibration – useful in real operations. Controls engaging in pre-test actor-photo familiarisation exercises made fewer false alarms than untrained controls, a method my team have used in subsequent police training courses. The test was adapted for online testing by collaborators, the Centre of Research and

Technology, Hellas (CERTH) (Durova et al., 2017), and revised for consultancy projects.

The 'Long-Term Face Memory Test' (e.g., Bretfelean & Davis, 2017; Davis et al., 2020) incorporated delays from 1 to 56 days. We demonstrated that whereas many super-recognisers (as assessed by short-term memory tests) achieved good long-term performances, a substantial minority scored poorly (see also Davis & Tamonytė, 2017 for similar results with disguised faces).

The main conclusions of the LASIE project were that a four-component test battery was required to identify super-recognisers possessing a range of skills for policing and security:

a. Short-term face memory
b. Simultaneous face matching
c. Long-term face memory
d. Spotting faces in a crowd

Faces of different ethnicities offset cross-ethnicity-effect influence (e.g., Meissner & Brigham, 2001). To reduce deductions or guessing, proportions of new/old and mismatched/matched trials are also varied. To optimise performances, testing is protracted to reduce fatigue, and because anyone can 'have a bad day at the office', anomalously poor single-test performances can be excluded. Some organisations have deployed existing staff to new super-recogniser roles. Other research has generated new jobs in the UK and internationally. More is planned. As such, the programme has generated social impact in terms of crime detection, but also economic impact in the UK and internationally – a major driver of the UK Government's Research Excellence Framework (2021).

Our super-recognition research is ongoing. Employing electroencephalography (EEG), Belanova et al. (2018) revealed differences in super-recogniser's brain activity; super-recognisers' superiority at adult *and* infant face recognition; and that super-recognisers' cross-age effect (the difference between scores on adult and infant face recognition tests) is slightly larger than controls. One super-recogniser who worked with infants displayed higher infant than adult face recognition scores, an opposite pattern to all other participants. This finding might have applications for child victim identification, as a super-recogniser with extensive child contact might be best placed to make decisions concerning child identity. This proposal has not been fully explored. However, as part of the MET project, police seconded to the National Crime Agency's Child Exploitation and Online Protection Command completed the tests described above in 2016/2017, although all images were of adults.

Further academic research on the analogous cross-ethnicity effect (Robertson, Black, Gilmour, Chamberlain, Megreya, & Davis, 2020), and super-recognisers' ability to recognise personality traits in 'selfies' (Satchell, Davis, Julle-Danière, Tupper, & Marshman, 2019), has been published, and one of my PhD students is investigating the relationship between super-face and super-voice recognition ability (e.g. Jenkins, Tsermentseli, Monks, Robertson, Stevenage, Symons, & Davis, 2020).

The transition from research to application

Unlike most research, in which attempts to transition to application may struggle to influence organisations that might most benefit, our super-recogniser research was driven by *prior* high MET super-recogniser ident rates. Our first research mainly aimed to explain successes (Davis et al., 2013, 2016). Subsequent projects assisted police in developing new procedures to replicate successes – first within the MET, and later in the wider UK and international communities. This required the usual dissemination activities (publications, conference presentations), as well as many worldwide media appearances, exhibits in museums (Germany, Switzerland, UK), and even providing acknowledged advice to fiction and screen writers (e.g. J. S. Monroe's, *The Other You*, 2020). One book was short-listed for a Waterstones Children's Book Prize (2019). Tracy Darnton's (2018), *The Truth About Lies*, contained a URL link to take one of our super-recogniser tests.

Table 2.1 depicts a summary of my dissemination activities. Super-recognition was not always the primary focus, although all related to policing or eyewitness identification. Most of all, however, because of substantial media interest, my research team answer a constant stream of emails – often followed by phone calls, video conferences or meetings – from members of the public, worldwide police or other organisations wishing to understand the super-recogniser phenomenon and to determine whether it might help their operations. I have rarely actively marketed services. However, most organisations have not followed quotes up. Resources not only need to be put aside for the identification of super-recognisers; career development planning is required, meaning human resources departments take an interest. Often, systematic operational changes are necessary to

TABLE 2.1 List of dissemination activities and academic impact involving Dr Josh P. Davis, his collaborators or supervised students (see www.superrecognisers.com for more details)

	Presentations and Meetings[1]		*TV/Radio Interviews*		*Other Media (newspapers, online)*		*Authored Articles*	*Citations*[2]	*Participants taking CYBAST*[3]
	UK	*International*[4]	*UK*	*International*	*UK*	*International*			
2019	15	10	1	2	1	6	4	88	529,019
2018	22	9	6	17	7	22	3	96	713,634
2017	22	18	4	1	3	5	3	70	1,945,492
2016	21	14	5	5	11	12	2	67	2,590,840
2015	7	8	8	3	7	6	8	79	1,366,053
2014	17	5	1	0	4	2	1	34	–
2013	7	0	2	2	2	6	2	25	–
2012	8	2	2	1	1	0	3	32	–
2011	6	1	-	-	1	0	0	14	–
2010	4	0	-	-	1	0	3	18	–

[1] Peer-reviewed and keynote conference presentations, seminars, workshops, research consultancy dissemination meetings
[2] Google Scholar: https://scholar.google.co.uk/citations?user=Yev5EfIAAAAJ&hl=en
[3] CYBAST: Could you be a Super-Recogniser Test online participant numbers (see text for further information, and Davis, 2019)
[4] International refers to presentations outside the UK, and presentations/meetings with international police visiting London

ensure super-recognisers' skills are effectively engaged. Many organisations simply do not have the resources.

With the MET, I initially attended internal briefings and strategy meetings with senior management (up to Deputy Commissioner level), to advise on restructuring visual image management systems. Indeed, our testing of the first police super-recognisers just before the 2011 London Riots occurred at the same time as the MET was centralising these structures anyway. This was not a coincidence. Improvements in the distribution of suspect images, particularly on 'Caught on Camera', led to idents. Initially, only the inner London boroughs with blanket surveillance camera cover contributed. Additional super-recogniser testing ran parallel with outer borough realignments. Local county forces were encouraged to engage, and I gave presentations to national, and international police forces at New Scotland Yard. With fewer resources, however, smaller forces require different structures.

Organisational change inevitably faces resistance. Most consultants will encounter communication difficulties within the institutions in which they engage, and the super-recogniser programme was no different. To start with there was very little published empirical evidence, and none funded until 2014. Nonetheless, the work was first picked up by the media after the London Riots (Grimston, 2011), probably because of the title 'super-recogniser' and the implied 'super-powers'. This was both a blessing and a curse. For the criminal justice system, there are troubling, potentially prejudicial issues associated with the label, particularly if a police super-recogniser announced their status in cross-examination in court – something I always advise against. No police super-recogniser has ever scored 100% on all face recognition tests, meaning there is always some if not 'reasonable doubt' in their identification accuracy (e.g., Bate et al., 2019; Davis et al., 2016; 2018; Durova et al., 2017; Robertson, Noyes, Dowsett, Jenkins, & Burton, 2016), and although this applies to any witness, no ident should ever be accepted without question (see Davis et al., 2016; 2018). Encouragingly, the MET shared data of known super-recogniser ident errors with the media (e.g., O'Keefe, 2016), demonstrating risk acknowledgement. Compared to the proportion of idents leading to criminal charges (73%), errors, often tentative idents from low-quality images, were far less common (13%), and were mostly addressed during initial case review, *before* investigating team involvement. The lack of a criminal charge in the remaining 14% of cases does not imply misidentifications.

Cases may be discontinued for many reasons, and idents may be of witnesses not involved in a crime.

Forensic and legal connotations

Later, the MET embedded image management within its forensic science department. This instituted a more cautious approach. This was not a surprise. Worldwide, forensic science has come under scrutiny from policy-makers because of miscarriages of justice (e.g., see Innocence Project, n.d.), as well as scientific advances discrediting techniques once thought reliable (e.g., hair matching; Houck & Budowle, 2002). Experienced fingerprint experts were shown to be susceptible to cognitive biases from task-irrelevant information (e.g., Dror, Charlton, & Peron, 2006). Their decision-making could be altered from claiming a match to a mismatch and vice versa to the same set of fingerprints. As forensic facial comparison methods used by expert witnesses have been criticised (e.g., Moreton & Morley, 2011), it is not surprising that scepticism surrounding super-recognisers was high. Social and contextual information available in facial images might heighten cognitive bias risk (Edmond et al., 2015). Regardless of face processing ability, a single video frame only provides limited individuating information, and I have always noted that risks of super-recogniser error should always be acknowledged (e.g., Davis et al., 2016, 2018).

Legal researchers have discussed best-practice use of super-recognisers (e.g., Evison, 2014; Edmond & Wortley, 2016), while interdisciplinary workshops for legal experts, police, forensic scientists, criminologists and psychologists have debated how super-recognisers' evidence should be defined in law.[1] For instance, if an ident is based on prior familiarity with a suspect, a witness may provide identification evidence in court in the manner of one present at the scene of the crime (Attorney General's Reference, No.2 of 2002, 2003). Cross-examination can test the nature of the familiarity and/or whether image quality supports recognition. However, MET super-recognisers made idents of suspects never met in person but matched across images of different crimes. Some argued that these idents might best be classified as a form of ad hoc expert opinion evidence, and in which case, different standards apply. However, an expert can be cross-examined on their professional credentials, training, and experience, and case relevance. Most MET super-recognisers had simply achieved high face recognition test scores and initially received no specialist training. This created a legal anomaly, as effectively their idents were based on claims that because of their heightened skills they could see (in)consistencies in two facial images that others might not see.

In the same vein, the UK Forensic Science Regulator (Tully, 2018) argued that although super-recognisers may assist investigations, their workplace practices could not be considered forensic science as:

> a) The work is generally carried out within an operational policing unit, with no separation to ensure independence and impartiality;
> b) Photographs of known suspects or offenders are studied prior to watching the footage containing unknown individuals, without implementing safeguards against cognitive bias; and
> c) Although there is scientific literature to support the fact that some people have a greater propensity to match faces, the 'super recogniser' process of attempting to match faces from photographs against CCTV footage is not based on scientifically validated methodology, nor are error rates known.
>
> *(Tully, 2018, p. 20)*

Societal and technological challenges

My team's research programme was developing at the same time as austerity-driven cuts to policing and crime prevention in the UK, as well as increasing computerised face recognition system deployment worldwide (Big Brother Watch, 2018; BBC, 2017; Department of Home Security, 2018). Some local authorities reduced CCTV budgets, while police numbers were cut by 20,000 between 2010 and 2018 (Full Fact, 2018). Plans by some UK forces to create super-recogniser teams were cancelled. Some had already been identified by our test procedures. The requirement to restructure systems and super-recognisers' ambiguous legal status perhaps made these programmes an easy target for policymakers to abandon. Therefore, all my recent public sector research consultancy projects have been with organisations outside the UK, where funding appears less of an issue.

Computerised systems

Mass installation of CCTV cameras was the perceived panacea to the problems associated with the reliability of eyewitness identifications, and algorithms are seen as the solution for the problems associated with camera monitoring and suspect identification. Algorithms work best at places like passport control, or for one-to-one identity verification with full-face still images taken in perfect lighting with compliant targets. The annual worldwide market for computerised systems is expected to be over $2 billion in 2019 (Biometric Technology Today, 2015), partly driven by mass CCTV surveillance culture in countries more intrusive than the UK. China has an estimated 170 million CCTV cameras, many fitted with artificial intelligence (BBC News, 2017). Media articles covering algorithms have almost all been negative and often evoke the spirit of George Orwell's *1984* (Big Brother Watch, 2018; Dodd, 2018, 2018). Freedom of information requests have revealed high false-alarm rates of UK police public pilots, when systems have been used to monitor large sporting or music events. The faces of many innocent people are stored on police databases. Criticisms might be slightly unfair as these were trials, designed to evaluate system limits (see Fussey & Murray, 2019). Nevertheless, super-recognisers are often contrasted in the media as epitomising old-fashioned 'Dixon of Dock Green' policing values, when officers were expected to know all the local offenders and their associates.

Unlike humans, algorithms never sleep, and they can provide a rapid, effective search engine for identifying individuals depicted in multiple CCTV feeds. This is often accomplished by pattern recognition from clothing or paraphernalia and estimates of movement between cameras covering different locations with gaps in the field of view. Accuracy at matching faces against very large databases is improving (National Institute of Science and Technology (NIST), n.d.). However, humans may still outperform algorithms with unconstrained images (O'Toole & Phillips, 2015).

The fundamental issue will probably always remain that, legally, a human being will likely be required to make final identity decisions. And this is an avenue for future super-recogniser employment. Algorithms generate an array of matches from databases. A human decides which is most likely to be the target. Recent NIST (Phillips et al., 2018) assessments comparing the most accurate commercial algorithms with super-recognisers revealed no differences. However, the fusion of decisions from both sources produced the highest accuracy. This joint approach may offset the high false-alarm rates described earlier.

In summary, despite the cautions outlined in this section, I do believe that super-recognisers can be highly beneficial to policing and security. They may enhance operations such as surveillance and crowd monitoring, but most of all, in conjunction with effective CCTV image distribution systems, as members of a pro-active intelligence team, they may provide the first vital clue towards solving a crime. A super-recogniser ident can then be followed up by the investigating team to secure additional incriminating evidence.

The impact and legacy of the Greenwich super-recogniser research programme

The impact and legacy of the super-recogniser research programme, which started in 2011, had its origins in my research on human recognition (i.e., voices: Wilding, Scott, & Davis, 2000), eyewitness identification (e.g., Valentine et al., 2012), facial composites (e.g., Davis, Gibson, & Solomon, 2014) and field research of police identification procedures (e.g., Davis, Valentine, Memon, & Roberts, 2015). My PhD, *The Forensic Identification of Unfamiliar Faces in CCTV Images*, studied at Goldsmiths, University of London (Davis, 2007) and supervised by Tim Valentine, was partly inspired by psychologists Vicki Bruce (e.g., Bruce et al. 1999), Mike Burton (e.g., Burton et al., 1999), Graham Davies (Davies & Thasen, 2000) and Richard Kemp (Kemp et al., 1997) who had first demonstrated the unreliability of unfamiliar face matching decisions. Most of my PhD participants' data (n = 3,000+) was collected at London's Science Museum (e.g., Davis & Valentine, 2009).

Metropolitan Police Service impact

Police have for decades deployed 'spotters' at events such as football matches to identify trouble-makers (College of Policing, n.d.). Some were probably super-recognisers. These factors are hard to capture in formal assessments of impact such as my Research Excellence Framework (REF) Case Impact Study (e.g., Davis, 2014; see also Johnson & Fletcher, 2015). Although we could describe the relationship between our research results, and the high London 2011 rioter ident rates by super-recognisers, this cannot be claimed as cause and effect. The first *planned* legacy resulted from uploading our pilot tests to the MET's intranet system in 2013, in that high scorers were subsequently deployed to the following operations. These established a model to capitalise on super-recognisers' skills.

Alice Gross (August 2014)

The MET super-recognisers' first post-London riots deployment was to a west London murder investigation. This operation started after a teenager,

Alice Gross, was reported missing by her family, and the MET had collected up to 500,000 hours of CCTV footage. The super-recognisers constructed a timeline of events leading to her death and her murderer's suicide. This required excluding very large numbers of innocent bystanders. The case was solved by the team realising that the unknown murderer and victim appeared in geographically and temporally separated clips at roughly the same time.

Hillsborough Inquest (September 2014)

Other super-recognisers assisted Greater Manchester Police, the lead force on Operation Resolve. They searched TV and CCTV footage to build individual victim timelines for the second Hillsborough Stadium Disaster Inquest that had already commenced in March 2014 into the deaths of 96 people at the 1989 FA Cup semi-final between Liverpool and Nottingham Forest. The longest-running jury case in British legal history delivered a final verdict of unlawful death on 26 April 2016 (Conn, 2017). Again, this required matching victims across gaps in the field of view, while discounting thousands of other football fans.

1970 River Thames Drowning (January 2015)

My team assisted in a MET River Police investigation (Davis, Maigut, & Forrest, 2019). For this, a photo of a drowned man recovered from the River Thames in 1970 was displayed alongside a photo line-up. One line-up photo was of a man who went missing at about the same time. The others were foils selected from a larger short-list of 1970s images. Police (n = 164) provided confidence ratings to each line-up member as to whether they matched the deceased man's photo. Using the 'Wisdom of the Crowd' procedure (e.g., Surowiecki, 2004; White, Burton, Kemp, & Jenkins, 2013), the amalgamated confidence ratings of police super-recognisers were higher to the missing man's image than to foils. This added support to proposals that the deceased man and the missing man were one and the same person, evidence accepted by the coroner for issuing a death certificate.

MET super-recognisers were also deployed to pop concerts to identify pickpockets, which reduced mobile phone theft rates (Davenport, 2015). Some attended Notting Hill Carnival, where they familiarised themselves with photos of suspects in advance, to later spot them in crowds of up to one million (Venkataramanan, 2015). At a January 2015 event at New

Scotland Yard, 72 super-recognisers made 150 idents from 3,000 images (Davenport, 2015).

These successes led the MET to create the world's first Proactive Super-Recognition Unit at New Scotland Yard, mainly made up of my undergraduate student project's highest test scorers (Maigut, 2014). Very high ident rates were soon recorded. The police described some of their work as 'snapping' (as in the card game) unknown suspects depicted in new and previously unconnected cold case images stored on a very large database. This sometimes created a 'domino effect', whereby criminal associates were identified. Some suspects had never been arrested before. Before the unit's establishment, most cases would probably never have been linked or investigated, particularly when crimes occurred in different London boroughs.

Austin Caballero (January 2016)

This thief was snapped in 40 different cold-case crime-scene images captured between 30 April 2013 and 22 December 2015 (Rice, 2016). Admitting guilt, he received a two-and-a-half-year prison sentence for theft of goods worth over £100,000. Collaborators were also charged with multiple crimes (Robertson, 2016).

Ilhan Karatepe (June 2016)

This man was filmed on three bus cameras committing serial child sexual assaults. He was coincidently spotted across a rush-hour crowd by a MET super-recogniser (O'Keefe, 2016). Prior to taking our tests and joining the unit, this officer had never made an ident, or possessed any insight into her superior skills.

Many cases were solved within months (e.g., ITV Report, 2016; Manzoor, 2016). The earliest cases were possibly the most brazen, and probably, the easiest to solve. The first *published* research on the unit independently confirmed their superior simultaneous face matching abilities (Robertson et al., 2016), and 18 months after its establishment, the unit had made 2,250 idents, one quarter of the MET total (Manzoor, 2016). Although not the most reliable measure of 'ground truth of guilt', most suspects (≈70%) confessed in interview when confronted by CCTV images.

These outcomes generated substantial publicity with super-recognisers winning 'Cop of the Year' awards (e.g., Hickey, 2016); and not only in

London (e.g., BBC, 2018). PCSO Andy Pope from West Midlands Police Force was accredited with 2,000 identifications alone by 2020 (Webber, 2020). They were praised by the Mayor of London, Sadiq Khan when announcing a new anti-knife crime initiative (Mayor's Office for Policing and Crime, 2017). In 2018, they identified two alleged Russian Novichok-poisoning spies from 5,000 hours of CCTV images from Salisbury and London Gatwick Airport (Brunt, 2018). All had contributed to our research and enterprise programme.

Public impact

The impact and legacy in terms of the public awareness of my team's research have also been publicised worldwide. This started when a BBC Future online article describing the MET Super-Recogniser Unit, together with our research was linked to a fun online test ('Could you be a Super-Recogniser?') (Venkataramanan, 2015). Within a month over one million participants had taken this test, later made available in different languages. The flow of participants continues, with spikes whenever a media article on super-recognition is published. Participants from 99% of countries have contributed (including $n > 26$ on Antarctic bases). In December 2018, numbers hit six million (Davis, 2019; see Table 2.1). Many contributed to follow-up projects ($n > 100{,}000$), or left details to be invited to future research ($n > 40{,}000$, including about 5,000 super-recognisers). This should result in a substantial legacy of high-impact journal articles.

Wider policing impact

Between 2015 and 2017, my team also generated research consultancy contracts with three UK police forces, and one UK security agency. Updated four-component tests replicating those used with the MET were employed in a two-phase process (Davis, 2019). For the first online phase, the entire workforce of an organisation was encouraged to complete eight face matching and recognition tests taking about 90 minutes. The highest scorers completed the second longer phase in examination conditions.

Since 2017, additional consultancy projects have been conducted for security and police forces in two European countries (e.g., Munich Police, Stuttgart Police), one Asian country and Australia (Queensland Police Service). Most requested no publicity. In contrast, the Polizeipräsidium München (Munich Police Department) super-recogniser programme was launched by the police president and me at a press conference. This was attended by at least 5 TV companies and over 20 other media organisations. More than 5,000 out of the 7,100 workforce had started the testing process, and over 35 were identified as scoring above our super-recogniser threshold (Crossland, 2018). Within a month, more than 100,000 members of the public had contributed to the German language version of the 'Could you be a Super-Recogniser?' test, a direct link from news items to public interest in psychology. Four months after initial training at Oktoberfest, Munich Police announced that their MET-modelled Super-Recogniser Unit had solved its first 200 crimes, a success given the relatively sparse CCTV coverage in Munich, meaning crime scene images are less common, in comparison to the blanket CCTV coverage in London (Sueddeutsche Zeitung, 24 January 2019; see also Abendzeitung, 18 March 2019). Media reports can only be considered anecdotal, and not empirical evidence, although they provide a pointer to test battery validity. Indeed, the Munich Super-Recogniser Unit became a permanent department in September 2019, generating new interest in the University of Greenwich tests from other German forces.

Economic impact

In terms of economic legacy, research consultancy contracts have been agreed with one retail organisation and two other businesses including Yoti (www.yoti.com), an identity verification company. Over 50 full-time jobs in the UK and India have been created. This was partly due to high media impact. Research participants who score in the super-recogniser range on our online test battery are provided with otherwise withheld information about potential jobs. Those interested take further recruitment tests. Some are directed to the tests by the company itself. By December 2019, over 10,000 Indians had taken 4 online simultaneous multi-ethnic face matching tests, with high scorers taking a fifth test in examination conditions, when applying for jobs in Bangalore.

Academic impact

Finally, it would be imprudent of any academic to suggest that their own research might have inspired empirical investigations by others. However, it is likely that the impact on police policy and practice has generated the growing body of inspirational research into super-recognition. This research would have been the focus of an alternative type of chapter. It has driven our police and business test battery design.

Some authors have been critical, suggesting claims of super-recognisers' superiority may be overstated (Ramon, Bobak, & White, 2019). Others have criticised the use of specific tests, and published details of alternatives (e.g., Bate et al., 2018). As was highlighted in a recent edition of the *British Journal of Psychology* (e.g., Ramon et al., 2019), one of the problems is that there is no widely agreed super-recogniser definition or minimum inclusion criteria. Some argue that task-specific recruitment tests should be employed (see Noyes, Hill, & O'Toole, 2018), and that field research should establish test validity (Ramon et al., 2019). However, task-specific tests provide no flexibility if new roles for super-recognisers are suddenly required, and I have always believed the multi-test highly flexible generic regime we employ is most likely to generate positive outcomes. The thousands of idents made by Greenwich-tested MET super-recognisers provide evidence of validity. Although more published field research would be useful, during the LASIE project we found most super-recogniser idents were based on a multiplicity of factors that were not readily amenable to categorisation and quantitative analyses. I have encountered similar issues when conducting field research on alternative police identification procedures (Davis et al., 2015). And once a super-recogniser unit is established, it is almost impossible to conduct a randomised control evaluation.

Some authors propose a moratorium on super-recogniser testing for legally critical roles until a consensus is agreed (Ramon et al., 2019). However, academic research progresses at a pedestrian pace, and almost always generates conflicting findings. I share some concerns but have a pragmatic attitude. Criminals will not wait, and such a moratorium would have meant thousands of crimes in London alone would not have been solved.

To counter this anticipated 'backlash', my team have always set an exceptionally high standard before describing someone as a super-recogniser (Davis, 2019). Well under 1% of the population would achieve this standard. This is far higher than in any published super-recogniser research paper, and because of the inexactness of any cognitive test, this inevitably means some genuine super-recognisers will have been excluded. On the other hand, some organisations have been so satisfied with the calibre of their super-recogniser staff, they have extended consultancy contracts (several times) in order to recruit more.

Lessons learnt

The impact and legacy of any research programme will continue to unfold for years or even decades. Traditionally for academics, impact has been valued in terms of publications in high-quality journals, citations, grants, awards and titles. However, the Government first embedded case impact studies in the 2014 Research Excellence Framework (REF2014) (e.g. Davis, 2014). As they are weighting this factor higher in the forthcoming REF2021, the perceived worth of an academic has changed. Status is increasingly linked to entrepreneurship and delivering benefit to wider society. This includes economic benefits, as well as benefits to the direct consumers – university students. I had a pre-university business management background. This shift was relatively comfortable, even if not expected when starting a PhD. Not all colleagues are equally sanguine.

Writing this chapter has provided a perfect outlet for reflection. Perhaps the strongest lesson I can impart, is that when my super-recogniser research started in 2011, there was no sense that it could provide a fruitful research career. For a few years, precious time was spent on applying for grants in parallel or different fields. Indeed, my 2014 REF Impact Statement (Davis, 2014), 'Enhancing Suspect Identification Rates from Facial Composites and CCTV', mainly focussed on facial composite research. This is still an ongoing research avenue, as with commercial partners, VisionMetric Ltd, we were awarded a grant of £370,000 by Innovate UK in 2019 (Solomon, Gibson, & Davis, 2019).

Therefore, the first recommendation to researchers working in a niche area that might generate impact is to direct focus immediately, and generate collaborations. The weakest part of my CV is the relatively small number of high-impact peer-reviewed publications. A large body of research is complete. However, I have had no time to write it up despite, like many academics, often working 50-hour-plus weeks. I have also applied for very large- and small-scale research grants to link the super-recogniser tests we use to workplace practices. Despite good reviews, none were successful, although cross-European applications with multiple police force partners were perhaps not helped by the political climate of Brexit. Funding bodies tend to argue that organisations benefiting from research should fund it themselves. Unfortunately, austerity impact on UK policing put paid to this. As such, attempting collaborative projects with UK police forces meant that energies were directed for a long time at what now appears to be a dead end. International police often possess more resources. It seems inevitable that in the UK if changes are not made, private super-recogniser enterprises will fill the gap (see, for instance, clients: Super-Recognisers International, http://superrecognisersinternational.com), and the Association of Super-Recognisers, www.associationofsuperrecognisers.org).

The second lesson learned from funding application failures in times of austerity was the necessity to apply business experiences into developing a sustainable model of research consultancy despite the competing requirements of an academic (lectures, supervision, ever-growing administration, external examination, reviews, pastoral care, etc.). Most of my projects have been short-term and hiring research fellows with PhDs who would need training each time would have been cost-prohibitive and time consuming. To avoid conflicts of interest, I do not financially benefit from any consultancy work. Until December 2019, I had also never bought out any teaching time, the usual solution for academics with research budgets. Instead, funds have mainly paid part-time undergraduate research assistants, on regularly updated contracts. Most of the day-to-day consultancy work, such as communications with clients, collaborations with other universities, updating and piloting new tests, managing volunteers who conduct face-to-face participant testing, and training replacement staff, all provide very rare opportunities for my exceptionally high-calibre student staff to develop their research skills. This is probably the biggest *hidden* impact of my research, as many progressed to careers/further academic programmes at high-status universities/businesses unavailable to most graduates. There are far too many to mention by name, but I must acknowledge and thank them for their contribution.

A further lesson to other researchers developing their own careers in super-recognition would be to employ a full battery of diverse tests. This is important for practical and theoretical perspectives. No test will perfectly predict how anyone will transfer their skills to real work in different environments. It should also be acknowledged that the use of 'face' in this chapter sometimes refers to identity in general. Although the face is most important (Burton et al., 1999), body shape and size (Noyes et al., 2018), gait (Yovel & O'Toole, 2016) and idiosyncratic facial movement (Davis et al., 2016) facilitate recognition. Face recognition tests are often designed to standardise conditions, and to reduce floor and ceiling effects. They allow only brief learning times for familiarisation to facial stimuli; and in test phases they often require a series of rapid identification decisions without opportunity to review and reflect. In contrast, a series of careful checks and balances are included within police identification protocols that bear little relationship to standardised tests (see for instance, Police and Criminal Evidence Act (1984), Codes of Practice (Code D) for proscribed police identification procedures in England and Wales).

Another lesson learned is that researchers hoping to work on super-recogniser projects with police must identify senior champions within each force. To ensure successes are sustained, a long-term business model needs agreement with Human Resources (HR) teams. Most public sector positions are created with an equal opportunities philosophy, and the expectation that staff development and training should equip most applicants to most roles. Super-recognition, however, is not amenable to training and does not fit standard HR and promotion models. For this reason, police forces are often wary of fixed-term funded projects initiated by academics. In addition, many people working within the criminal justice system have a natural aversion to the term 'super-recogniser'. Outside policing and security, however, there are many opportunities for super-recognisers in which the recognition of infrequently encountered people might enhance job efficiency (e.g., casinos, marketing, hospitality, identity verification, public relations, media and even politics). I have provided keynote addresses at professional conferences for all these groups, and I hope these avenues generate opportunities.

This edited volume is partly concerned with how universities support staff who will likely produce research impact case studies for REF2021, as well as the REF to follow. Currently, my own institution, the University of Greenwich, supports research, teaching and enterprise career pathways. However, to maintain league-table position and to retain high-calibre staff, it might be argued that funds in future might need to be directed towards sustaining impact. This might prove politically sensitive in institutions with strong equal opportunities philosophies. I have been fortunate, and I am grateful that my employer has supported my activities. However, I have also had my fair share of hidden failures (internal and external research funding bids rejected, consultancy quotes rejected, peer-reviewed publications rejected).

To conclude, I must thank the many hundreds, if not thousands, of super-recognisers and the millions of controls who have contributed to my research. Some may have inherited their skills (e.g., Shakeshaft & Plomin, 2015), which appear to be driven by an underlying face-specific processing mechanism (Verhallen, Bosten, Goodbourn, Lawrance-Owen, Bargary, & Mollon, 2017). However, they are still affected by the cross-age (Belanova et al., 2018) and cross-ethnicity effects (Robertson et al., 2020), suggesting environmental influence. It is unlikely to be trainable. Ramon et al. (2016) demonstrated that world-record-holder memory-competition winners, the so called 'super-memorisers', performed within the typical range on face recognition tests. As such, super-recognisers may be the Usain Bolts of the cognitive world. The skill may be innate, but super-recognition may need continued experiential tuning to sustain ability. How super-recognisers do this is still a mystery.

Note

1 Interdisciplinary workshops debating super-recognisers' legal status and evidence reliability:

Unfamiliar Face Identification Group Conference 2019. *University of New South Wales, Sydney*, 8 February 2019, http://forensic.psy.unsw.edu.au/ufig_programs/UFIG 2019.pdf

Face Recognition at its Best Workshop. *University of Notre Dame (USA)*, *London*, 19 October 2017.

Super-Recognisers Workshop, *Edinburgh Napier University, Scotland*, 28 May 2016.

The Theory of 'Super Recognisers': Practice, Law and Policy. *Northumbria School of Law, University of Northumbria*, 14 April 2015.

The 10th Annual Forensic Research and Teaching Conference: Interfaces: Law and Science. *Northumbria School of Law University of Northumbria,* 3 July 2014.

References

Abendzeitung (Germany). (2019, March 18). Hooligan-Prügelei in München: 29 Schläger identifiziert. Retrieved from https://www.abendzeitung-muenchen.de/inhalt.spezialbeamte-ermitteln-hooligan-pruegelei-in-muenchen-29-schlaeger-identifiziert.cf15039c-9db7-4c76-963a-670e9658a5d6.html.

Attorney General's Reference, No.2 of 2002. (2003). EWCA Crim 2373. Retrieved from https://www.casemine.com/judgement/uk/5b46f1ed2c94e0775e7ee3e9.

Bate, S., Frowd, C., Bennetts, R., Hasshim, N., Murray, E., Bobak, A. K., … Richards, S. (2018). Applied screening tests for the detection of superior face recognition. *Cognitive Research: Principles and Implications*, *3*, 1–19.

Bate, S., Frowd, C., Bennetts, R., Hasshim, N., Portch, E., Murray, E., & Dudfield, G. (2019). The consistency of superior face recognition skills in police officers. *Applied Cognitive Psychology*, *33*(5), 828–842.

Bate, S., Haslam, C., Jansari, A., & Hodgson, T. L. (2009). Covert face recognition relies on affective valence in congenital prosopagnosia. *Cognitive Neuropsychology*, *26*(4), 391–411.

BBC News. (2009, August 24). 1,000 Cameras 'solve one crime'. Retrieved from http://news.bbc.co.uk/1/hi/8219022.stm 2009.

BBC News. (2017, December 10). In your face: China's all-seeing state. Retrieved from https://www.bbc.co.uk/news/av/world-asia-china-42248056/in-your-face-china-s-all-seeing-state.

BBC News. (2018, July 23). 'Memory cop' honored for identifying 1,000 suspects. Retrieved from https://www.bbc.co.uk/news/uk-england-birmingham-44926492.

Behrman, B. W., & Richards, R. E. (2005). Suspect/foil identification in actual crimes and in the laboratory: A reality monitoring analysis. *Law and Human Behavior, 29*(3), 279–301.

Belanova, E., Davis, J. P., & Thompson, T. (2018). Cognitive and neural markers of super-recognisers' face processing superiority and enhanced cross-age effect. *Cortex, 98*, 91–101.

Big Brother Watch. (2018). Face off: The lawless growth of facial recognition in UK policing. Retrieved from https://bigbrotherwatch.org.uk/wp-content/uploads/2018/05/Face-Off-final-digital-1.pdf.

Biometric Technology Today. (2015). Market analysts predict biometric boom. *Biometric Technology Today, 1*, 1–2.

Bobak, A. K., Bennetts, R. J., Parris, B. A., Jansari, A., & Bate, S. (2016). An in-depth cognitive examination of individuals with superior face recognition skills. *Cortex, 82*, 48–62.

Bobak, A. K., Dowsett, A. J., & Bate, S. (2016). Solving the border control problem: Evidence of enhanced face matching in individuals with extraordinary face recognition skills. *PLoS One, 11*(2), 1–13.

Bobak, A. K., Parris, B. A., Gregory, N. J., Bennetts, R. J., & Bate, S. (2017). Eye-movement strategies in developmental prosopagnosia and "super" face recognition. *The Quarterly Journal of Experimental Psychology, 70*(2), 201–217.

Bowcott, O. (2008, May 6). CCTV boom has failed to slash crime, say police. *The Guardian*. Retrieved from https://www.theguardian.com/uk/2008/may/06/ukcrime1.

Bretfelean, L.-D., & Davis, J. P. (2017, August 30). Super-recognition: Long term reliable memory of unfamiliar faces following a 'fleeting glimpse'. *Undergraduate prize winner, British Psychological Society: Cognitive section (poster presentation),* Newcastle, England.

British Security Industry Association. (n.d.). Overview. Retrieved November 16, 2018, from https://www.bsia.co.uk/Portals/4/Publications/302-bsia-overview.pdf.

Bruce, V., Henderson, Z., Greenwood, K., Hancock, P. J. B., Burton, A. M., & Miller, P. (1999). Verification of face identities from images captured on video. *Journal of Experimental Psychology: Applied, 5*(4), 339–360.

Bruce, V., Henderson, Z., Newman, C., & Burton, A. M. (2001). Matching identities of familiar and unfamiliar faces caught on CCTV images. *Journal of Experimental Psychology: Applied*, 7(3), 207–218.

Brunt, M. (2018, August 28). Super recogniser squad tracks Skripal novichok attackers. *Sky News.* Retrieved from https://news.sky.com/story/super-recognisers-help-identify-skripal-suspects-11483995.

Burton, A. M., White, D., & McNeill, A. (2010). The Glasgow face matching test. *Behavior Research Methods, 42*(1), 286–291.

Burton, A. M., Wilson, S., Cowan, M., & Bruce, V. (1999). Face recognition in poor-quality video: Evidence from security surveillance. *Psychological Science, 10*(3), 243–248.

Clark, S. E., Moreland, M. B., & Rush, R. A. (2015). Lineup composition and lineup fairness. In T. Valentine & J. P. Davis (Eds.), *Forensic facial identification: Theory and practice of identification from eyewitnesses, composites and CCTV* (pp. 211–238). Chichester: Wiley-Blackwell.

College of Policing. (n.d.). Football spotter. Retrieved December 3, 2018, from https://profdev.college.police.uk/professional-profile/football-spotter/.

Conn, D. (2017, June 28). The long road to justice: Hillsborough disaster timeline. *The Guardian.* Retrieved from https://www.theguardian.com/football/2017/jun/28/long-road-justice-hillsborough-inquest-timeline.

Crossland, D. (2018, September 22). 'Super recognisers' to spot guilty faces at Oktoberfest. *The Times.* Retrieved from https://www.thetimes.co.uk/article/super-recognisers-to-spot-guilty-faces-atoktoberfest-06tkfhbjp.

Darnton, T. (2018). *The truth about lies.* London: Stripes.

Davenport, J. (2015, July 17). Met's squad of super-recognisers is putting pickpockets out of business. *Evening Standard.* Retrieved from https://www.standard.co.uk/news/crime/mets-squad-of-super-recognisers-is-putting-pickpockets-out-of-business-10396368.html.

Davies, G., & Thasen, S. (2000). Closed-circuit television: How effective an identification aid? *British Journal of Psychology, 91*(3), 411–426.

Davis, J. P. (2007). *The forensic identification of unfamiliar faces in CCTV images* (Unpublished Doctoral Dissertation). University of London, London.

Davis, J. P. (2014). Enhancing suspect identification rates from facial composites and CCTV. *Research Excellence Framework Case Impact Study.* Retrieved from http://impact.ref.ac.uk/CaseStudies/CaseStudy.aspx?Id=64.

Davis, J. P. (2019). The worldwide public impact of identifying super-recognisers for police and business. *Cognitive Bulletin, Journal of the British Psychological Society: Cognitive Section, 4,* 17–22.

Davis, J. P., Bretfelean, D., Belanova, E., & Thompson, T. (2020). Super-recognisers: face recognition performance after variable delay intervals. *Applied Cognitive Psychology,* DOI:10.1002/acp.3712

Davis, J. P., Gibson, S., & Solomon, C. (2014). The positive influence of creating a holistic facial composite on video lineup identification. *Applied Cognitive Psychology, 28*(5), 634–639.

Davis, J. P., Lander, K., Evans, R., & Jansari, A. (2016). Investigating predictors of superior face recognition ability in police super-recognisers. *Applied Cognitive Psychology, 30*(6), 827–840.

Davis, J. P., Lander, K., & Jansari, A. (2013). I never forget a face. *The Psychologist, 26*, 726–729. Retrieved from https://thepsychologist.bps.org.uk/volume-26/edition-10/i-never-forget-face.

Davis, J. P., Maigut, A., & Forrest, C. L. D. (2019). The wisdom of the crowd: A case of post- to ante-mortem face matching by superior face matchers. *Forensic Science International, 302*, 1–6.

Davis, J. P., & Tamonytė, D. (2017). Masters of disguise: Super-recognisers' superior memory for concealed unfamiliar faces. *Proceedings of the from the seventh international conference on emerging security technologies (EST)*, Canterbury, UK.

Davis, J. P., Treml, F., Forrest, C., & Jansari, A. (2018). Identification from CCTV: Assessing police super-recognisers ability to spot faces in a crowd and susceptibility to change blindness. *Applied Cognitive Psychology, 32*(3), 337–353.

Davis, J. P., & Valentine, T. (2009). CCTV on trial: Matching video images with the defendant in the dock. *Applied Cognitive Psychology, 23*(4), 482–505.

Davis, J. P., & Valentine, T. (2015). Human verification of identity from photographic images. In T. Valentine & J. P. Davis (Eds.), *Forensic facial identification: Theory and practice of identification from eyewitnesses, composites and CCTV* (pp. 211–238). Chichester: Wiley-Blackwell.

Davis, J. P., Valentine, T., & Davis, R. E. (2010). Computer assisted facial comparison of photographic images taken from full-face and profile viewpoints. *Forensic Science International, 200*(1–3), 165–176.

Davis, J. P., Valentine, T., Memon, A., & Roberts, A. J. (2015). Identification on the street: A field comparison of police street identifications and video line-ups in England. *Psychology, Crime and Law, 1*(1), 9–27.

Davis, J. P., Valentine, T., & Wilkinson, C. (2012). Facial image comparison. In C. Wilkinson & C. Rynn (Eds.), *Craniofacial identification* (pp. 136–153). Cambridge, UK: Cambridge University Press.

De Haan, E. H., Young, A. W., & Newcombe, F. (1987). Face recognition without awareness. *Cognitive Neuropsychology, 4*(4), 385–415.

De Haan, E. H., Young, A. W., & Newcombe, F. (1991). Covert and overt recognition in prosopagnosia. *Brain, 114*(6), 2575– 2591.

Department of Home Security. (2018). *Facial recognition pilot* (DHS/USSS/PIA-024). Washington, DC: Department of Home Security. Retrieved from https://www.dhs.gov/publication/dhsussspia-024-facial-recognition-pilot.

Ditton, J., & Short, E. (1998). Evaluating Scotland's first town centre CCTV scheme. In C. Norris, J. Moran & G. Armstrong (Eds.), *Surveillance, closed circuit television and social control* (pp. 155–174.). Aldershot: Ashgate.

Dodd, V. (2011, October 24). Cost of English riots much higher than first thought, Met police report suggests. *The Guardian*. Retrieved from https://www.theguardian.com/uk/2011/oct/24/england-riots-cost-police-report.

Dodd, V. (2018, May 15). UK police use of facial recognition technology a failure, says report. *The Guardian*. Retrieved from https://www.theguardian.com/uk-news/2018/may/15/uk-police-use-of-facial-recognition-technology-failure.

Dodd, V. (2018, August 24). Facial recognition out, knife arches in at Notting Hill carnival. *The Guardian*. Retrieved from https://www.theguardian.com/culture/2018/aug/24/knife-arches-to-be-set-up-at-notting-hill-carnival.

Dror, I. E., Charlton, D., & Peron, A. (2006). Contextual information renders experts vulnerable to making erroneous identifications. *Forensic Science International, 156*(1), 74–78.

Durova, M. D., Dimou, A., Litos, G., Daras, P., & Davis, J. P. (2017). TooManyEyes: Super-recogniser directed identification of target individuals on CCTV. Proceedings from the 8th IET *international conference on imaging for crime detection and pr*evention (ICDP-17), IET *digital library*, 43–48.

Edmond, G., Davis, J. P., & Valentine, T. (2015). Expert analysis: Facial image comparison. In T. Valentine & J. P. Davis (Eds.), *Forensic facial identification: Theory and practice of identification from eyewitnesses, composites and CCTV* (pp. 239–262). Chichester: Wiley-Blackwell.

Edmond, G., & Wortley, N. (2016). Interpreting image evidence: Facial mapping, police familiars and super-recognisers in England and Australia. *Journal of International and Comparative Law, 3*(2), 473–522.

Evison, M. P. (2014). The third forensics: Images and allusions. *Policing and Society: An International Journal of Research and Policy, 1*, 1–19.

Full Fact. (2018, 11 September). Police Officer numbers in England and Wales. Retrieved from https://fullfact.org/crime/police-numbers/.

Fussey, P., & Murray, D. (2019). *Independent report on the Metropolitan Police Service's trial of live face recognition technology.* University of Essex. Retrieved from https://48ba3m4eh2bf2sksp43rq8kk-wpengine.netdna-ssl.com/wp-content/uploads/2019/07/London-Met-Police-Trial-of-Facial-Recognition-Tech-Report.pdf.

Garrett, B. L. (2011). *Convicting the innocent: Where criminal prosecutions go wrong.* Cambridge, MA: Harvard University Press.

Gill, M., Allen, J., Bryan, J., Kara, D., Little, R., Waples, S., … Swain, D. (2005). *The impact of CCTV: Fourteen case studies* (Home Office, Research Development and Statistics Directorate. Online Report 15/05). London: Home Office.

Gill, M., & Loveday, K. (2003). What do offenders think about CCTV? In M. Gill (Ed.), *CCTV* (pp. 81–91). Leicester: Perpetuity Press.

Gill, M., Smith, P., Spriggs, A., Argomaniz, J., Allen, J., Follett, M., … Swain, D. (2003). *National evaluation of CCTV: Early findings on scheme implementation – Effective practice guide* (Home Office Research, Development and Statistics Directorate: Development and Practice Report, 7). London: Home Office.

Gobbini, M. I., & Haxby, J. V. (2007). Neural systems for recognition of familiar faces. *Neuropsychologia, 45*(1), 32–41.

Grimston, J. (2011, November 20). Eagle Eye of the Yard can spot rioters by their ears. *The Times*. Retrieved from https://www.thetimes.co.uk/article/eagle-eye-of-the-yard-can-spot-rioters-by-their-ears-0568803ktdj.

H. M. Coroner for the Inner South District of Greater London. (2009). Coroner's Inquest into the death of Jean Charles de Menezes. Retrieved from http://web

archive.nationalarchives.gov.uk/20090317235546/http://www.stockwellinquest.org.uk/hearing_transcripts/index.htm.

Haxby, J. V., Hoffman, E. A., & Gobbini, M. I. (2000). The distributed human neural system for face perception. *Trends in Cognitive Sciences, 4*(6), 223–233.

Henderson, Z., Bruce, V., & Burton, A. M. (2001). Matching the faces of robbers captured on video. *Applied Cognitive Psychology, 15*(4), 445–464.

Hickey, H. (2016, February 13). Super-recogniser picks up top award at prestigious ceremony. *Police Oracle.* Retrieved from https://www.policeoracle.com/news/criminal_justice/2016/Feb/09/-super-recogniser--picks-up-top-award-at-prestigious-ceremony-_90853.html/news.

Horry, R., Memon, A., Wright, D., & Milne, R. (2012). Predictors of eyewitness identification decisions from video lineups in England: A field study. *Law and Human Behavior, 36*(4), 257–265.

Houck, M., & Budowle, B. (2002). Correlation of microscopic and mitochondrial DNA hair comparisons. *Journal of Forensic Sciences, 47*(5), 964–967.

Innocence Project. (n.d.). Innocence project. Retrieved November 16, 2018, from https://www.innocenceproject.org/.

ITV Report. (2016, June 12). Thief who stole thousands in 39 thefts finally jailed. *ITV.* Retrieved from https://www.itv.com/news/london/2016-06-10/thief-who-stole-thousands-in-39-thefts-finally-jailed/.

Jenkins, R., Tsermentseli, S., Monks, C. P., Robertson, D. J., Stevenage, S. V., Symons, A. E., & Davis, J. P. (2020, January 3). I remember you: Super-recognisers of faces display superior cross-modal skills with voices. doi:10.31234/osf.io/7xdp3.

Johnson, S., & Fletcher, B. (2015). Evaluating the economic impact of social science: Case studies of REF impact projects. Retrieved from https://esrc.ukri.org/files/research/research-and-impact-evaluation/hull-valuation-report/.

Kemp, R., Towell, N., & Pike, G. (1997). When seeing should not be believing: Photographs, credit cards and fraud. *Applied Cognitive Psychology, 11*(3), 211–222.

Kennerknecht, I., Grueter, T., Welling, B., Wentzek, S., Horst, J., Edwards, S., & Grueter, M. (2006). First report of prevalence of non-syndromic hereditary prosopagnosia (HPA). *American Journal of Medical Genetics, 140*(15), 1617–1622.

Kennerknecht, I., Ho, N. Y., & Wong, V. C. (2008). Prevalence of hereditary prosopagnosia (HPA) in Hong Kong Chinese population. *American Journal of Medical Genetics Part A, 146A*(22), 2863–2870.

Lander, K., Bruce, V., & Hill, H. (2001). Evaluating the effectiveness of pixilation and blurring on masking the identity of familiar faces. *Applied Cognitive Psychology, 15*(1), 101–116.

LASIE Partners. (2014, May 2014). Large scale information exploitation of forensic data (LASIE). *European Commission 7th Framework Programme. SEC-2013.1.6-1: 607480*, €8,406,523.35. Retrieved from http://www.lasie-project.eu/.

Maigut, A. (2014). *Individual differences in face recognition, face matching and object recognition.* (Unpublished BSc Dissertation). University of Greenwich, UK.

Manzoor, S. (2016, November 5). You look familiar: On patrol with the Met's super-recognisers. *The Guardian*. Retrieved from https://www.theguardian.com/uk-news/2016/nov/05/metropolitan-police-super-recognisers.

Mayor's Office for Policing and Crime (MOPAC). (2017). The London knife crime strategy. Retrieved from https://www.london.gov.uk/sites/default/files/mopac_knife_crime_strategy_june_2017.pdf.

McCahill, M., & Norris, C. (2003). *CCTV in Britain* (Urban Eye Working Paper No. 3). Retrieved from http://www.urbaneye.net/results/results.htm.

Meissner, C. A., & Brigham, J. C. (2001). Thirty years of investigating the own-race bias in memory for faces: A meta-analytic review. *Psychology, Public Policy, and Law*, 7(1), 1–35.

Monroe, J. S. (2020). *The other you*. London: Head of Zeus.

Moreton, R., & Morley, J. (2011). Investigation into the use of photoanthropometry in facial image comparison. *Forensic Science International*, *212*(1–3), 231–237.

Munsterberg, H. (1908). *On the witness stand: Essays on psychology and crime*. New York, NY: Doubleday.

National Institute of Science and Technology (NIST). (n.d.). Face recognition vendor test (FRVT) ongoing. Retrieved December 8, 2018, from https://www.nist.gov/programs-projects/face-recognition-vendor-test-frvt-ongoing.

Norris, C., McCahill, M., & Wood, D. (2004). The growth of CCTV: A global perspective on the international diffusion of video surveillance in publicly accessible space. *Surveillance and Society*, *2*(2/3), 110–135.

Noyes, E., Hill, M. Q., & O'Toole, A. J. (2018). Face recognition ability does not predict person identification performance: Using individual data in the interpretation of group results. *Cognitive Research: Principles and Implications*, *3*(1), 23.

O'Keefe, P. (2016, August 22). The detectives who never forget a face. *The New Yorker*. Retrieved from http://www.newyorker.com/magazine/2016/08/22/londons-super-recognizer-police-force.

O'Toole, A., & Phillips, P. J. (2015). Evaluating automatic face recognition systems with human benchmarks. In T. Valentine & J. P. Davis (Eds.), *Forensic facial identification: Theory and practice of identification from eyewitnesses, composites and CCTV* (pp. 263–283). Chichester: Wiley-Blackwell.

Phillips, P. J., Yates, A. N., Hu, Y., Hahn, C. A., Noyes, E., Jackson, K., … O'Toole, A. J. (2018). Face recognition accuracy of forensic examiners, super-recognizers, and face recognition algorithms. *Proceedings of the National Academy of Science (PNAS)*, *115*(24), 6171–6176.

Police and Criminal Evidence Act. (1984). *PACE code D 2017*. London: Home Office. Retrieved May 29, 2019, from https://www.gov.uk/government/publications/pace-code-d-2017.

R v Clarke [1995] 2 Cr App R 425 (England and Wales).

Ramon, M., Bobak, A., & White, D. (2019). Super-recognizers: From the lab to the world and back again. *British Journal of Psychology*, *110*(3), 461–479.

Ramon, M., Miellet, S., Dzieciol, A. M., Konrad, B. N., Dresler, M., & Caldara, R. (2016). Super-memorizers are not super-recognizers. *PLoS One*, *11*(3), 1–24.

Research Excellence Framework 2021. (n.d.). Retrieved from https://www.ref.ac.uk/.

Rice, X. (2016, August 2). The super-recognisers of Scotland Yard. *New Statesman*. Retrieved from http://www.newstatesman.com/politics/uk/2016/08/super-recognisers-scotland-yard.

Robertson, A. (2016, April 2). Serial thief who pilfered more than £100,000 in jewellery, handbags, clothes and antiques from luxury London boutiques is finally caught after Scotland Yard brings in its team of 'super recognisers'. *Daily Mail*. Retrieved from https://www.dailymail.co.uk/news/article-3520488/Serial-thief-pilfered-100-000-jewellery-handbags-clothes-antiques-luxury-London-boutiques-finally-caught-Scotland-Yard-brings-team-super-recognisers.html.

Robertson, D., Black, J., Chamberlain, B., Megreya, A. M., & Davis, J. P. (2020). Super-recognisers show an advantage for other race face identification. *Applied Cognitive Psychology*, *34*(1), 205–216.

Robertson, D. J., Noyes, E., Dowsett, A. J., Jenkins, R., & Burton, A. M. (2016). Face recognition by Metropolitan Police super-recognisers. *PLoS One*, *11*(2), 1–8.

Rossion, B., Caldara, R., Seghier, M., Schuller, A. M., Lazeyras, F., & Mayer, E. (2003). A network of occipitotemporal face-sensitive areas besides the right middle fusiform gyrus is necessary for normal face processing. *Brain*, *126*(11), 2381–2395.

Russell, R., Chatterjee, G., & Nakayama, K. (2012). Developmental prosopagnosia and super-recognition: No special role for surface reflectance processing. *Neuropsychologia*, *50*(2), 334– 340.

Russell, R., Duchaine, B., & Nakayama, K. (2009). Super-recognizers: People with extraordinary face recognition ability. *Psychonomic Bulletin and Review*, *16*(2), 252–257.

Satchell, L., Davis, J. P., Julle-Danière, E., Tupper, N., & Marshman, P. (2019). Recognising faces but not traits: Accurate personality judgment from faces is unrelated to superior face memory. *Journal of Research in Personality*, *79*, 49–58.

Security News Desk. (2013, September 24). Conference report: Police embracing CCTV as a forensic discipline. *Security News Desk*. Retrieved from http://www.securitynewsdesk.com/conference-report-police-embracing-cctv-as-a-forensic-discipline/.

Shakeshaft, N. G., & Plomin, R. (2015). Genetic specificity of face recognition. *Proceedings of the National Academy of Sciences of the United States of America*, *112*(41), 12887–12892.

Solomon, C., Gibson, S., & Davis, J. P. (2019). Deep learning strategies for accurate identification from facial composite images (E2ID). *Innovate UK*. February 2019.

Sueddeutsche Zeitung (Germany). (2019, January 24). "Super-recogniser" helfen bei 200 Fällen. Retrieved from https://www.sueddeutsche.de/muenchen/super-recogniser-polizei-gesichtserkenner-1.4301590.

Surowiecki, J. (2004). *The wisdom of crowds.* New York, NY: Random House.

Tardif, J., Duchesne, X. M., Cohan, S., Royer, J., Blais, J., Fiset, D., … Gosselin, F. (2019). Use of face information varies systematically from developmental prosopagnosics to super-recognizers. *Psychological Science, 30*(2), 300.

Tully, G. (2018). Forensic science regulator annual report (November 2016–November 2017). Retrieved from https://assets.publishing.service.gov.uk/government/uploads/system/uploads/attachment_data/file/674761/FSRAnnual_Report_2017_v1_01.pdf.

Valentine, T., & Davis, J. P. (2015). *Forensic facial identification: Theory and practice of identification from eyewitnesses, composites and CCTV.* Chichester: Wiley-Blackwell.

Valentine, T., Davis, J. P., Memon, A., & Roberts, A. (2012). Live showups and their influence on a subsequent video lineup. *Applied Cognitive Psychology, 26*(1), 1–23.

Venkataramanan, M. (2015, June 11). The super power police now use to tackle crime. *BBC future.* Retrieved from http://www.bbc.com/future/story/20150611-the-superpower-police-now-use-to-tackle-crime.

Verhallen, R. J., Bosten, J. M., Goodbourn, P. T., Lawrance-Owen, A. J., Bargary, G., & Mollon, J. D. (2017). General and specific factors in the processing of faces. *Vision Research, 141,* 217–222.

Webber, E. (2020, February 16). Eagle-eyed police super recogniser spotted a record 406 wanted suspects in 2019 including 16 in one day to help solve attempted murder, sex assault and theft cases. *Daily Mail.* Retrieved from https://www.dailymail.co.uk/news/article-8010123/Eagle-eyed-police-super-recogniser-spotted-record-406-wanted-suspects-2019.html.

White, D., Burton, A. M., Kemp, R. I., & Jenkins, R. (2013). Crowd effects in unfamiliar face matching. *Applied Cognitive Psychology, 27*(6), 769–777.

White, D., Dunn, J. D., Schmid, A. C., & Kemp, R. I. (2015). Error rates in users of automatic face recognition software. *PLoS One, 10*(10), 1–14.

White, D., Kemp, R. I., Jenkins, R., Matheson, M., & Burton, A. M. (2014). Passport officers' errors in face matching. *PLoS One, 9*(8), 1–6.

Wilding, J., Cook, S., & Davis, J. P. (2000). Sound familiar? *Psychologist, 13*(11), 558–562. Retrieved from https://thepsychologist.bps.org.uk/volume-13/edition-11/sound-familiar.

Wilmer, J. B., Germine, L., Chabris, C. F., Chatterjee, G., Williams, M., Loken, E., … Duchaine, B. (2010). Human face recognition ability is specific and highly heritable. *Proceedings of the National Academy of Sciences of the United States of America, 107*(11), 5238–5241.

Yoti. (2018, 22 November). Yoti launched a year ago! So what's next? Retrieved December 2, 2018, from https://www.yoti.com/blog/yoti-launched-a-year-ago-so-whats-next/.

Young, A. W., & Noyes, E. (2019). We need to talk about super-recognisers. *British Journal of Psychology, 110*(3), 492–494.

Yovel, G., & O'Toole, A. J. (2016). Recognizing people in motion. *Trends in Cognitive Sciences, 20*(5), 383–395.

3

FORENSIC QUESTIONING

Ching-Yu S. Huang, Samantha J. Andrews, Sarah J. Krähenbühl and Megan Hermolle

Introduction: the context of forensic questioning research and practice

Since a series of day care sex abuse scandals in the 1980s and early 1990s, it has been recognised that child witnesses have dispositional vulnerabilities that affect the quality of evidence they provide to the police and the courts. Such vulnerabilities present serious issues with regard to the effective operation of justice in these very important types of crime. In order for witnesses, especially vulnerable ones, to provide the best evidence, the practice of forensic questioning plays a pivotal role in criminal justice proceedings. Therefore, since the 1980s, the field of forensic questioning has received increasing attention from psychological researchers with the aim of improving the quality of evidence elicited from vulnerable witnesses and suspects.

Forensic questioning refers to the structured conversations between legal professionals and victims, witnesses and suspects to gather and/or present testimonial evidence. In the context of an alleged personal crime, in most adversarial countries, questioning of parties occurs at the investigation stage of the process during forensic interviews conducted primarily by police officers, and, should the case proceed to trial, during direct- and cross-examination of parties in court by prosecutors and defence lawyers, respectively. The core theoretical foundations of this field are multifaceted, drawing primarily from developmental, cognitive, and social psychology, and have been used to underpin basic research that drives applied recommendations to legal practice and policy. As such, forensic questioning has been able to make large advances in developing evidence-based best-practice techniques for practitioners to aid vulnerable victims/witnesses, and suspects in giving their best evidence in legal settings, and ultimately improving the chances that justice is achieved (see Clarke & Milne, 2001; Lamb, Brown, Hershkowitz, Orbach, & Esplin, 2018; Spencer & Lamb, 2012). Such developments showcase how theory and basic research can effectively translate into impactful changes. However, despite these achievements, there remains a number of ongoing applied challenges within the field.

This chapter begins by outlining the underpinning research and theories around forensic questioning, then describes how such research has been applied in the field to inform its best practice. Thereafter, some of the issues faced with its implementation and maintenance over time will be discussed. These pertinent challenges to the preservation of best practice are then identified in the impact and legacy of the research section, including 1) the difficulties in translating research to practice, 2) the use and efficacy of interpreters in forensic questioning, 3) the effectiveness of special measures for vulnerable witnesses, and 4) public attitudes towards victimisation and perpetration that influence practice and policy. The theory and research contextualising and underpinning each of these challenges are outlined, before discussion of how the research has been applied in practice, as well as the impact and legacy of the research. The chapter concludes by drawing together the lessons we have learnt in the field, providing advice to applied researchers, practitioners and policymakers on the basis of our reviews and experiences.

Underpinning research and theory for forensic questioning

The field of forensic questioning has received increasing attention within the past four decades from researchers as well as practitioners. As such, a 'best-practice' forensic questioning approach, seeking to achieve optimal methods to elicit productive and reliable accounts from those being interviewed, has been developed and implemented in many jurisdictions around the world. With detailed and consistent accounts from victims and suspects, triers of fact (e.g., police officers in forensic interviews; jurors and judges in courtroom examinations) are more accurately able to assess the testimony for veracity (see Henderson & Andrews, 2017), thus contributing to the better attainment of just decisions. Whilst what constitutes best practice is somewhat dependent on the purpose and requirements of the context and the role of the person under questioning, the general emphasis remains the same; to provide victims, witnesses and/or suspects with the opportunity to give their best evidence (Victims and Witnesses (Scotland) Act, 2014). In order to ensure equality within the justice system, best practice should be endorsed for all witnesses and suspects in all contexts, as opposed to merely vulnerable and intimidated witnesses (Home Office, 1999).

Nonetheless, it has been recognised that some witnesses, such as children and those with intellectual disabilities, have dispositional vulnerabilities that can significantly affect the quality of evidence they provide in forensic questioning. For example, younger children have typically been found to have poorer language abilities than older children (see Walker, Kenniston, & Inada, 2013 for a review), can have difficulties distinguishing between fantasy and reality (e.g., Roberts & Lamb, 2009), struggle with monitoring the source of their memories (e.g., Earhart & Roberts, 2014; Thierry & Spence, 2002) and are typically viewed as more suggestible than older children and adults (e.g., Ceci, Ross, & Toglia, 1987; Otgaar, Candel, Smeets, & Merckelbach, 2010, but see Otgaar, Howe, Merckelbach, & Muris, 2018). At the time, these findings led young children, in particular, to be viewed as unreliable witnesses, contributing to the difficulties with successfully prosecuting cases that relied in large part on children's testimony (e.g., child sex abuse cases, see Ceci & Bruck, 1995). However, experimental research, where baseline account accuracy can be established, has since shown that these issues can be circumvented by changing questioning practices to accommodate dispositional vulnerabilities, and this has been confirmed by subsequent field research (see Lamb et al., 2018 for a review).

Adults who are deemed to be vulnerable may present as having a mental or physical disorder or disability, or an impairment of intelligence and social functioning. These vulnerable adults are over-represented in the criminal justice system, both as defendants (Baldry, Dowse, & Clarence, 2011; Woodbury-Smith & Dein, 2014) and as victims (Browning & Caulfield, 2011; Petersilia, 2001; Vanny, Levy, Greenberg, & Hayes, 2009). One area of vulnerability that has received considerable research attention has been that of witnesses with autism spectrum disorder. Such vulnerable witnesses may have memory deficits that adversely affect their ability to provide free recall (Boucher, Mayes, & Bigham, 2012; Bowler, Gaigg & Gardiner, 2008) in investigative contexts. The majority of this research has been conducted with child witnesses and victims (for example see Henry et al., 2017; Mattison, Dando & Ormerod, 2018) exploring the use of additional or alternative means of support for such witnesses that can in theory be utilised in certain types of investigative interviews with such vulnerable adults.

From research to application

The accumulated research knowledge has led to the construction of evidence-informed best-practice guidance for questioning vulnerable witnesses, such as the revised National Institute of Child Health and Human Development (NICHD) Investigative Interview Pl (Hershkowitz, Lamb, & Katz, 2014) and Achieving Best Evidence (ABE) Guidelines (Ministry of Justice, 2011) for forensic interviews, and The Inns of Court College of Advocacy (ICCA) revised 20 principles of questioning national training programme (ICCA, 2019) for courtroom questioning. Within these protocols and/or the bodies of work that underpin the continual development of this guidance, there is general consensus of what best practice for vulnerable witnesses consists of.

Identify the key vulnerabilities

Before conducting any questioning, it is important to know what dispositional vulnerabilities the witness may possess and how these may affect interactions and responses to questioning. Vulnerability is legally considered to be a characteristic wherein the quality of evidence is likely to be diminished due to the witness, 1) being under the age of 18 years old, 2) suffering from a mental disorder within the meaning of the Mental Health Act (1983), 3) has significant impairment of intelligence and social functioning, 4) has a physical disability or is suffering from a physical disorder, or is 5) an intimidated witnesses (i.e., involved in an offence falling with section 35(3)(a) (sexual offences etc.), or an offence falling within section 35(3)(b), (c) or (d) (kidnapping, assaults, etc.) (Home Office, 1999). Of course, there are less adverse forms of vulnerability that may not be picked up by forensic interviewers or courts under this Act, or even not be visible or known to the witness and their guardians, but which still affect the witnesses' ability to give their best evidence. Examples may include undiagnosed mental health disorders or even having to give evidence in a second language (Bartels, 2011).

Importance of planning

Planning the structure and content of the prompts to be asked of witnesses in advance of questioning has been identified as one of the most important aspects of forensic questioning (Smith & Milne, 2011, but see a review of blind interviewing to reduce interview bias and expectancy effects, Rohrabaugh, London, & Hall, 2016). Many guidelines emphasise common features of interview preparation, including consideration of information about the child, such as any vulnerabilities they possess, consideration of information about the alleged event in order to generate and test hypotheses during questioning (Poole & Lamb, 1998), the context of the interview, such as the location, time of day, and presence of any support persons in the room, as well as any practical considerations, such as the use of video and audio recording equipment (see Rohrahbaugh et al., 2016). Careful forward planning encourages interviewers to think about the key issues that they need to question the witnesses about and the appropriate form that those questions should take (e.g., the 'ask, don't talk' premise, ICCA, 2019), as well as ensures the questioning is paced at a suitable level, chronological and signposted, thus easier for witnesses to understand and engage with (Dando, Ormerod, Wilcock, & Milne, 2011; Fisher & Geiselman, 2010). Planning may also aid in alleviating potential situations where question content may cause witnesses to become particularly distressed or behaviourally difficult.

Rapport-building and supportiveness

Best-practice guidance emphasises that rapport, that is, the development of mutual trust, respect and affinity between interviewer and interviewee, should be established before any substantive abuse-related questioning occurs, and should be maintained during the course of the interaction (Hershkowitz, Lamb, Katz, & Malloy, 2013). This can be achieved by discussing neutral events at the beginning of the interaction, maintaining eye contact and engagement throughout the interview, empathising during periods of emotion, and facilitating speech with supportive utterances and open body language (Lamb, Hershkowitz, Orbach & Esplin, 2011). Building and maintaining rapport has been found to improve the quantity and quality of the evidence that witnesses provide, improve witness concentration and cooperation (Abbe & Brandon, 2014; Roberts, Lamb, & Sternberg, 2004; Teoh & Lamb, 2010) and lower the proportion of misinformation and inaccurate information (Vallano & Schreiber Compo, 2011; Goodman-Delahunty & Martschuk, 2016).

Ground rules

It is important that all those that are to be questioned are well informed about practical matters relating to the interview, such as the need for video and/or audio-recording, that the interviewer may take notes during the interview and, in court, the importance of not talking to other witnesses before they have testified, to avoid collusion. Furthermore, forensic questioning can be unusual and difficult for children, in particular, who are accustomed to being tested by knowledgeable adults (Lyon, 2010), and often feel pressured to answer adults' questions (Earhart, La Rooy, Brubacher, & Lamb, 2014). Lawyers may also question children using complicated prompts about events that occurred long ago (Andrews, Lamb, & Lyon, 2015; Hanna, Davies, Crothers, & Henderson, 2012; Spencer & Lamb, 2012), making it critical to prepare children for their unique roles as witnesses by providing them with ground rules, which includes instructing them not to guess and to express uncertainty when they do not understand or know the answers to questions (i.e., the 'I don't know' ground rule).

Studies have shown that pre-interview instructions encouraging children to use ground rules lead them to use the rules appropriately more often, though the instruction did not affect responses to non-misleading questions (Mulder & Vrij, 1996; Waterman & Blades, 2011). This lack of impact was particularly true when children practised using ground rules prior to substantive questioning (Danby, Brubacher, Sharman, & Powell, 2015; see Brubacher, Poole, & Dickinson, 2015, for a review). As such, this guidance is expressly written into forensic interview guidance (e.g., ABE Guidelines; the NICHD Protocol). However, these recommendations have not been translated into practice in court. In one courtroom study analysing rates of children's uncertainty (Andrews, Ahern, & Lamb, 2017), it was found that lawyers rarely stated the 'I don't know' ground rule, and never practised it with children. Therefore, as in Earhart et al.'s (2014) study, the presentation of the don't know/remember ground rule was not associated with a significant increase in the frequency with which children expressed uncertainty. It has therefore been emphasised that lawyers should practise the use of ground rules to check children's understanding of its use, and ground rules should be reiterated throughout proceedings (Andrews et al., 2017).

Question types

The types of questions used to elicit accounts of vulnerable witnesses' experiences affect both the quantity and quality of the information they provide (Lamb, Malloy, Hershowitz, & La Rooy, 2015). On the one hand, when questioned with open-ended free-recall invitations (e.g., 'Tell me what happened'; 'You mentioned X. Tell me more about that') and cued-recall directive (wh-) prompts (e.g., 'What did he do?'; 'Where did this happen?'), young witnesses provide accounts that may be brief but are more likely to be accurate, whereas the probability that responses will be erroneous increases considerably when children are questioned using closed-ended recognition prompts (e.g., 'Did he touch you with his fingers?'), due to the false recognition of details and response biases (Lamb, Orbach, Hershkowitz, Horowitz, & Abbott, 2007). Suggestive prompts (e.g., 'He hurt you, didn't he?') are most problematic because witnesses, especially young children, may change details in their accounts and thus respond inconsistently, either by incorporating suggested information or acquiescing to perceived interviewer coercion (London & Kulkofsky, 2010). Interviewing guidelines therefore emphasise the need to utilise open-ended, free- and cued-recall questions as far as possible, and avoid the use of suggestive questions, particularly leading tag questions (e.g., 'He hurt you, didn't he?') and questions phrased as statements (e.g., 'He hit you?') (Lamb et al., 2018).

Question repetition

Repeated questions provide witnesses with opportunities to change their initially correct or incorrect responses and are common in forensic interviews (Krähenbühl, Blades, & Westcott, 2010; La Rooy & Lamb, 2011) and courtroom examinations (Andrews, Lamb, & Lyon, 2015). Experimental studies indicate that children are more likely to contradict their answers when closed-ended questions are repeated than when open-ended questions are repeated (e.g., Krähenbühl & Blades, 2009; Quas, Davis, Goodman, & Myers, 2007). Children may change details in their accounts and thus respond inconsistently (Lamb & Fauchier, 2001; Zajac, Gross, & Hayne, 2003), perhaps believing that the questioners were unsatisfied with their initial answers or that their initial answers were incorrect (e.g., Howie, Kurukulasuriya, Nash, & Marsh, 2009; Howie, Nash, Kurukulasuriya, & Bowman, 2012; Melinder, Scullin, Gravvold, & Iversen, 2007). Since triers of fact often place emphasis on report consistency when assessing the credibility of oral testimony (Bruer & Pozzulo, 2014; Myers, Redlich, Goodman, Prizmich, & Imwinkelried, 1999; Semmler & Brewer, 2002), the adverse effects that inappropriate question repetition may have on children's testimony is concerning.

However, repeated questions do not necessarily degrade the accuracy of children's accounts (see Lyon, 2002). For example, in experimental studies, children provide additional accurate information that was not reported earlier when asked repeated open-ended prompts (Memon & Vartoukian, 1996; Poole & White, 1991). Furthermore, in forensic settings questions may need to be repeated to make the requests clear, to clarify details previously mentioned by the children (e.g., ambiguous or unclear responses) or to encourage children who are anxious or reluctant (Andrews & Lamb, 2014; La Rooy & Lamb, 2011). It is therefore recommended, though not incorporated in all guidance, that the need to sometimes repeat questions is emphasised when explaining the ground rules to witnesses, that questions are only repeated using open-ended prompts, and that witnesses are provided with a rationale for any question repetition (Andrews & Lamb, 2017).

The impact and legacy of the research

There is no doubt that the field has made considerable advances in improving the quality of evidence that witnesses are afforded to give when questioned in forensic settings due to the development of best-practice guidelines. The research has profoundly impacted the way forensic questioning is conducted in the field (for an overview, see Newlin et al., 2015). However, several challenges remain when attempting to translate research into practice and policy improvements. These include 1) difficulties in translating research into practice, 2) the use and efficacy of interpreters in forensic questioning, 3) the effectiveness of special measures for vulnerable witnesses and 4) public attitudes towards victimisation and perpetration.

The difficulties in translating research into practice

Take courtroom questioning, for example; a growing body of evidence has suggested that the linguistic complexity and content of questions can affect the quality of evidence elicited from vulnerable witnesses. One major concern is that children may not possess the linguistic capacity and psychological competence necessary to effectively comprehend and respond to courtroom questioning (Hanna, Davies, Henderson, Crothers, & Rotherham, 2010; Zajac, O'Neill, & Hayne, 2012). Indeed, children seldom request clarification of grammatically complex and/or nonsensical questions (Carter, Bottoms, & Levine, 1996; Zajac, Gross, & Hayne, 2003), perhaps because they have difficulty detecting whether or not they have understood the requests. Worryingly, field research has confirmed that many of the questions that lawyers ask are linguistically complex (Andrews & Lamb, 2017). In terms of content, research further demonstrates that witnesses are asked a large proportion of questions that prompt temporal information (Andrews & Lamb, 2018), that children in particular struggle to comprehend and answer accurately (e.g., Droit-Volet & Izaute, 2005; Wandrey, Lyon, Quas, & Friedman, 2012; Zélanti & Droit-Volet, 2011). Furthermore, it has been found that lawyers typically ask many questions focused on peripheral (non-plot) aspects of the alleged event, rather than central (plot-relevant) details. This is concerning since in both laboratory and analogue contexts, central details are more accessible in memory than peripheral details (Ibabe & Sporer, 2004), and thus children respond more accurately to questions about central features than questions about peripheral details (e.g., Almerigogna, Ost, Akehurst, & Fluck, 2008; Candel, Merckelbach, Jelicic, Limpens, & Widdershoven, 2004; Saywitz, Goodman, Nicholas, & Moan, 1991).

Despite these findings being well supported, they have yet to be systematically incorporated into best-practice guidance. Moreover, another poignant and controversial difficulty is the resistance in the translation of evidence-based best-practice for suspects and for questioning in the courtroom. As readers may have noticed above, best-practice guidelines are overwhelmingly focused on supporting vulnerable witnesses giving evidence in forensic interview settings. Guidance of substantive evidence-based questioning practices and conduct is sparser when interviewing suspects (see the Police and Criminal Evidence Act, 1984), and when witnesses and defendants are direct- and cross-examined. This is partially due to there being considerably more research conducted on witnesses than suspects, and on forensic interview than courtroom settings, but also due to concerns that best-practices may interfere with the adversarial justice system (the defence and the prosecution each collect and present evidence, and argue in front of the judge at court on behalf of the side they represent) and prevent defendants from suitably challenging the evidence put against them (European Court of Human Rights (1953) Article 6 (3d), of the European Convention on Human Rights). However, because triers-of-fact must determine guilt or innocence based on the evidence presented, it is necessary to provide them with the most reliable evidence possible (Henderson & Andrews, 2017). Veracity can be assessed more accurately when children provide narrative accounts in the course of examinations adhering to the best-practice guidelines (see Earhart, La Rooy, & Lamb, 2016; Henderson & Andrews, 2017; Hershkowitz, Fisher, Lamb, & Horowitz, 2007).

We would suggest that for a trial to be fair, evidence needs to be elicited in accordance with research-informed best-practice guidelines. However, even where guidance is in force, there is evidence to suggest that practice is still not optimal. For example, a recent study of prosecutors in the United States found substandard rapport-building between prosecutors and child witnesses (Ahern, Stolzenberg, & Lyon, 2015). Research in British courts has further found that the linguistic and cognitive demands made by lawyers' questions continued to exceed the developmental capabilities of vulnerable witnesses, to the detriment of their testimonial credibility (Andrews & Lamb, 2017; Henderson, Andrews, & Lamb, 2018). There is also a systematic failure of practitioners to maintain best practice once its premise is understood and implemented into forensic interviewer training (Lamb, Sternberg, Orbach, Hershkowitz, Horowitz, & Esplin, 2002). Together, this suggests that there are serious problems not only in implementing best practices, but, despite decades of intervention and training, practitioners and institutions routinely fail to maintain best practice (see Lamb, 2016, for a detailed discussion on the difficulties in translating research to practice).

The use and efficacy of interpreters in forensic questioning

Legal professionals often come across people who do not speak the same languages (Mulayim, Lai, & Norma, 2014). In such circumstances, the service of an interpreter is required to facilitate and enable communication. Whilst research-informed best-practice guidelines exist for investigators to guide the forensic questioning practice, practical guidelines pertaining to how the interpreters should be involved in the interview as well as research on how interpreters affect the interview are still lacking. Non-native speakers are faced with a range of communication barriers, placing them in a vulnerable position in the criminal justice system. For instance, native speakers, compared to non-native speakers, have a larger vocabulary and thus can better express themselves when being questioned (Ullman, 2001), thus they often give longer and more detailed responses (Ewens,

Vrij, Leal, Mann, Jo, & Fisher, 2016). Non-native speakers may show 'message reduction' (Dornyei & Scott, 1995) – leaving out important information when reporting – simply due to lack of vocabulary and knowledge on how to convey these details in the target language (Huang, 2010). Non-native speaking interviewees may choose to provide a shorter statement which includes less detail in order to lower the cognitive demand, as speaking in a foreign language is cognitively demanding (Evans, Michael, Meissner, & Brandon, 2013). Neurologically speaking, people say less when speaking in a foreign language because they need to actively inhibit neural control mechanisms that would otherwise automatically make them respond in their first language (Wang, Xue, Chen, Xue, & Dong, 2007). Socio-cultural factors can also contribute to such 'message reduction'. For instance, cultural self-construal can affect the processes of how one remembers and determines the perceived importance of autobiographical memory during self and identity construction (Wang, 2001; 2004). This then influences how, what and whether personal experiences are remembered (e.g., Peterson, Wang, & Hou, 2009; Wang, 2004; Wang & Conway, 2004), and these cultural linguistic differences can be seen in children as young as three to four years of age (Wang, 2006).

Other than communication barriers, there are also practical challenges in interpreted interviews. The first major challenge with interpreter-mediated interviews is the accuracy/impartiality of the interpretation (Salaets & Balogh, 2015). Public service interpreters are expected to remain neutral and interpret everything that has been said with a high degree of accuracy. The perception of interpreter simply being a computer – which merely calculates what the corresponding words are in the alternate language and transmits them directly – prevails amongst the service users in the legal sectors (Böser, 2013; Smith, 2016). However, languages do not have a one-to-one correspondence with each other, thus interpreters must bring their subjective judgement into their work. Although professional interpreters strive to adhere to the principle of accuracy, in practice, whether and how much this can be maintained is subject to influence by various factors (Berk-Seligson, 2002). Findings from many studies reveal that the linguistic content of the utterances within the interaction is not always accurately replicated and that interpretations are often edited (Angelelli, 2004; Aranguri, Davison, & Ramirez, 2006; Nakane, 2008). Sometimes interpreters violate the principle of accuracy by 'repairing' originally ambiguous or poorly worded utterances (Nakane, 2008), motivated to appear more competent or to improve communication between both parties.

Such repairs are sometimes justifiable and can indeed bridge gaps between expectations arising from different cultural norms. However, this may be problematic if the interviewer intentionally asks leading (Berk-Seligson, 1999) or ambiguous questions (Wadensjö, 1998).

The interpretation inaccuracy can be further magnified by untrained or unqualified bilinguals (Hale, Goodman-Delahunty, & Martschuk, 2017a), due to lack of proficiency in the target language or legal/technical vocabulary (Goodman-Delahunty, Hale, Dhami, & Martschuk, 2015). Trained interpreters outperformed untrained bilinguals on a range of professional skills and were rated as more confident, knowledgeable and trustworthy by service users (Hale et al., 2017a), but professional interpreters may not be accessible. Although policies and best-practice guidelines do recommend the use of professional interpreters, they may not always be used (e.g., Valero Garcés & Lázaro Gutiérrez, 2016), potentially due to constraints on costs, staffing and time (Wakefield et al., 2014). A survey (Shaffer & Evans, 2018) conducted among the US law enforcement reported using colleagues more often than professional interpreters, and that they used interpreters more often with suspects and in certain crimes (e.g., domestic violence). Moreover, interpreters were usually at least partially informed about case details before interpreting (Shaffer & Evans, 2018), which is problematic and can jeopardise the impartiality of an investigation. As a result, legal practitioners experienced with interpreter-mediated interviews have expressed concerns over the accuracy of interpretation as well as the potential risk of biases and partiality of interpreted interviews (Goodman-Delahunty & Martschuk, 2016).

Another challenge is in the mode of interpretation. When the investigator solicits the service of an interpreter, the interpreter may be involved in mediating the communication either in person (onsite) or remotely, and their interpretation can be conducted consecutively or simultaneously. Simultaneous interpretation refers to the modality of interpretation when the interpreter interprets at the same time as the individual they are interpreting. Consecutive interpretation is when the interpreter translates what the individual has said after the s/he has finished talking (Viezzi, 2012). More research is still needed to examine which mode of interpretation is the most appropriate to adopt in what situation and for whom. Simultaneous interpretation in investigative settings is less time-consuming (Ewens et al., 2016), more cognitively demanding for the interpreter (Moser-Mercer, Kunzli, & Korac, 1998) but less tiring for both the interviewer and interviewee (Hale, Martschuk, Ozolins, & Stern,

2017b). Research with mock-jurors shows that simultaneous interpreting achieved the same levels of credibility and culpability ratings of the defendant as those in a monolingual version of the same trial (Hale et al, 2017a); whereas consecutive interpreting increased the credibility rating of the defendant but decreased culpability rating. Despite the advantages of simultaneous interpreting, in legal and medical interpreting, consecutive is commonly recommended over simultaneous interpreting when accuracy is the priority (Mikkelson, 2010). Research comparing consecutive and simultaneous interpreting has yielded contradicting results, with some findings suggesting higher accuracy for consecutive (e.g., Russell, 2000) and others for simultaneous (e.g., Gile, 2001). Practitioners generally agree that consecutive interpreting holds higher 'practical' appeal for precision, as consecutive allows interpreters to consider the meaning of the entire utterance, and thus is less likely to create the need for correction, and it is less likely to interrupt the flow of the other members of the conversation, particularly in the courtroom.

Moreover, compared to onsite interpretation, a lower level of accuracy (with more additions and expansions) was achieved in remote interpreting through videoconference in legal settings (Braun & Taylor, 2011), and interpreters disliked working remotely (Rozinger & Shlesinger, 2010). Whilst favourable research outcomes of simultaneous and onsite interpretation suggest practitioners should prioritise the use of simultaneous onsite interpretation over consecutive and remote interpretation, this may not be practically possible.

The effectiveness of special measures for vulnerable witnesses

Other than best-practice guidance for the questioning itself, there are also Special Measures available for a court to enhance the quality of testimony. The Youth Justice and Criminal Evidence Act (1999), Sections 16–30, present a series of Special Measures Directions ('SMDs') that are available for the court to select to enhance the quality of testimony of vulnerable witnesses. Witnesses considered eligible on the basis of criteria include the sexual nature of the offence charged, a mental disorder, an impairment of intelligence and social functioning, a physical disability or physical disorder. The SMDs available include video-recording of testimony to provide evidence in chief, pre-trial video-recorded cross-examination or re-examination, use of screens so that the witness does not see the defendant, the removal of wigs and gowns by judges and advocates, providing evidence without the presence of the public or press, allowing the witness to use communication aids and allowing for the use of an intermediary to support communication. Whilst all children under 18 are deemed to be eligible for SMDs, rulings related to adult witnesses must be evidence-based – and there are concerns that this facility is underused for vulnerable adult witnesses and victims (Ewin, 2015).

The existing research on the effect of SMD implementation for vulnerable adults provides generally positive results, especially in relation to child witnesses and victims (e.g., see Plotnikoff & Woolfson, 2004, 2007a, 2009). For instance, studies on the SMD implementation found the facility of video-recording evidence-in-chief highly supportive, whilst the use of measures (such as the screens or remote communication) in cross-examination led to reduced distress (Burton, Evans & Sanders, 2006, 2007; Hamlyn, Phelps, Turtle & Sattar 2004, Kebbel, O'Kelly & Gilchrist, 2007). Additionally, in general terms, those who had access to SMDs were more likely to believe that the Criminal Justice System was effective in meeting the needs of victims, treating them fairly and with respect and ultimately being more effective in bringing criminals to justice.

However, victim anxiety levels remained high and there were concerns regarding the levels of appropriate access to SMD for all eligible victims (Burton et al., 2006, 2007; Hamlyn et al., 2004; Kebbel et al., 2007), and the limited research predominantly focused on the victims. Even the policies, such as the ABE protocol (Ministry of Justice, 2011), are focused on vulnerable witnesses but do little to consider conditions associated with vulnerable defendants. Under the Mental Health Act 2007, there are provisions for the assessment and treatment of those defendants who are too mentally unwell to engage in the criminal justice system – but there are concerns about the efficacy of those provisions (Department of Health, 2009; Forrester et al., 2009). There is recognition of the risks associated with policing vulnerable defendants and this has led to guidance for police officers (College of Policing: Authorised Professional Practice, 2019); whilst helpful in supporting recognition of vulnerable defendants, this provides no additional interview guidance than what is recommended in the ABE (Herrington & Roberts, 2012).

Concerns regarding the use of SMD on jury decisions have also been raised (Payne, 2009; Stern, 2010); some juries may prefer live evidence to video evidence, but whilst this may be potentially beneficial to the victim, it may, at the same time, be detrimental for convictions. More recent examination on the influence of the live-link, video-recorded evidence-in-chief followed by live-link cross-examination, and protective screens on mock jurors' deliberations of adult sexual offence complainants, found no clear or consistent impact of these different SMD evidence presentation modes on juror decisions (Ellison & Munro, 2014). This suggests that some jurors are becoming more aware of the use of SMD as being a neutral and appropriate measure, or that, at least, concerns regarding the use of SMD, may be overstated or no longer relevant in current proceedings.

Another available support resource outlined by the ABE protocol to facilitate communication is the use of a Registered Intermediary. The Registered Intermediary (RI) scheme is available across England and Wales (Cooper & Mattison, 2017) with similar schemes initiated in Austria, New Zealand, Australia, Norway, Israel and South Africa (Spencer & Lamb, 2012). All RIs in England and Wales are specialists in communication who follow the procedural guidance manual (Ministry of Justice, 2015). The role of the RI is an impartial facilitator for communication between the witness, defendant and other legal professionals, through assessment and provision of recommendations in accordance with the individual needs of the witnesses (Ministry of Justice, 2015; O'Mahoney, Smith, & Milne, 2011). A RI may be involved in witness and victim interviews and cross-examination, and in ground rules hearings for witnesses and defendants (Cooper, Bracken & Marchant, 2015) in order to ensure fair treatment of all. The scheme has been met with considerable approval from both the legal professionals (Henderson, 2015) and RIs (O'Mahoney, 2009; Plotnikoff & Woolfson, 2007b) and is being recommended for use in other countries, such as Australia (Hepner, Woodward, & Stewart, 2015).

However, implementation of the RI scheme has also met with issues such as the willingness and/or ability of advocates to adapt their questioning appropriately (Plotnikoff & Woolfson, 2011), or that the involvement of RIs takes place only later in the legal process (Cooper, 2012). The impact of the support of RIs to vulnerable adult witnesses on legal professionals and/or juries remains unexamined (though see O'Mahoney, 2012, for an examination of the interaction between a RI, vulnerable defendant, barristers and a judge), as research in this area predominantly pertains to child witnesses. Moreover, despite working together to establish appropriate questioning strategies, RIs and advocates did not share an understanding of what constituted a leading question (Krähenbühl, Blades, & Cherryman, 2015). Mock jurors rated the quality of the mock cross-examination and the child witness' behaviour more positively when a RI was involved (Collins, Harker, & Antonopoulos, 2017; Krähenbühl, 2019). Additionally, Krähenbühl (2019) found disturbing results relating to juror perceptions of the intervention provided. With the intervention provided by the RI, the jurors rating of expectation of a guilty verdict was lower than when the same intervention was provided by the judge. These findings suggest that whilst the RI's role is appropriately neutral, there may be unexpected impact of their interventions on others involved in legal proceedings, which needs to be examined in greater detail to prevent inappropriate conclusions.

Public attitudes towards victimisation and perpetration

Public attitudes and reactions towards the handling of child abuse investigations have been changing for over 40 years, in what has been called 'cycles of discovery and suppression' (Olafson, Corwin, & Summit, 1993). With each new scandal comes a wave of public reaction driven by the media, and a backlash that often has an impact on future practices.

An example of this is the Cleveland child abuse scandal, in the north-east of England, that came to public attention in 1987–1988 when two paediatricians diagnosed 121 children as having been sexually abused. The children concerned were removed from their homes and taken into foster care, before media outlets began to run articles in support of the parents, and which strongly criticised local authorities. The subsequent Butler-Sloss (1988) inquiry outlined criticisms about professionals' handling of the cases, although it also acknowledged that there had been serious concerns about many of the children involved before they had been examined. Due to public and parental concerns around medical examinations and 'disclosure work', Butler-Sloss (1988) gave a series of recommendations regarding listening to children and interviewing them, which included taking their allegation seriously, and making the purposes of interview clear. Her report resulted in the Children's Act (Department of Health, 1989), which put children's welfare at the forefront of any decisions made by local authorities. Somewhat surprisingly, there were no specific guidelines for interviewing children within the Act.

In the case of Cleveland, as in the case of similar incidents in the years following, such as Nottingham (1989), Rochdale (1990) and Orkney (1991), the public's perceptions of authorities' handling of these cases were generally that of sympathy for the families and support for the accused. Social workers were portrayed as both 'fools and wimps' for failing to protect children, and 'villain and bully' for being overly heavy handed (Franklin & Parton, 1991, p. 16, 19).

After the large media backlash surrounding Orkney, the government ordered an inquiry under Lord Clyde (1992). When published, Clyde included 30 recommendations relating to interviewing children, which included thorough planning, full and comprehensive training and the development of dedicated facilities suitable for interviewing children in the context of abuse. These, and other recommendations, influenced the subsequent Children (Scotland) Act (1995), in which guidelines were set out for interviewing both disabled and non-disabled children.

It is clear from these examples that public attitudes can have pertinent effects on influencing changes to policy. But to what extent are attitudes and beliefs from jury-eligible populations accurate and why would they affect forensic questioning practices?

As discussed in Prince, Andrews, Lamb, and Foster (2018), child sexual abuse (CSA) misconceptions are incorrect beliefs regarding sexual abuse, victims and perpetrators (Cromer & Goldsmith, 2010). Survey research conducted in the United States (Quas, Thompson, & Clarke-Stewart, 2005) and Scotland (Andrews, Lamb, & Foster, under review) found that jury-eligible laypeople have limited and often incorrect knowledge of children's competencies and ability to testify (Antrobus, McKimmie, & Newcombe, 2012; Andrews, Lamb, & Foster, under review). Quas et al. (2005) and Andrews, Lamb, and Foster (under review) found that laypeople generally believe, inaccurately, that children can easily be coerced into making false allegations of sexual assault, and that children who are sexually abused often show bizarre sexual behaviour. Such prejudicial views about CSA might influence how juries assess complainants' evidence (Cossins, 2008).

For example, juror misconceptions about adolescent sexual activity can affect beliefs about the extent to which adolescents may have consented to alleged sexual abuse, reducing defendant responsibility (Klettke & Mellor, 2012). Because many direct- and cross-examinations in CSA cases rely on victim and perpetrator stereotypes (O'Connor, 2008; Westcott & Page, 2002), and the majority of potential jurors hold beliefs that are incongruent with empirical evidence (Andrews, Lamb, & Foster, under review; Cossins, 2008; Quas et al., 2005), it is important to investigate the prevalence of such misconceptions, and to examine whether particular misconceptions feature in examinations more frequently than others (McGee, O'Higgins, Garavan, & Conroy, 2011). Such findings could allow practitioners to better protect alleged victims and defendants against miscarriages of justice.

Mock jurors' pre-existing (incorrect) beliefs and stereotypes about sexual assault, which often have no bearing on criminal liability (Temkin, 2010), can influence verdicts more than the facts of the case (Goodman & Melinder, 2007), suggesting that the ways in which lawyers present their arguments affect case outcomes (Bottoms, Golding, Stevenson, Wiley, & Yozwiak, 2007). Thus, defence lawyers might attempt to discredit witnesses by reinforcing beliefs and/or stereotypes (Cossins, 2012). Whilst lawyers cannot ask witnesses to draw inferences from the facts (Henderson, 2016), they can encourage juries to make inferences that comply with their predetermined views about such crimes by directing the narratives and referring to common misconceptions.

In adversarial jurisdictions, the defence lawyer's responsibility is to convince a jury and/or judge of their client's innocence and they are thus motivated to construct narratives of alleged events to persuade juries that their client's version of events is true (Cederborg, 1999). To achieve this, lawyers question child witnesses in ways that maintain their control of the discourse (Westcott & Page, 2002) by limiting the extent to which witnesses can provide information (by asking closed-ended questions) and leading them to co-construct a convincing narrative (Henderson, 2002, 2016). Through the construction of lawyers' narratives, jurors are encouraged to perceive events in the light of personal and societal conceptions (Howarth, 2006; Willig, 2008).

This reasoning is supported by social representations theory, which suggests that, when attempting to understand an unusual situation, individuals draw upon socially shared conventions that are previously 'known' via the process of anchoring (Moscovici, 1998). These narratives can be integrated into common discourse via the media and the use of anecdotes, assuming the status of truth or common sense (Marecek, Crawford, & Popp, 2004). Such narratives provide societies with a structure within which to interpret unusual or novel situations (Burns, 2004), allowing these situations to be understood or even excused (Westcott & Page, 2002). The most credible accounts of abusive episodes are thus likely to be those that adhere to recognised or expected social vocabularies (Weiss, 2009).

Media reports focus on the most extreme cases of CSA (Weatherred, 2015). Any deviations from those unrepresentative portrayals, such as cases including lack of medical evidence or lack of corroborating witnesses, could be used by defence lawyers. Social representations may further create stereotypes of 'ideal' victims and 'ideal' defendants (Lindholm & Cederborg, 2016). Any deviations from these ideals may be highlighted by lawyers seeking to suggest that the abuse may not have occurred (Peace, Shudra, Forrester, Kasper, Harder, & Porter, 2015). Common narratives thus include defence lawyers presenting children as 'un-childlike' and 'wicked liars' (Westcott & Page, 2002), perhaps appealing to familiar examples in stories such as 'Lolita' or 'The Boy Who Cried Wolf'. Narratives encouraging jurors to consider the alleged events in reference to such beliefs are both tangible and logical, allowing prosecutors and defence lawyers to differentially communicate particular beliefs about the perpetration of CSA persuasively.

At the personal level, narratives involve expressions of the narrators' lived experiences, whereas at the societal level they involve socially shared stories that are characteristic of certain communities (Flick, 2014). Because children are not given the opportunity to construct their own narratives in court, lawyers can guide them to help create reports that will convince jurors. By using socially constructed stereotypes and stories to structure their narratives, lawyers disrupt the children's personal narratives, and compromise their lived experiences for the benefit of their respective clients (Prince et al., 2018). Whilst the right to cross-examine witnesses is a fundamental aspect of adversarial legal systems, issues of relevance and humiliation become salient when lawyers rely on common misconceptions to construct their narratives in order to affect perceptions of credibility. Jurors need to be made aware of the myths and stereotypes that may influence their decision-making and consequently disrupt the pursuit of justice.

Lessons learnt and the future of impact

It is clear that research has profoundly impacted the way forensic questioning is conducted in the field; nevertheless, there remain difficulties in translating evidence-informed guidance into practice, particularly for suspects and those with non-visible and/or unknown vulnerabilities; more needs to be done by both researchers and practitioners to monitor and enhance the maintenance of best practice.

Initiatives to enhance the implementation and maintenance of best practice

As discussed in detail in the previous section, research suggests that there are serious problems not only in implementing best practices, but, despite decades of intervention and training, practitioners and institutions routinely fail to maintain best practice (Lamb, 2016). As Lamb (2016) emphasises, traditional intensive classroom training models on the use of best practice are ineffective (e.g., Lamb et al., 1996; Wolfman, Brown, & Jose, 2016). By contrast, intensive courses that involve distributed training and intensive ongoing peer and/or supervisor feedback are associated with continued improvements in interviewing quality and adherence to best practices (e.g., Lamb et al., 2002; Lindholm, Cederborg, & Winerdal, 2016; Powell, Fisher, & Hughes-Scholes, 2008). This type of training, however, is time-intensive and costly, and so does not routinely accompany the use of best-practice guidelines.

More recently, training initiatives have begun to circumvent these accessibility issues by using computer-assisted technology training (Lamb, 2016). Trainees are typically required to remotely access modules via personal computers and are tested on their knowledge with regular quizzes (e.g., Powell, Guadagno, & Benson, 2016). Follow-up mock Skype interviews demonstrated skill acquisition and maintenance over a 6- (Powell et al., 2016) to 12-month period (Benson & Powell, 2015). However, as Lamb (2016) emphasises, performance in mock interviews does not reliably reflect the quality of questioning in real forensic interviews (Lamb et al., 2002), therefore advance skills are unlikely to develop without the opportunity to receive feedback on forensic interviews conducted with real alleged victims (Lamb, 2016).

Recommendations and future directions of interpreted forensic questioning

Being interviewed in a foreign language can be a cognitively taxing and anxiety-inducing experience, especially in a forensic/investigative context. The language and culture barriers faced by non-native speakers are exacerbated by poor practice of interpretation and violation of recommended policies (e.g., not using a professional interpreter). Legal practitioners should adhere to recommended best practice and solicit the service from professional interpreters. Despite the lack of consensus on the modality of interpretation to use, given the decreased level of interpreting accuracy (Braun & Taylor, 2011), onsite (face-to-face) interpreting should be prioritised, and the interpreter should be placed adjacent to the investigator during the interview to increase interviewee's level of comfort (Houston, Russano & Ricks, 2017). Additional time should be allocated for conducting interpreter-assisted interviews, given it is typically more time-consuming than regular interviews (e.g., Fontes & Tishelman, 2016; Shaffer & Evans, 2018). It is also critical for the interpreters to establish rapport with the interviewee (Houston, Russano & Ricks, 2017) to optimise the interview outcome.

Policies and guidelines on the use of professional interpreters need to be strictly enforced, and the inclusion of information on appropriate briefing and interviewing strategies for professionals working with interpreters also needs to be developed. Stipulations on the exceptional circumstances where non-professional (ad hoc) interpreters may be considered must be established. Ad hoc interpreters should at least be given an information briefing on basic rules of such interpretation before the interpretation takes place.

Given the highly sensitive nature as well as the legal implications of forensic questioning, and the fact that the interpreter has to participate in this interaction, interpreters need to receive training on principles of forensic interviewing in addition to their standard interpreting training, highlighting the pivotal importance of accuracy in translating different types of questions, rapport building and maintenance. Where the interviewee is a child, the interpreter, just like the interviewer s/he is assisting, needs to receive training on children's developmental, cognitive and socio-emotional characteristics to safeguard best practice.

Future research needs to empirically examine the accuracy of interpretation, especially because the investigative interview content and outcomes have important legal and practical implications. Research on how interpreters mediate the interaction within the investigative interview also need to be assessed, and the potential use of alternative technologies (such as using computer or other smart devices) for interpretation should also be explored.

Implementation and further challenges with special measures

The research conducted has highlighted issues with enabling vulnerable witnesses to engage with and provide best evidence in legal proceedings. This has led to the development of support in the form of advocacy resources and training, such as the Inns of Court College of Advocacy training programme, The Advocates Gateway (n.d.) and the Achieving Best Evidence (ABE) interviewing protocol (Ministry of Justice, 2011). The ABE guidance provides an interviewing structure, with advice on optimal and appropriate questioning strategies and techniques to support eliciting best evidence from vulnerable witnesses (see Milne & Bull, 2006). However, the ABE protocol is focused on vulnerable witnesses but does little to consider conditions associated with vulnerable defendants.

Ongoing challenges remain in the implementation of these special measures. One of the future challenges is to increase the understanding and interactions of vulnerable witness experiences with the recall and reporting of those experiences. Such research has been conducted by Leander, Christianson, and Granhag (2007) with children. It is recognised that children may have difficulties in reporting sexual abuse when the perpetrator is familiar (e.g., due to dependency on the perpetrator, concerns for consequences of disclosure on the family, and loyalty conflicts). Leander's research demonstrated that children also had difficulties in reporting details of sexual abuse when the perpetrator was a stranger. The authors are not aware of comparable research undertaken with adult victims or defendants in relation to sexual abuse. The ethical implications of such studies are considerable, especially if the findings contrast with legal proceeding outcomes, and may lead to increased concerns regarding the reliability of the evidence of such witnesses – a research and ethical minefield!

A second challenge is to ensure that the support given to vulnerable witnesses, and those professionals who engage with them in legal proceedings is firmly based on established theoretical frameworks and empirical evidence. It is apparent (for a recent study see Maras et al., 2017) that there is little research conducted on the involvement of vulnerable witnesses during court proceedings. Specifically, there has been little research conducted regarding the theoretical or evidential basis for the underlying principles of advocacy training (Cooper, Dando, Ormerod, Mattison, Marchant, Milne, & Bull, 2018), professional understanding and preconceived assumptions as to the impact of the approaches taken with vulnerable witnesses (Westera, McKimmie, Kebbell, Milne & Masser, 2015) and to the impact of approaches and interventions not only on the witnesses themselves but also on those who take influential decisions regarding case progression and outcome (Krähenbühl, 2019). To date, the authors of this chapter are unaware of any research regarding the impact of vulnerability of differing forms on the CPS decision-making process.

Conclusions

To summarise, the field of forensic questioning has made considerable advances in informing best practices in the field, though these practices are not implemented for all populations nor across all contexts, and there is an issue in maintaining best practices once implemented. Other ongoing challenges to best-practice questioning are presented, including the use and efficacy of interpreters in forensic interview settings, the effectiveness of special measures designed to facilitate the communication of vulnerable witnesses, and public attitudes towards victimisation and perpetration that influence practice and policy.

Whilst there has been considerable progress in supporting individuals within the legal system it has also become apparent that factors that may be seen to be positive in one context may have an inadvertent detrimental effect in another context – either within, or outside of, the legal proceedings. Accordingly, it is for all engaged in legal proceedings, from witnesses to legal professionals (police, advocacy, RIs), to volunteers and academic researchers to take a holistic approach to all of the issues raised. It is ill-conceived and counter-productive for research to be undertaken in a context that is devoid of practical application within the legal system as it stands. Such research may help lead to changes within the legal system that many researchers and practitioners believe to be necessary and overdue – however, it does little to appropriately support those engaging with the legal system either currently, or in the near future. In order to facilitate this holistic approach, there needs to be more open dialogue between all parties regarding the issues faced, the approaches taken, the impact of those approaches, and the provision of resources (data in the form of statistics, evidential material, access to potential participants) under stringent ethical guidelines – which is not generally characteristic of current ethos and practices.

References

Abbe, A., & Brandon, S. (2014). Building and maintaining rapport in investigative interviews. *Police Practice and Research*, *15*(3), 207–220.

Advocates Gateway. (n.d.). Retrieved from https://www.theadvocatesgateway.org.

Ahern, E., Stolzenberg, S., & Lyon, T. (2015). Do prosecutors use interview instructions or build rapport with child witnesses? *Behavioural Sciences and the Law*, *33*(4), 476–492.

Almerigogna, J., Ost, J., Akehurst, L., & Fluck, M. (2008). How interviewers' nonverbal behaviours can affect children's perceptions and suggestibility. *Journal of Experimental Child Psychology*, *100*(1), 17–39.

Andrews, S. J., Ahern, E., & Lamb, M. E. (2017). Children's expressions of uncertainty when testifying about alleged sexual abuse in Scottish courts. *Behavioural Sciences and the Law*, *35*(3), 204–224.

Andrews, S. J., & Lamb, M. E. (2014). The effects of age and delay on responses to repeated questions in forensic interviews with children alleging sexual abuse. *Law and Human Behaviour, 38*(2), 171–180.

Andrews, S. J., & Lamb, M. E. (2017). The structural linguistic complexity of lawyers' questions and children's responses in Scottish criminal courts. *Child Abuse and Neglect, 65*, 182–193.

Andrews, S. J., & Lamb, M. E. (2018, accepted). Lawyers' question content and children's responses in Scottish Criminal courts. *Psychology, Crime, and Law.*

Andrews, S. J., Lamb, M. E., & Foster, J. L. H. (Under review). Beliefs about sexual abuse in Scotland: A qualitative analysis.

Andrews, S. J., Lamb, M. E., & Lyon, T. D. (2015). The effects of question repetition on responses in direct- and cross-examinations of children alleging sexual abuse in court. *Law and Human Behaviour, 39*(6), 559–570.

Angelelli, C. V. (2004). *Revisiting the interpreter's role: A study of conference, court, and medical interpreters in Canada, Mexico, and the United States.* Amsterdam; Philadelphia, PA: John Benjamins.

Antrobus, E., McKimmie, B., & Newcombe, P. (2012). Community members' beliefs about children in Australian courts. *Psychiatry, Psychology and Law, 19*(4), 497–516.

Aranguri, C., Davidson, B., & Ramirez, R. (2006). Patterns of communication through interpreters. *Journal of General Internal Medicine, 21*(6), 623–629.

Baldry, E., Dowse, L., & Clarence, M. (2011). People with mental and cognitive disabilities: Pathways into prison. *Background paper for the national legal aid conference,* Darwin, Australia. Retrieved from https://www.mhdcd.unsw.edu.au/sites/.../MHDCDbackgroundOutlaws%20Conf1.pdf.

Bartels, L. (2011). *Police interviews with vulnerable adult suspects. Research in practice* (Report No. 21). Australian Government: Australian Institute of Criminology. Retrieved from http://www.aic.gov.au/publications/current%20series/rip/21-40/rip21.html.

Benson, M., & Powell, M. (2015). Evaluation of a comprehensive interactive training system for investigative interviewers of children. *Psychology, Public Policy, and Law, 21*(3), 309–322.

Berk-Seligson, S. (1999). The impact of court interpreting on the coerciveness of leading questions. *The Journal of Forensic Linguistics, 6*(1), 30–56.

Berk-Seligson, S. (2002). *The bilingual courtroom: Court interpreters in the judicial process.* Chicago, IL: University of Chicago Press.

Böser, U. (2013). "So tell me what happened!" Interpreting the free recall segment of the investigative interview. *Translation and Interpreting Studies, 8*(1), 112–136.

Bottoms, B., Golding, J., Stevenson, M., Wiley, T., & Yozwiak, J. (2007). A review of factors affecting jurors' decisions in child sexual abuse cases. In M. Toglia, J. Read, D. Ross & R. Lindsay (Eds.), *The handbook of eyewitness psychology, vol. 1. Memory for events* (pp. 509–543). Mahwah, NJ: Lawrence Erlbaum Associates Publishers.

Boucher, J., Mayes, A., & Bigham, S. (2012). Memory in autistic spectrum disorder. *Psychological Bulletin, 138*(3), 458–496.

Bowler, D. M., Gaigg, S. B., & Gardiner, J. M. (2008). Effects of related and unrelated context on recall and recognition by adults with high-functioning autism spectrum disorder. *Neuropsychologia, 46*(4), 993–999.

Braun, S., & Taylor, J. L. (2011). Video-mediated interpreting: An overview of current practice and research. In S. Braun & J. L. Taylor (Eds.), *Video conference and remote interpreting in criminal proceedings* (pp. 25–57). Guildford, UK: University of Surrey.

Browning, A., & Caulfield, L. (2011). The prevalence and treatment of people with Asperger's syndrome in the criminal justice system. *Criminology and Criminal Justice, 11*(2), 165–180.

Brubacher, S., Poole, D., & Dickinson, J. (2015). The use of ground rules in investigative interviews with children: A synthesis and call for research. *Developmental Review, 36*, 15–33.

Bruer, K., & Pozzulo, J. (2014). Familiarity and recall memory for environments: A comparison of children and adults. *Journal of Applied Developmental Psychology, 35*(4), 318–325.

Burns, C. (2004). Constructing rape: Judicial narratives on trial. *Japanese Studies, 24*(1), 81–96.

Burton, M., Evans, R., & Sanders, A. (2006). *An evaluation of the use of special measures for vulnerable and intimidated witnesses.* London: Home Office. Retrieved from library.college.police.uk/docs/hofindings/r270.pdf.

Burton, M., Evans, R., & Sanders, A. (2007). Vulnerable and intimidated witnesses and the adversarial process in England and Wales. *The International Journal of Evidence and Proof, 11*(1), 1–23.

Butler-Sloss, E. (1988). *The report of the inquiry into child abuse in Cleveland.* London: HMSO.

Candel, I., Merckelbach, H., Jelicic, M., Limpens, M., & Widdershoven, K. (2004). Children's suggestibility for peripheral and central details. *The Journal of Credibility Assessment and Witness Psychology, 5*(1), 9–18.

Carter, C., Bottoms, B., & Levine, M. (1996). "Linguistic and socioemotional influences on the accuracy of children's reports": Erratum. *Law and Human Behaviour, 20*(5), 579–579.

Ceci, S. J., & Bruck, M. (1995). *Jeopardy in the courtroom: A scientific analysis of children's testimony.* Washington, DC: American Psychological Association.

Ceci, S., Ross, D., & Toglia, M. (1987). Suggestibility of children's memory: Psycholegal implications. *Journal of Experimental Psychology: General, 116*(1), 38–49.

Cederborg, A. (1999). The construction of children's credibility in judgements of child sexual abuse. *Acta Sociologica, 42*(2), 147–158.

Children (Scotland) Act. (1995). *Regulations and guidance.* Edinburgh: The Stationery Office. Retrieved from http://www.legislation.gov.uk/ukpga/1995/36/contents.

Clarke, C., & Milne, R. J. (2001). *National evaluation of the PEACE investigative interviewing course* (PRAS, No. 149). London: Home Office.

Clyde, J. (1992). *The report of the inquiry into the removal of children from Orkney in February 1991*. Edinburgh: HMSO.

College of Policing: Authorised Professional Practice. (2019). *Mental health index*. Retrieved January 2, 2019, from https://www.app.college.police.uk/mental-health-index-2/.

Collins, K., Harker, N., & Antonopoulos, G. A. (2017). The impact of Registered Intermediary presence on adults' perceptions of child witnesses: Evidence from a mock cross-examination. *European Journal on Criminal Policy and Research, 23*(2), 211–225.

Cooper, P. (2012). *Tell me what's happening 3: Registered Intermediary survey*. Retrieved January 2, 2019, from https://www.city.ac.uk/__data/.../30-April-FINAL-Tell-Me-Whats-Happening-3.pdf.

Cooper, P., Bracken, P., & Marchant, R. (2015). Getting to grips with ground rules hearings: A checklist for judges, advocates and intermediaries to promote the fair treatment of vulnerable people in court. *Criminal Law Review, 6*, 420–435.

Cooper, P., Dando, C., Ormerod, T., Mattison, M., Marchant, R., Milne, R., & Bull, R. (2018). One step forward and two steps back? The "20 Principles" for questioning vulnerable witnesses and the lack of an evidence-based approach. *The International Journal of Evidence and Proof, 22*, 392–410.

Cooper, P., & Mattison, M. (2017). Intermediaries, vulnerable people and the quality of evidence: An international comparison of three versions of the English intermediary model. *The International Journal of Evidence and Proof, 21*(4), 351–370.

Cossins, A. (2008). Children, sexual abuse and suggestibility: What laypeople think they know and what the literature tells us. *Psychiatry, Psychology and Law, 15*(1), 153–170.

Cossins, A. (2012). Cross-examining the child complainant in Australia. In J. R. Spencer & M. E. Lamb (Eds.), *Children and cross-examination: Time to change the rules?* Oxford, UK: Hart Publishing.

Cromer, L., & Goldsmith, R. (2010). Child sexual abuse myths: Attitudes, beliefs, and individual differences. *Journal of Child Sexual Abuse, 19*(6), 618–647.

Danby, M., Brubacher, S., Sharman, S., & Powell, M. (2015). The effects of practice on children's ability to apply ground rules in a narrative interview. *Behavioural Sciences and the Law, 33*(4), 446–458.

Dando, C., Ormerod, T., Wilcock, R., & Milne, R. (2011). When help becomes hindrance: Unexpected errors of omission and commission in eyewitness memory resulting from change temporal order at retrieval? *Cognition, 121*(3), 416–421.

Department of Health. The Children Act. (1989). *Guidance and Regulations*. London: HMSO (1991).

Department of Health. (2009). *The Bradley report; Lord Bradley's review of people with mental health problems or learning disabilities in the Criminal Justice System*. London: Department of Health.

Dornyei, Z., & Scott, M. L. (1995). Communication strategies in a second language: Definitions and taxonomies. *Language Learning, 47*(1), 173–210.

Droit-Volet, S., & Izaute, M. (2005). The effect of feedback on timing in children and adults: The temporal generalization task. *The Quarterly Journal of Experimental Psychology Section A, 58*(3), 507–520.

Earhart, B., La Rooy, D., Brubacher, S., & Lamb, M. (2014). An examination of "don't know" responses in forensic interviews with children. *Behavioural Sciences and the Law, 32*(6), 746–761.

Earhart, B., La Rooy, D., & Lamb, M. (2016). Assessing the quality of forensic interviews with child witnesses. In W. O'Donohue & M. Fanetti (Eds.), *Forensic interviews regarding child sexual abuse: A guide to evidence-based practice* (pp. 317–335). New York, NY: Springer.

Earhart, B., & Roberts, K. (2014). The role of executive function in children's source monitoring with varying retrieval strategies. *Frontiers in Psychology, 5*, 1–12.

Ellison, L., & Munro, V. E. (2014). A 'Special' delivery? Exploring the impact of screens, live-links and video-recorded evidence on mock juror deliberation in rape trials. *Social and Legal Studies, 23*(1), 3–29.

European Court of Human Rights. (1953). *European Convention of Human Rights (ECHR)* (Art, 6, d.3). Rome: Council of Europe.

Evans, J. R., Michael, S. W., Meissner, C. A., & Brandon, S. E. (2013). Validating a new assessment method for deception detection: Introducing a psychologically based credibility assessment tool. *Journal of Applied Research in Memory and Cognition, 2*(1), 33–41.

Ewens, S., Vrij, A., Leal, S., Mann, S., Jo, E., & Fisher, R. P. (2016). The effect of interpreters on eliciting information, cues to deceit and rapport. *Legal and Criminological Psychology, 21*(2), 286–304.

Ewin, R. (2015). The vulnerable and intimidated witness: A socio-legal analysis of Special Measures. *Journal of Applied Psychology and Social Science, 1*, 31–54.

Fisher, R., & Geiselman, R. (2010). The Cognitive Interview method of conducting police interviews: Eliciting extensive information and promoting Therapeutic Jurisprudence. *International Journal of Law and Psychiatry, 33*(5–6), 321–328.

Flick, U. (2014). Using narrative data. In U. Flick (Ed.), *An introduction to qualitative research* (pp. 263–291). New York, NY: Sage Publications.

Fontes, L. A., & Tishelman, A. C. (2016). Language competence in forensic interviews for suspected child sexual abuse. *Child Abuse and Neglect, 58*, 51–62.

Forrester, A., Henderson, C., Wilson, S., Cumming, I., Spyrou, M., & Parrott, J. (2009). A suitable waiting room? Hospital transfer outcomes and delays from two London prisons. *Psychiatric Bulletin, 33*(11), 409–412.

Franklin, B., & Parton, N. (Eds.) (1991). *Social work, the media and public relations.* London: Routledge.
Gile, D. (2001). Consecutive vs. simultaneous: Which is more accurate? *Interpretation Studies, 1*(1), 8–20.
Goodman, G., & Melinder, A. (2007). Child witness research and forensic interviews of young children: A review. *Legal and Criminological Psychology, 12*(1), 1–19.
Goodman-Delahunty, J., Hale, S., Dhami, M., & Martschuk, N. (2015). *Effects of situational and relational variables on interpreting in high stakes police interviews.* United States: Federal Bureau of Investigation.
Goodman-Delahunty, J., & Martschuk, N. (2016). Risks and benefits of interpreter-mediated police interviews 1. *Varstvoslovje, 18*(4), 451–471.
Hale, S., Goodman-Delahunty, J., & Martschuk, N. (2017a). Interactional management in a simulated police interview: Interpreters' strategies. In M. Mason & F. Rock (Eds.), *The discourse of police investigation.* Chicago, IL: University of Chicago Press.
Hale, S., Martschuk, N., Ozolins, U., & Stern, L. (2017b). The effect of interpreting modes on witness credibility assessments. *Interpreting, 19*(1), 69–96.
Hamlyn, B., Phelps, A., Turtle, J., & Sattar, G. (2004). *Are Special Measures working? Evidence from surveys of vulnerable and intimidated witnesses.* London: Home Office.
Hanna, K., Davies, E., Crothers, C., & Henderson, E. (2012). Questioning child witnesses in New Zealand's criminal justice system: Is cross-examination fair? *Psychiatry, Psychology and Law, 19*(4), 530–546.
Hanna, K., Davies, E., Henderson, E., Crothers, C., & Rotherham, C. (2010). *Child witnesses in the New Zealand criminal courts: A review of practice and implications for policy.* Auckland: Institute of Public Policy.
Henderson, E. (2002). Persuading and controlling: The theory of cross-examination in relation to children. In H. L. Westcott, G. M. Davies & R. H. C. Bull (Eds.), *Children's testimony, A handbook of psychological research and forensic practice* (pp. 279–294). Chichester: John Wiley & Sons.
Henderson, E. (2015). "A very valuable tool": Judges, advocates and intermediaries discuss the intermediary system in England and Wales. *Evidence & Proof, 19,* 154–171.
Henderson, E. (2016). Best evidence or best interests? What does the case law say about the function of criminal cross-examination? *The International Journal of Evidence and Proof, 20*(3), 183–199.
Henderson, H. M., & Andrews, S. J. (2017). Assessing the veracity of children's forensic interviews: Implications for the courtroom. In H. Otgaar & M. L. Howe (Eds.), *Finding the truth in the courtroom: Dealing with deception, lies, and memories* (pp. 103–135). Oxford, UK: Oxford University Press.
Henderson, H., Andrews, S., & Lamb, M. (2018). Examining children in English High Courts with and without implementation of reforms authorized in Section 28 of the Youth Justice and Criminal Evidence Act. *Applied Cognitive Psychology, 33*(2), 252–264.

Henry, L. A., Crane, L., Nash, G., Hobson, Z., Kirke-Smith, M., & Wilcock, R. (2017). Verbal, visual, and intermediary support for child witnesses with autism during investigative interviews. *Journal of Autism and Developmental Disorders, 47*(8), 2348–2362.

Hepner, I., Woodward, M. N., & Stewart, J. (2015). Giving the vulnerable a voice in the criminal justice system: The use of intermediaries with individuals with intellectual disability. *Psychiatry, Psychology and Law, 22*(3), 453–464.

Herrington, V., & Roberts, K. (2012). Addressing psychological vulnerability in the police suspect interview. *Policing, 6*(2), 177–186.

Hershkowitz, I., Fisher, S., Lamb, M., & Horowitz, D. (2007). Improving credibility assessment in child sexual abuse allegations: The role of the NICHD investigative interview protocol. *Child Abuse and Neglect, 31*(2), 99–110.

Hershkowitz, I., Lamb, M., & Katz, C. (2014). Allegation rates in forensic child abuse investigations: Comparing the revised and standard NICHD protocols. *Psychology, Public Policy, and Law, 20*(3), 336–344.

Hershkowitz, I., Lamb, M., Katz, C., & Malloy, L. (2013). Does enhanced rapport-building alter the dynamics of investigative interviews with suspected victims of intra-familial abuse? *Journal of Police and Criminal Psychology, 30*(1), 6–14.

Home Office. (1999). *The youth justice and criminal evidence Act*. Retrieved January 2, 2019, from http://www.legislation.gov.uk/ukpga/1999/23/contents.

Houston, K. A., Russano, M. B., & Ricks, E. P. (2017). 'Any friend of yours is a friend of mine': Investigating the utilization of an interpreter in an investigative interview. *Psychology, Crime and Law, 23*(5), 413–426.

Howarth, C. (2006). A social representation is not a quiet thing: Exploring the critical potential of social representations theory. *British Journal of Social Psychology, 45*(1), 65–86.

Howie, P., Kurukulasuriya, N., Nash, L., & Marsh, A. (2009). Inconsistencies in children's recall of witnessed events: The role of age, question format and perceived reason for question repetition. *Legal and Criminological Psychology, 14*(2), 311–329.

Howie, P., Nash, L., Kurukulasuriya, N., & Bowman, A. (2012). Children's event reports: Factors affecting responses to repeated questions in vignette scenarios and event recall interviews. *British Journal of Developmental Psychology, 30*(4), 550–568.

Huang, C. P. (2010). Exploring factors affecting the use of oral communication strategies. Retrieved from https://pdfs.semanticscholar.org/468a/7212e4d3bb4e359f84160c32fe3ef253bfa8.pdf.

Ibabe, I., & Sporer, S. (2004). How you ask is what you get: On the influence of question form on accuracy and confidence. *Applied Cognitive Psychology, 18*(6), 711–726.

Inns of Court College of Advocacy. (2019). The 20 principles of questioning: A guide to the cross-examination of vulnerable witnesses. Retrieved from https://www.icca.ac.uk/wp-content/uploads/2019/05/20-Principles-of-Questioning.pdf.

Kebbell, M. R., O'Kelly, C. M. E., & Gilchrist, E. L. (2007). Rape victims' experiences of giving evidence in English courts: A survey. *Psychiatry, Psychology and Law, 14*(1), 111–119.

Klettke, B., & Mellor, D. (2012). At what age can females consent to sexual activity? A survey of jury-eligible Australians. *Psychiatry, Psychology and Law, 19*(2), 198–208.

Krahenbuhl, S. (2019). Mock jurors' perceptions of a child witness: The impact of the presence and/or intervention of a registered intermediary during cross-examination. *Psychology, Crime and Law, 25*(7), 713–728.

Krähenbühl, S. J., & Blades, M. (2009). Does the form of question repetition have an effect on children's recall accuracy and consistency? *International Journal of Police Science and Management, 11*(4), 460–475.

Krähenbühl, S. J., Blades, M., & Cherryman, J. (2015). A qualitative examination of "Ground Rules" implementation practice in investigative interviews with children. *Psychiatry, Psychology and Law, 22*(6), 830–841.

Krähenbühl, S. J., Blades, M., & Westcott, H. (2010). 'What else should I say?' an analysis of the question repetition practiced in police interviews of 4–11-year-olds. *Police Practice and Research, 11*(6), 473–476.

La Rooy, D., & Lamb, M. (2011). What happens when interviewers ask repeated questions in forensic interviews with children alleging abuse? *Journal of Police and Criminal Psychology, 26*(1), 20–25.

Lamb, M. (2016). Difficulties translating research on forensic interview practices to practitioners: Finding water, leading horses, but can we get them to drink? *American Psychologist, 71*(8), 710–718.

Lamb, M. E., Brown, D. A., Hershkowitz, I., Orbach, Y., & Esplin, P. W. (2018). *Tell me what happened: Questioning children about abuse.* Hoboke, NJ: John Wiley & Sons Inc.

Lamb, M., & Fauchier, A. (2001). The effects of question type on self-contradictions by children in the course of forensic interviews. *Applied Cognitive Psychology, 15*(5), 483–491.

Lamb, M., Hershkowitz, I., Orbach, Y., & Esplin, P. (2011). *Tell me what happened: Structured investigative interviews of child victims and witnesses.* Hoboken, NJ: John Wiley & Sons.

Lamb, M., Hershkowitz, I., Sternberg, K., Esplin, P., Hovav, M., Manor, T., & Yudilevitch, L. (1996). Effects of investigative utterance types on Israeli children's responses. *International Journal of Behavioural Development, 19*(3), 627–637.

Lamb, M., Malloy, L., Hershkowitz, I., & La Rooy, D. (2015). Children and the law. In M. Lamb & R. Lerner (Eds.), *Handbook of child psychology and developmental science: Socioemotional processes* (pp. 464–512). Hoboken, NJ: John Wiley & Sons Inc.

Lamb, M., Orbach, Y., Hershkowitz, I., Horowitz, D., & Abbott, C. (2007). Does the type of prompt affect the accuracy of information provided by alleged victims of abuse in forensic interviews? *Applied Cognitive Psychology, 21*(9), 1117–1130.

Lamb, M., Sternberg, K., Orbach, Y., Hershkowitz, I., Horowitz, D., & Esplin, P. (2002). The effects of intensive training and ongoing supervision on the quality of investigative interviews with alleged sex abuse victims. *Applied Developmental Science, 6*(3), 114–125.

Leander, L., Christianson, S. A., & Granhag, P. A. (2007). A sexual abuse case study: Children's memories and reports. *Psychiatry, Psychology and Law, 14*(1), 120–129.

Lindholm, J., & Cederborg, A. (2016). Legal assessments of child victims of human trafficking for sexual purposes. *Behavioural Sciences and the Law, 34*(1), 218–233.

Lindholm, J., Cederborg, A., & Winerdal, U. (2016). An evaluation of the training programme for investigative interviewers in Sweden. *Presentation, American psychology-law society annual conference*, Atlanta, GA.

London, K., & Kulkofsky, S. (2010). Factors affecting the reliability of children's reports. In G. M. Davies & D. B. Wright (Eds.), *New frontiers in applied memory* (pp. 119–141). New York, NY: Psychology Press.

Lyon, T. D. (2002). Scientific support for expert testimony on child sexual abuse accommodation. In J. R. Conte (Ed.), *Critical issues in child sexual abuse* (pp. 107–138). Newbury Park, CA: Sage.

Lyon, T. D. (2010). Investigative interviewing of the child. In D. N. Duquette & A. N. Haralambie (Eds.), *Child welfare law and practice* (2nd ed., pp. 87–109). Denver, CO: Bradford.

Maras, K. L., Crane, L., Mulcahy, S., Hawken, T., Cooper, P., Wurtzel, D., & Memon, A. (2017). Autism in the courtroom: Experiences of legal professionals and the autism community. *Journal of Autism and Developmental Disorders, 47*(8), 2610–2620.

Marecek, J., Crawford, M., & Popp, D. (2004). On the construction of gender, sex, and sexualities. In A. H. Eagly, A. E. Beall & R. J. Sternberg (Eds.), *The psychology of gender* (pp. 192–216). New York, NY: Guilford Press.

Mattison, M., Dando, C. J., & Ormerod, T. C. (2018). Drawing the answers: Sketching to support free and probed recall by child witnesses and victims with autism spectrum disorder. *Autism, 22*(2), 181–194.

McGee, H., O'Higgins, M., Garavan, R., & Conroy, R. (2011). Rape and child sexual abuse. *Journal of Interpersonal Violence, 26*(17), 3580–3593.

Melinder, A., Scullin, M., Gravvold, T., & Iversen, M. (2007). The stability and generalizability of young children's suggestibility over a 44-month interval. *Psychology, Crime and Law, 13*(5), 459–468.

Memon, A., & Vartoukian, R. (1996). The effects of repeated questioning on young children's eyewitness testimony. *British Journal of Psychology, 87*(3), 403–415.

Mental Health Act. (1983). *Mental Health Act 1983*. Retrieved from http://www.legislation.gov.uk/ukpga/1983/20/contents.
Mental Health Act. (2007). *Mental Health Act 2007*. Retrieved from http://www.legislation.gov.uk/ukpga/2007/12/contents.
Mikkelson, H. (2010). Consecutive or simultaneous? An analysis of their use in the judicial setting. *Across the Board, Australian Sign Language Interpreters Association, 5*(1), 4–7.
Milne, B., & Bull, R. (2006). Interviewing victims of crime, including children and people with intellectual disabilities. In M. E. Kebbell & Davies, G. M. (Eds.), *Practical psychology for forensic investigations and prosecutions* (pp. 7–23). London: John Wiley & Sons, Ltd.
Ministry of Justice. (2011). *Achieving best evidence in criminal proceedings: Guidance on interviewing victims and witnesses, and guidance on using special measures*. London: Ministry of Justice.
Ministry of Justice. (2015). *The registered intermediary procedural guidance manual*. London: Ministry of Justice.
Moscovici, S. (1998). Social consciousness and its history. *Culture and Psychology, 4*(3), 411–429.
Moser-Mercer, B., Künzli, A., & Korac, M. (1998). Prolonged turns in interpreting: Effects on quality, physiological and psychological stress (Pilot study). *Interpreting, 3*(1), 47–64.
Mulayim, S., Lai, M., & Norma, C. (2014). *Police investigative interviews and interpreting: Context, challenges, and strategies*. Boca Raton, FL: CRC Press.
Mulder, M., & Vrij, A. (1996). Explaining conversation rules to children: An intervention study to facilitate children's accurate responses. *Child Abuse and Neglect, 20*(7), 623–631.
Myers, J., Redlich, A., Goodman, G., Prizmich, L., & Imwinkelried, E. (1999). Jurors' perceptions of hearsay in child sexual abuse cases. *Psychology, Public Policy, and Law, 5*(2), 388–419.
Nakane, I. (2008). Politeness and gender in interpreted police interviews. *Monash University Linguistics Papers, 6*(1), 29–40.
Newlin, C., Steele, L. C., Chamberlin, A., Anderson, J., Kenniston, J., Russell, A., ... & Vaughan-Eden, V. (2015). *Child forensic interviewing: Best practices*. US: Department of Justice, Office of Justice Programs, Office of Juvenile Justice and Delinquency Prevention. Laurel, MD.
O'Connor, D. (2008). Attributions and cognitive closure: Stereotypes of perpetrators and victims of child sexual abuse, 7. Retrieved from https://digitalcommons.unf.edu/ojii_volumes/13/.
Olafson, E., Corwin, D., & Summit, R. (1993). Modern history of child sexual abuse awareness: Cycles of discovery and suppression. *Child Abuse and Neglect, 17*(1), 7–24.
O'Mahoney, B. M. (2009). The emerging role of the Registered Intermediary with the vulnerable witness and offender: Facilitating communication with

the police and members of the judiciary. *British Journal of Learning Disabilities, 38*, 232–237.

O'Mahoney, B. M. (2012). Accused of murder: Supporting the communication needs of a vulnerable defendant at court and at the police station. *Journal of Learning Disabilities and Offending Behaviour, 3*, 77–84.

O'Mahoney, B. M., Smith, K., & Milne, B. (2011). The early identification of vulnerable witnesses prior to an investigative interview. *British Journal of Forensic Practice, 13*(2), 114–123.

Otgaar, H., Candel, I., Smeets, T., & Merckelbach, H. (2010). 'You didn't take Lucy's skirt off': The effect of misleading information on omissions and commissions in children's memory reports. *Legal and Criminological Psychology, 15*(2), 229–241.

Otgaar, H., Howe, M., Merckelbach, H., & Muris, P. (2018). Who is the better eyewitness? Sometimes adults but at other times children. *Current Directions in Psychological Science, 27*(5), 378–385.

Payne, S. (2009). *Redefining justice: Addressing the individual needs of victims and witnesses.* London: Home Office. Retrieved from library.college.police.uk/docs/moj/sara-payne-redefining-justice.pdf.

Peace, K., Shudra, R., Forrester, D., Kasper, R., Harder, J., & Porter, S. (2015). Tall tales across time: Narrative analysis of true and false allegations. *Journal of Investigative Psychology and Offender Profiling, 12*(2), 171–184.

Petersilia, J. R. (2001). Crime victims with developmental disabilities: A review essay. *Criminal Justice and Behaviour, 28*(6), 655–694.

Peterson, C., Wang, Q., & Hou, Y. (2009). "When I was little": Childhood recollections in Chinese and European Canadian grade-school children. *Child Development, 80*(2), 506–518.

Plotnikoff, J., & Woolfson, R. (2004). *In their own words: The experiences of 50 young witnesses in criminal proceedings.* London: NSPCC.

Plotnikoff, J., & Woolfson, R. (2007a). *Evaluation of young witness support: Examining the impact on witnesses and the criminal justice system.* London: Ministry of Justice.

Plotnikoff, J., & Woolfson, R. (2007b). *The "Go-Between": Evaluation of intermediary pathfinder projects.* London: Ministry of Justice.

Plotnikoff, J., & Woolfson, R. (2009). *Measuring up? Evaluating implementation of Government commitments to young witnesses in criminal proceedings.* Nuffield Foundation. Retrieved from https://www.nuffieldfoundation.org/wp-content/uploads/2019/11/Measuring20Up20executive20summary.pdf.

Plotnikoff, J., & Woolfson, R. (2011). Registered intermediaries in action. Retrieved January 2, 2019, from lexiconlimited.co.uk/wp-content/uploads/.../Registered-Intermediaries-in-Action.pdf.

Police and Criminal Evidence Act. (1984). *Police and Criminal Evidence Act 1984.* Retrieved from http://www.legislation.gov.uk/ukpga/1984/60/contents.

Poole, D. A., & Lamb, M. E. (1998). *Investigative interviews of children: A guide for helping professionals*. Washington, DC: American Psychological Association.

Poole, D., & White, L. (1991). Effects of question repetition on the eyewitness testimony of children and adults. *Developmental Psychology, 27*(6), 975–986.

Powell, M., Fisher, R., & Hughes-Scholes, C. (2008). The effect of intra- versus post-interview feedback during simulated practice interviews about child abuse. *Child Abuse and Neglect, 32*(2), 213–227.

Powell, M., Guadagno, B., & Benson, M. (2016). Improving child investigative interviewer performance through computer-based learning activities. *Policing and Society, 26*(4), 365–374.

Prince, E., Andrews, S., Lamb, M., & Foster, J. (2018). The construction of allegedly abused children's narratives in Scottish criminal courts. *Psychology, Crime and Law, 24*(6), 621–651.

Quas, J., Davis, E., Goodman, G., & Myers, J. (2007). Repeated questions, deception, and children's true and false reports ofbody touch. *Child Maltreatment, 12*(1), 60–67.

Quas, J. A., Thompson, W. C., & Clarke-Stewart, K. A. (2005). Do jurors "know" what isn't so about child witnesses? *Law and Human Behaviour, 29*(4), 425–456.

Roberts, K., & Lamb, M. (2009). Reality-monitoring characteristics in confirmed and doubtful allegations of child sexual abuse. *Applied Cognitive Psychology, 24*(8), 1049–1079.

Roberts, K., Lamb, M., & Sternberg, K. (2004). The effects of rapport-building style on children's reports of a staged event. *Applied Cognitive Psychology, 18*(2), 189–202.

Rohrabaugh, M., London, K., & Hall, A. K. (2016). Planning the forensic interview. In W. T. O'Donohue & M. Fanetti (Eds.), *Forensic interviews regarding child sexual abuse: A guide to evidence-based practice* (pp. 197–218). Cham, Switzerland: Springer International Publishing.

Rozinger, I., & Shlesinger, M. (2010). Much ado about something remote: Stress and performance in remote interpreting. *Interpreting, 12*(2), 214–247.

Russell, D. (2000). *Interpreting in legal contexts: Consecutive and simultaneous interpreting* (Doctoral Dissertation). University of Calgary, Calgary, Alberta.

Salaets, H., & Balogh, K. (2015). *Children and justice: Overcoming language barriers*. Cambridge: Intersentia Uitgevers N V.

Saywitz, K., Goodman, G., Nicholas, E., & Moan, S. (1991). Children's memories of a physical examination involving genital touch: Implications for reports of child sexual abuse. *Journal of Consulting and Clinical Psychology, 59*(5), 682–691.

Semmler, C., & Brewer, N. (2002). Using a flow-chart to improve comprehension of jury instructions. *Psychiatry, Psychology and Law, 9*(2), 262–270.

Shaffer, S., & Evans, J. (2018). Interpreters in law enforcement contexts: Practices and experiences according to investigators. *Applied Cognitive Psychology, 32*(2), 150–162.

Smith, S. W. (2016). *Roles, conflicts, and disclosures: American Sign language/English interpreters' adherence to best practices in Legal settings*. Retrieved from https://digitalcommons.wou.edu/cgi/viewcontent.cgi?article=1034&context=theses.

Smith, K., & Milne, R. (2011). Planning the interview. In M. Lamb, D. La Rooy, L. C. Malloy & C. Katz (Eds.), *Children's testimony, A handbook of psychological research and forensic practice* (pp. 87–107). Chichester, England: Wiley.

Spencer, J. R., & Lamb, M. E. (2012). *Children and cross-examination: Time to change the rules?* Oxford, UK: Hart Publishing.

Stern, V. (2010). *The Stern review: A report by Baroness Stern CBE of an independent review into how rape complaints are handled by public authorities in England and Wales*. London: Home Office. Retrieved from https://webarchive.nationalarchives.gov.uk/20110608162919/http:/www.equalities.gov.uk/pdf/Stern_Review:acc_FINAL.pdf.

Temkin, J. (2010). "And always keep a-hold of nurse, for fear of finding something worse": Challenging rape myths in the courtroom. *New Criminal Law Review, 13*(4), 710–734.

Teoh, Y., & Lamb, M. (2010). Preparing children for investigative interviews: Rapport-building, instruction, and evaluation. *Applied Developmental Science, 14*(3), 154–163.

Thierry, K., & Spence, M. (2002). Source-monitoring training facilitates preschoolers' eyewitness memory performance. *Developmental Psychology, 38*(3), 428–437.

Ullman, M. T. (2001). The neural basis of lexicon and grammar in first and second language: The declarative/procedural model. *Bilingualism: Language and Cognitive, 4*(2), 105–122.

Valero Garcés, C., & Lázaro Gutiérrez, R. (2016). Perceptions from the outside in cases of gender violence. 'What are you [the interpreter] doing here?' *European Journal of Applied Linguistics, 4*(1), 57–72.

Vallano, J. P., & Schreiber Compo, N. (2011). A comfortable witness is a good witness: Rapport-building and susceptibility to misinformation in an investigative mock-crime interview. *Applied Cognitive Psychology, 25*(6), 960–970.

Vanny, K. A., Levy, M. H., Greenberg, D. M., & Hayes, S. C. (2009). Mental illness and intellectual disability in Magistrates Courts in New South Wales. *Journal of Intellectual Disability Research, 53*(3), 289–297.

Victims and Witnesses (Scotland) Act. (2014). HMSO. Retrieved from http://www.legislation.gov.uk/asp/2014/1/pdfs/asp_20140001_en.pdf.

Viezzi, M. (2012). Simultaneous and consecutive interpreting (non-conference settings). In C. Millan & F. Bartrina (Eds.), *The Routledge handbook of translation studies* (pp. 377–388). Abingdon: Routledge.

Wadensjö, C. (1998). *Interpreting as interaction*. London; New York, NY: Longman.

Wakefield, S., Kebbell, M., Moston, S., & Westera, N. (2014). Perceptions and profiles of interviews with interpreters: A police survey. *Australian and New Zealand Journal of Criminology, 48*(1), 53–72.

Walker, A. G., Kenniston, J., & Inada, S. S. (2013). *Handbook on questioning children: A linguistic perspective* (3rd ed.). Washington DC: American Bar Association.
Wandrey, L., Lyon, T., Quas, J., & Friedman, W. (2012). Maltreated children's ability to estimate temporal location and numerosity of placement changes and court visits. *Psychology, Public Policy, and Law, 18*(1), 79–104.
Wang, Q. (2001). Cultural effects on adults' earliest childhood recollection and self-description: Implications for the relation between memory and the self. *Journal of Personality and Social Psychology, 81*(2), 220–233.
Wang, Q. (2004). The emergence of cultural self-constructs: Autobiographical memory and self-description in European American and Chinese children. *Developmental Psychology, 40*(1), 3–15.
Wang, Q. (2006). Earliest recollections of self and others in European American and Taiwanese young adults. *Psychological Science, 17*(8), 708–714.
Wang, Q., & Conway, M. A. (2004). The stories we keep: Autobiographical memory in American and Chinese middle-aged adults. *Journal of Personality, 72*(5), 911–938.
Wang, Y. P., Xue, G. M., Chen, C. S., Xue, F., & Dong, Q. (2007). Neural bases of asymmetric language switching in second-language learners: An ER-fMRI study. *NeuroImage, 35*(2), 862–870.
Waterman, A., & Blades, M. (2011). Helping children correctly say "I don't know" to unanswerable questions. *Journal of Experimental Psychology: Applied, 17*(4), 396–405.
Weatherred, J. (2015). Child sexual abuse and the media: A literature review. *Journal of Child Sexual Abuse, 24*(1), 16–34.
Weiss, K. (2009). "Boys will be boys" and other gendered accounts. *Violence Against Women, 15*(7), 810–834.
Westcott, H., & Page, M. (2002). Cross-examination, sexual abuse and child witness identity. *Child Abuse Review, 11*(3), 137–152.
Westera, N., McKimmie, B., Kebbell, M., Milne, R., & Masser, B. (2015). Does the narrative style of video evidence influence judgements about rape complainant testimony? *Applied Cognitive Psychology, 29*(5), 637–646.
Willig, C. (2008). Memory work. In C. Willig (Ed.), *Introducing qualitative research in psychology: Adventures in theory and method* (pp. 125–138). Philadelphia, PA: Open University Press.
Wolfman, M., Brown, D., & Jose, P. (2016). Examining forensic interviewers' perceptions of practice-focused supervision. *Australian and New Zealand Journal of Criminology, 50*(4), 566–581.
Woodbury-Smith, M., & Dein, K. (2014). Autism Spectrum Disorder (ASD) and unlawful behaviour: Where do we go from here? *Journal of Autism and Developmental Disorders, 44*(11), 2734–2741.
Zajac, R., Gross, J., & Hayne, H. (2003). Asked and answered: Questioning children in the courtroom. *Psychiatry, Psychology and Law, 10*(1), 199–209.

Zajac, R., O'Neill, S., & Hayne, H. (2012). Disorder in the courtroom? Child witnesses under cross-examination. *Developmental Review, 32*(3), 181–204.

Zélanti, P., & Droit-Volet, S. (2011). Cognitive abilities explaining age-related changes in time perception of short and long durations. *Journal of Experimental Child Psychology, 109*(2), 143–157.

4

DETECTING DECEPTION

Aldert Vrij and Ronald Fisher

Research developments in nonverbal and verbal lie detection

The two aims of an investigative interview are (1) to obtain a full account from an interviewee and (2) to determine whether the provided information is true or deceptive (Loftus, 2011). Two extensive research areas have emerged to underpin these aims (Vrij, Hope, & Fisher, 2014). One area examines how to obtain the most accurate information from truthful, cooperative interviewees. The two most influential techniques on investigative interviewing practice to date are the Cognitive Interview, used with adult interviewees (Fisher & Geiselman, 1992), and the National Institute of Child Health and Human Development (NICHD) interview protocol (Lamb, Hershkowitz, Orbach, & Esplin, 2008), used with child interviewees.

Another area of research, relevant for this chapter, focuses on deception and, in particular, on the following two questions: 1) What are the differences in behaviour or speech between truth-tellers and liars? 2) How good are people at distinguishing between truth-tellers and liars when paying attention to these behaviours and speech? Two comprehensive meta-analyses summarised research addressing these questions. One meta-analysis summarised more than 150 studies examining nonverbal and verbal cues to deception (DePaulo et al., 2003) and the other meta-analysis summarised the lie detection performance of more than 24,000 observers (Bond & DePaulo, 2006). The outcomes of the two meta-analyses gave a bleak picture: Differences in behaviour and speech between truth-tellers and liars are weak and unreliable (DePaulo et al., 2003) and the average deception-detection accuracy was 54%, which was only just above the level of chance (50%) (Bond & DePaulo, 2006).

In the nonverbal and verbal cues to deception studies summarised by DePaulo et al. (2003), truth-tellers and liars typically gave responses to open-ended questions (e.g., 'Please tell me what happened when you were in that room just now'), without any further interventions from the interviewer. We consider this to be a passive interview style (Vrij & Granhag, 2012). After publication of the two meta-analyses introduced above, researchers started to examine whether a more active interview style, with interventions from the investigator that take into account the mental processes of truth-tellers and liars, would yield better results. To date, four approaches have emerged that resulted in improved ability to distinguish between truth-tellers and liars (around 70–75% detection accuracy) (Vrij, 2018, 2019). They have two important similarities. First, they are verbal lie detection tools that analyse speech content and ignore nonverbal behaviours. Second, they are cognitive-based approaches and focus on differences in mental processes or strategies between truth-tellers and liars, and ignore possible differences in arousal or nervousness between them. The four approaches represent something fundamentally different from what has been employed in the past where mainly nonverbal behaviours were analysed based on the assumption that they would differ between truth-tellers and liars, because liars were supposed to be more nervous than truth-tellers (Vrij, 2019). This assumption has proven to be false (Vrij, 2019). These four approaches are: strategic use of evidence, assessment criteria indicative of deception, verifiability approach and cognitive credibility assessment. We briefly outline them in a similar way as we have done elsewhere (Vrij, 2018, 2019; Vrij & Fisher, 2016).

Strategic use of evidence (SUE)

During interviews truth-tellers are generally forthcoming, whereas liars are inclined to be avoidant (e.g., in a free recall, avoiding mentioning where they were at a specific time), or use denials (e.g., denying having been at a certain place at a specific time when asked directly; Granhag & Hartwig, 2008). When investigators ask questions related to the evidence without making the interviewee aware that they possess this evidence, the different strategies used by truth-tellers and liars result in truth-tellers' accounts being more consistent with the available evidence than liars' accounts (Hartwig, Granhag, & Luke, 2014). In addition, when liars realise during an interview that the interviewer may hold some incriminating evidence against them, they are inclined to change their statement and try to provide an innocent explanation for the evidence. These changes in statements are called within-statement inconsistencies in SUE research and truth-tellers have more of these inconsistencies than liars (Hartwig, Granhag, & Luke, 2014).

Verifiability approach (VA)

In principle, liars prefer to provide many details, because detailed accounts are more likely to be believed (Bell & Loftus, 1989; Nahari, Vrij, & Fisher, 2012). Liars also prefer to avoid mentioning too many details out of fear that investigators will check such details, which could subsequently give the lie away (Nahari, Vrij, & Fisher, 2012). A strategy that incorporates both goals is to provide details that cannot be verified. Liars use this strategy and typically report fewer details that can be checked than truth-tellers (Nahari, Vrij, & Fisher, 2014a). This effect becomes stronger when interviewees are asked to include, where possible, details in their statement that the investigator can check, as truth-tellers, more than liars, add checkable details in their accounts following such a request (Harvey, Vrij, Nahari, & Ludwig, 2017; Nahari, Vrij, & Fisher, 2014b).

Assessment criteria indicative of deception (ACID)

The core of ACID is the use of mnemonics, which are interview techniques that facilitate memory recall (Colwell, Hiscock-Anisman, & Fede, 2013; Colwell, Hiscock-Anisman, Memon, Taylor, & Prewett, 2007). An example is describing the event from the perspective of another person present during the event (e.g., 'What could that person see?'). These mnemonics are derived from the Cognitive Interview (Fisher & Geiselman, 1992), a well-established protocol to elicit more information from cooperative witnesses. The ACID interview procedure starts with an initial free recall in which an interviewee is invited to describe, in as much detail as possible, everything that happened during a specific period of time. This is followed by the use of mnemonics. Truth-tellers provide more additional details than liars when exposed to the mnemonics.

Cognitive credibility assessment (CCA)

The CCA technique comprises three elements: (i) Imposing cognitive load; (ii) Encouraging interviewees to say more and (iii) Asking unexpected questions.

Imposing cognitive load

In interview settings, lying is typically more mentally taxing than truth-telling (see fMRI research, Christ et al., 2009). Investigators can exploit truth-tellers' and liars' different mental states by making the interview setting cognitively more difficult through additional requests. Liars, whose mental resources are more depleted, are less able than truth-tellers to cope with such additional requests (Debey, Verschuere, & Crombez, 2012), which impairs their storytelling (Evans, Michael, Meissner, & Brandon, 2013).

Encouraging interviewees to say more

Words carry the information that allows others to distinguish between liars and truth-tellers (Vrij, Mann, Kristen, & Fisher, 2007). Therefore, encouraging interviewees to say more should provide more cues/opportunities to distinguish between truth-tellers and liars. This is particularly relevant as truth-tellers typically do not provide spontaneously all the information they know (Fisher, 2010; Vrij, Hope, & Fisher, 2014). However, they will provide more information after prompting. Liars are unable or unwilling to provide the same amount or same type of information as truth-tellers do after receiving such prompts.

Asking unexpected questions

Liars typically prepare themselves for interviews by considering answers to possible questions (Hartwig, Granhag, & Strömwall, 2007). This strategy can be successful as planned lies contain fewer cues to deceit than spontaneous lies (DePaulo et al., 2003). However, the strategy has a weakness: Liars cannot know which questions will be asked. Investigators can exploit this weakness by asking a mixture of anticipated and unanticipated questions. Liars have more difficulties in answering the unanticipated questions than the anticipated questions, whereas truth-tellers can answer these questions with similar ease (Lancaster, Vrij, Hope, & Waller, 2012).

We have mainly worked on the CCA approach, which is the focus of the remainder of the chapter.

Underpinning research of CCA

Research has been carried out with all three elements of CCA: Imposing cognitive load, encouraging interviewees to say more, and asking unexpected questions.

Imposing cognitive load

One way to impose cognitive load is by asking interviewees to tell their stories in reverse order. This increases cognitive load because (1) it runs counter to the natural forward-order coding of sequentially occurring events (Gilbert & Fisher, 2006; Kahana, 1996), and (2) it disrupts reconstructing events from a schema (Geiselman & Callot, 1990). In one experiment interviewees (truth-tellers and liars) were requested to report the activities they carried out last Saturday night (Evans et al., 2013). They were asked to do this either in the normal order or in reverse order (e.g., start the story with going to bed and work your way back in time). Observers who watched the videotaped interviews were more accurate in classifying truth-tellers and liars in the reverse order condition (67% accuracy) than in the standard condition (37% accuracy). Another technique is the use of forced turn-taking which can be employed when two or more interviewees are interviewed together (Vernham, Vrij, Mann, Leal, & Hillman, 2014). In forced turn-taking, after asking the question, the investigator determines who starts answering a question. The investigator then interrupts that person after a short period of time and asks a second interviewee to continue with the story. After a short period of time, that person is interrupted and the third person (or the first person again in case of interviewing a pair) is asked to continue, etc. Compared to truth-tellers, liars wait longer with continuing after forced turned taking. And once they continue, they are more likely than truth-tellers to first repeat what the earlier speaker(s) had said.

Encouraging interviewees to say more

There are two reasons why interviewees do not spontaneously report all the information that is stored in their memory. First, because memory retrieval, like most cognitive processes, is imperfect, people cannot recall all the information spontaneously. Memory-enhancement tools, called mnemonics, have been designed to address this (Fisher & Geiselman, 1992). Asking interviewees to sketch while talking is such a mnemonic. Sketching while narrating elicits additional information in truth-tellers (Dando, Wilcock, & Milne, 2009; Leins, Fisher, Pludwinsky, Robertson, & Mueller, 2014; Mattison, Dando, & Omerod, 2015). This happens for several reasons (Vrij et al., 2018a). First, sketching serves to reinstate context, which itself enhances recall (encoding specificity principle, Thomson & Tulving, 1970 and Tulving & Thomson, 1973). Second, sketching, a visual output, is more compatible with visually experienced events. This facilitates recalling visual or spatial information in alignment with the Cognitive Interview principle of 'code compatible output' (Fisher & Geiselman, 1992). Third, sketching slows down the output process, which then affords the interviewee more time to think about the event. More time for retrieval is likely to enhance recall. Fourth, sketching implies a subtle request for more precise information than a verbal response. That is, when drawing a sketch, one must locate the sketched person/object in a specific location, a fact that might not be included in a verbal response (Vrij, Mann, Leal, & Fisher, 2012). In the only deception experiment that examined sketching while narrating (Vrij et al., 2018a), sketching while narrating resulted in more additional details from truth-tellers than from liars. Truth-tellers' memory of the event is likely to be richer than the made-up story liars have prepared to tell in advance or can spontaneously fabricate, which may lead to truth-tellers reporting more details when requested to sketch than liars.

A second reason why interviewees do not spontaneously report all they know is that they are unaware of how much information to provide (Fisher, 2010). An effective way to change truth-tellers' idea about how much information to provide is to expose them to a Model Statement, which is an example of a detailed account unrelated to the topic of the interview (Leal, Vrij, Warmelink, Vernham, & Fisher, 2015). A Model Statement likely works better than the verbal request 'to provide all the details someone can remember', because the former is a concrete example whereas the latter is an abstract instruction. It may be easier for people to follow concrete examples than abstract instructions (Leal, Vrij, Deeb, & Jupe, 2018).

Asking unexpected questions

Asking a mixture of expected and unexpected questions reveals differences between truth-tellers and liars. In all likelihood, liars will have prepared themselves for the expected questions and should be able to answer them in sufficient detail. However, they may struggle to answer in detail the unexpected questions. In Warmelink, Vrij, Mann, Jundi, and Granhag (2012) truth-tellers and liars were interviewed about their alleged forthcoming trip. Expected questions about the purpose of the trip (e.g., 'What is the main purpose of your trip?') were followed by unexpected questions about transport (e.g., 'How are you going to travel to your destination?'), planning ('What part of the trip was easiest to plan?') and the core event ('Keep in mind an image of the most important thing you are going to do on this trip. Please describe this mental image in detail.'). Liars gave significantly more details than truth-tellers to the expected questions, but significantly fewer details to the unexpected questions.

Two recent meta-analyses examined the CCA approach (Vrij, Fisher, & Blank, 2017: 34 studies; Vrij, Fisher, Blank, Leal, & Mann, 2016: 14 studies). Vrij et al. (2016) examined the cues that emerged as diagnostic to deceit in the CCA conditions and in the standard conditions (in which a passive interview technique was employed). In the CCA conditions, 65% of the cues that were examined differentiated truth-tellers from liars, whereas the same cues were indicative of truth or deceit in only 30% in the standard condition. In other words, CCA interview protocols elicited twice as many cues indicative of truth-telling or deceit than the standard protocols.

Vrij, Fisher, and Blank (2017) examined accuracy rates, the correct classifications of truth-tellers and liars. They were based either on observers' judgements or on computer software (statistical algorithms). In the studies, CCA protocols resulted in 71% accuracy compared to 56% accuracy in the standard interview protocols (accuracy rates based on human observers and computer software combined). This difference represented a medium effect size, $d = .42$. These findings may not seem too impressive but three factors should be taken into account. First, the observer did not know the truth-teller/liar (i.e., sender) and had no background information about the case. Thus, the observer could rely only on the nonverbal and verbal cues displayed by the sender, which is a particularly challenging task (Bond & DePaulo, 2006; Vrij, 2008). Second, in the studies the efficacy of one

CCA technique was tested at the time. It could well be that a combination of techniques would yield better results, which we found in the CCA lie detection training we gave to practitioners (see later). Third, improvement could be made when different dependent variables are introduced. In the studies summarised in the two meta-analyses, the dependent variable was typically the total number of details. This is a limited variable because it does not take into account the different strategies truth-tellers and liars use. Take, for example, the Model Statement. Both truth-tellers and liars realise that they need to provide more details after exposure to a Model Statement (Ewens et al., 2016), which they both do to a similar extent (Vrij, Leal, & Fisher, 2019). A difference between truth-tellers and liars emerges, however, when more nuanced dependent variables are used that take into account the different strategies truth-tellers and liars use. Two examples of this emerged in the literature to date, the use of complications (Vrij, Leal et al., 2017; Vrij, Leal, Jupe, & Harvey, 2018b) and the distinction between core and peripheral details (Leal, Vrij, Deeb, & Jupe, 2018). Complications are 'occurrences that affect the story-teller and make a situation more difficult' ('We got lost on the way to the cinema') (Vrij et al., 2020, pp. 26–27). Truth-tellers report more complications than liars. Liars prefer to keep their stories simple (Hartwig, Granhag, & Strömwall, 2007), but adding complications makes the story more complex. A Model Statement increases the number of complications reported, particularly by truth-tellers (Vrij, Leal et al., 2017; Vrij et al., 2018b). Complications are details that truth-tellers generally leave out when describing key aspects of activities as a story often makes perfect sense and is easily understood without reporting complications. However, exposure to a Model Statement encourages truth-tellers to report more of these complications.

Core details are details that, if changed, can result in changes in the basic and most important part of the story; details that have no such impact are considered peripheral (Heuer & Reisberg, 1990). Thus, if someone describes attending an Adele pop concert, all details about the actual concert are core details whereas information about, for example, drinks in the pub after the concert, are peripheral details. Truth-tellers, who have actually experienced an event (e.g., attending an Adele pop concert), will easily be able to provide many core and peripheral details, by employing a 'tell it all strategy' (Hartwig, Granhag, & Strömwall, 2007). For liars, who have not experienced an event (e.g., did not attend an Adele concert), providing core details is more difficult because they have to make up information, and is risky because the details may provide leads to investigators that can be checked. Thus, liars may avoid providing too many core details in an attempt to minimise the risk of presenting incriminating information (Granhag & Hartwig, 2008; Nahari et al., 2014a), but may compensate for this by providing peripheral details in an attempt to provide a sufficient amount of detail. This assumption was supported in Leal, Vrij, Deeb, and Jupe's (2018) experiment, where, after exposure to the Model Statement, truth-tellers provided more peripheral details than liars; however, no differences were found for total number of details.

Transition from research to practice

Lie detection tools become pragmatically valuable only when they are frequently used in real life. There are at least four challenges when introducing lie detection tools into interviewing practice. The first challenge is availability. Academics, who carry out most of the research, spend most of their time teaching and doing research rather than providing training to practitioners. Unless they are linked to commercial training companies – we do not know a single academic who is – the time they can spend on training is sporadic. This will have a negative impact on the number of practitioners they can reach. It is also disadvantageous to being invited to provide training. Organisations often prefer trainers who are frequently and at short notice available instead of trainers whose availability is limited to just a few weeks a year.

The second challenge is speaking the right language. Academics are used to conference presentations in which they describe their studies in fine detail. They feel this is important because only then can the audience judge the quality of the research. Academics realise that less research detail is required when speaking to practitioners. However, in meetings where academics and practitioners meet, we often notice that academics give talks, which are still far too technical. We often get the impression that practitioners do not understand what is going on, neither do they look particularly interested. They often are ready to believe that the quality of the work is good without having seen the evidence and just want to know how the technique works and how to use it. It took us many try-outs to make our lie detection presentation suitable for practitioners. We have taken out all the graphs, percentages and other numbers.

The third challenge is to find sufficient time for practitioners to practise the techniques in the training. People mainly learn from practice and our experience is that a lot of practice is required to become familiar with the CCA techniques. We started our CCA training as a one-day training which we gave to police detectives (Vrij, Leal, Mann, Vernham, & Brankaert, 2015). After the one-day training, we asked the police detectives to interview our mock suspects using our CCA techniques. We video-recorded these interviews. These videos showed that the detectives experienced problems with implementing the CCA techniques in the way we taught them in the training. We therefore decided to add more exercises to the training. The training now lasts three days and the two additional days are filled with practical exercises.

The fourth challenge is how practitioners can use the taught lie detection tool in their interviewing work. Lie detection training typically focuses on the lie detection aspect only but to make practitioners willing to use a lie detection tool in real life other issues become relevant. Elsewhere (Vrij, 2018; Vrij & Fisher, 2016) we discuss several questions that we think are relevant in this context. We summarise them here.

Is the technique easy to incorporate in a typical information-gathering interview?

If a technique can be easily incorporated in a typical information-gathering interview, investigators are more likely to consider it to be helpful; if not, investigators may become reluctant or even threatened by it. CCA adheres to the principles of a standard investigative interview but adds a more active interviewing element to it. The already strong link between CCA and a standard investigative interview makes CCA easy to implement in standard interviews.

Will the technique affect the response of a truthful interviewee?

The aim of an investigative interview is to elicit from an interviewee a complete and accurate account of what s/he knows. It is important to consider whether a technique has the potential to block this aim. Some requests to impose cognitive load (e.g., carrying out a secondary task at the same time as story-telling) will hamper eliciting information because the interviewees' cognitive resources are being directed to something other than searching through memory. Such requests also could make a truth-teller feel uncomfortable, which will subsequently hamper eliciting information (Vrij, Meissner et al., 2017). The unanticipated questions technique could make a truth-teller feel uncomfortable in case the questions are seen as odd. The remaining techniques are not expected to have a negative influence on the amount and accuracy of the information truth-tellers report.

Does the technique have within-subjects measurements?

Practitioners often stress the importance of 'within-subjects' lie detection tools (Vrij, 2016). That is, they wish to make a decision about the veracity status of an interviewee by comparing different responses made by the same interviewee during a single interview. This request makes perfect sense. There are large individual differences in people's verbal and nonverbal behaviours and physiological responses (DePaulo & Friedman, 1998). For example, some people are eloquent, others are not. Therefore, simple decision rules such as 'He does not say much, so he must be lying' will not work. The reverse-order technique (part of imposing cognitive load) can be used as a within-subjects lie detection tool (Vrij, 2016). Interviewees are first asked in an open-ended question to describe in as much detail as possible what they have experienced and are then invited to report it again, but this time in reverse order. This instruction invites truth-tellers to think about the event again, but from a different perspective and this often leads to reminiscences. Liars include fewer reminiscences than truth-tellers (Ewens et al., 2016; Shaw et al., 2014; Vrij, Leal, Mann, & Fisher, 2012). One reason for this is that liars are very concerned about consistency, more so than truth-tellers (Vrij, Fisher, Blank, Leal, & Mann, 2016). They therefore may see this as a test ('Can I report again what I just reported, but now in reverse order?'). Adding new information in the reverse order recall makes this recall less consistent with the initial chronological recall, so, from a consistency perspective, liars are unlikely to add new detail.

The Model Statement technique (part of the 'encouraging interviewees to say more' approach) allows investigators to make within-subjects comparisons. In this method the interviewer starts the interview with inviting the interviewee to report in as much detail as possible what s/he has experienced. After this initial recall, the investigator lets him/her listen to a Model Statement and invites him/her again to report in as much detail as possible what s/he has experienced. From a lie detection perspective, it is then relevant to observe the number of new complications the interviewee has mentioned or the amount of new peripheral detail provided.

Asking unexpected questions can also be used as a within-subjects measure. For liars, expected questions should be easier to answer than unexpected questions, because liars can give their planned and rehearsed answers to the expected questions, but they need to fabricate answers to the unexpected questions. In contrast, truth-tellers experience similar levels of cognitive load while answering expected and unexpected questions. This difference between truth-tellers and liars becomes evident because truth-tellers produce more comparable answers to the expected and unexpected questions than liars (Lancaster, Vrij, Hope, & Waller, 2012; Leins, Fisher, & Vrij, 2012; Roos af Hjelmsäter, Ohman, Granhag, & Vrij, 2014; Vrij et al., 2009).

Is the technique easy to use?

Investigators may be less receptive to techniques that require a lot of skill, training, equipment or resources. The 'imposing cognitive load' and 'asking unanticipated questions' techniques need some practice. For imposing cognitive load, skills are required to introduce an additional request that introduces cognitive load to interviewees. For example, the request to report a story in reverse chronological is seen as odd if no justification for this question is given. For 'asking unanticipated questions', training is required about which questions to ask during the interview. The 'encouraging interviewees to say more' techniques can be introduced without much training.

Does the technique sufficiently protect truth-telling interviewees against appearing suspicious?

The errors lie detection tools generate are not random; some tools are prone to false-positive errors (judging a truth-teller as a liar), whereas other tools are prone to false-negative errors (judging a liar as a truth-teller). Which error is most serious depends on the situation, but when an investigator mistakenly believes that an innocent suspect is lying (false-positive error), the investigator often is inclined to use an aggressive, accusatory style of interview methods to make the suspect admit that s/he is lying (Kassin, Goldstein, & Savitsky, 2003). Truth-tellers can easily struggle when cognitive load is imposed on them, which will make them look like liars. The other techniques probably protect truth-tellers sufficiently well enough against being seen as liars.

Is the technique sufficiently protected against countermeasures?

Countermeasures are attempts by liars to beat the lie detection tool and to make a convincing impression on investigators. The 'asking unanticipated questions' technique is difficult to counteract because of the surprise element of the questions that will be asked. The challenge liars face in counteracting the 'imposing cognitive load' and 'encouraging interviewees to say more' techniques is to look like truth-tellers. That is, truth-tellers should find it easier to cope with the additional imposing cognitive load requests; and truth-tellers can typically provide more details than liars when encouraged to do so because liars are restricted by the fact that the more information they volunteer, the more leads they provide to investigators, which can give away that they are lying. As we discussed earlier in this chapter, the verifiability approach is resistant against countermeasures because liars cannot provide verifiable details for their made-up stories.

The impact and legacy of the research

We have provided CCA training in countries all over the world (e.g., Canada, USA, Mexico, UK, Italy, Singapore). Our training is based on theory and has an empirical foundation, presented earlier. Training based on theory and research is scarce in the lie detection world (Vrij, Hartwig, & Granhag, 2018). The problem is that delivering lie detection training is unprotected, meaning that literally everyone can design and deliver lie detection training. This is in sharp contrast to, for example, bringing medication on to the market. Prior to this, these medicines need to be thoroughly tested. It needs to be demonstrated that it works and what the side effects are. No testing is needed to bring lie detection training onto the market.

Take for example the Behavior Analysis Interview (BAI). It is part of the Reid school of interrogation and consists of a list of 15 questions (e.g., 'Did you commit the crime?') to which truth-tellers and liars are supposed to give different nonverbal and verbal responses. The Reid interrogation technique has been taught to more than 500,000 practitioners world-wide according to the Reid website. The Reid interrogation manual (Inbau, Reid, Buckley, & Jayne, 2013) refers to a field study as support for the BAI (Horvath, Jayne, & Buckley, 1994). The problem with this field study, also acknowledged by Horvath et al. (1994), was a lack of ground truth because the researchers actually did not know which of the 60 suspects were telling the truth and which were lying. In the only laboratory experiment to date that tested the BAI, the liars and truth-tellers did not display the nonverbal responses predicted in the BAI (Vrij, Mann, & Fisher, 2006).

Ekman (1985) has long argued that deceptive emotional information is leaked by micro-expressions, fleeting but complete facial expressions that are thought to reveal the felt emotion during emotional concealment. This idea has enjoyed popularity in the media (Henig, 2006) and scientific community (Schubert, 2006) and, as our contacts revealed, is frequently taught to practitioners. Porter and ten Brinke (2008) conducted the first and, to date, only published experiment examining the relationship between micro-expressions and deception. They found micro-expressions in only 14 video fragments (2% of the video fragments included in the study), and 6 were displayed by truth-tellers rather than by liars.

When we discuss with practitioners the importance of demonstrating through evidence that a lie detection technique works, they sometimes say that they have heard trainers claim that the evidence is available but that it cannot be shared with trainees because it is confidential. We would like to caution against this. We could understand why how a tool works is sometimes confidential. That is, when someone claims to have developed a sophisticated machine that can detect lies through analysing voice patterns, they do not have to tell their clients what that machine is measuring exactly. However, showing that the machine works cannot be confidential.

We therefore consider the unclassified, USA government-funded research program on the science of interviewing and interrogation a welcome development (Meissner, Surmon-Böhr, Oleszkiewicz, & Alison, 2017). This High-Value Detainee Interrogation Group (HIG) Research Program started in 2010 and has identified effective approaches for developing cooperation and rapport, eliciting information, challenging inconsistencies by presenting evidence or information strategically, and assessing credibility using cognitive cues and strategic questioning tactics. Based on those findings, the HIG has developed training programs in a series of specialised areas (Meissner et al., 2017).

Lessons learnt for applied researchers

Earlier in this chapter we mentioned that setting up a good training package is not always easy for researchers because they tend to emphasise the research elements too much in their training. We finish this chapter by raising five more points we believe are worthwhile to think about for applied researchers.

First, realise that working together with practitioners can be very fruitful. Practitioners can give researchers information about how they work and what difficulties they face. Researchers, together with practitioners, can translate this information into innovative studies. Practitioners can also give feedback about how techniques developed in the lab work in real life and can point out some weaknesses of techniques. Collaboration with practitioners has moved lie detection research forward. Prime examples of this are: (1) the development from passive to active interviewing to detect deception research that is currently dominating the field; and (2) the development of within-subjects measures.

Second, realise that good applied research is always theory-based. Sometimes we hear applied researchers say that they 'hate theory'. We sincerely hope that they are joking when they say so, because that statement makes no sense. Good applied research should always be embedded in theory, because only then it can be established why something works and also when it will work (and when it will not). Also, good theory gives practitioners insight into how to adapt a technique when the conditions vary.

Third, realise that carrying out research takes time and it could easily create frictions with practitioners if this is not properly communicated. It takes us typically one year to carry out a study from start (coming up with the idea) to finish (writing up the report). This is a much longer time period than many practitioners expect, because they often believe that a study can be completed in a few months. We are aware that this can easily lead to impatience or disappointment amongst practitioners. We therefore present them at the earliest opportunity with a timeline outlining all stages of the research project.

Fourth, realise that quality research involves good research designs to ensure that meaningful conclusions can be drawn. Two aspects are hereby particularly relevant. It is crucial to always include a control group in the research design to compare the intervention with. This sometimes can be seen as a 'boring' condition, but without a control condition an intervention cannot be evaluated. In addition, if an intervention consists of multiple components – as often happens – it is important to examine the effect of each component separately, because only then can meaningful conclusions be drawn about the exact working of the intervention.

Finally, realise that trying to represent real life in laboratory experiments can be challenging – laboratory settings have natural limitations

- but it has substantial advantages: The more a researcher succeeds in introducing real-life experiences into laboratory settings, the more the findings emerging from these laboratories tell us about real life and the more likely practitioners are to take up the conclusions.

Conclusion

Intensive collaborations between academics and practitioners have resulted in much progress in nonverbal and verbal lie detection. They resulted in theory-based interview protocols, which obtain 70–75% accuracy in correctly classifying truth-tellers and liars. Teaching those tools to practitioners is currently ongoing but is a slow process. First, it requires academics to present their work in a different way than they are used to (e.g., presenting their work to fellow academics and under- or postgraduate students). Second, it requires spending a lot of time on training, and academics typically lack such time.

References

Bell, B. E., & Loftus, E. F. (1989). Trivial persuasion in the courtroom: The power of (a few) minor details. *Journal of Personality and Social Psychology, 56*(5), 669–679.

Bond, C. F., & DePaulo, B. M. (2006). Accuracy of deception judgements. *Personality and Social Psychology Review, 10*(3), 214–234.

Christ, S. E., Van Essen, D. C., Watson, J. M., Brubaker, L. E., & McDermott, K. B. (2009). The contributions of prefrontal cortex and executive control to deception: Evidence from activation likelihood estimate meta-analyses. *Cerebral Cortex, 19*(7), 1557–1566.

Colwell, K., Hiscock-Anisman, C. K., & Fede, J. (2013). Assessment criteria indicative of deception: An example of the new paradigm of differential recall enhancement. In B. S. Cooper, D. Griesel & M. Ternes (Eds.), *Applied issues in investigative interviewing, eyewitness memory, and credibility assessment* (pp. 259–292). New York, NY: Springer.

Colwell, K., Hiscock-Anisman, C. K., Memon, A., Taylor, L., & Prewett, J. (2007). Assessment criteria indicative of deception (ACID): An integrated system of investigative interviewing and detecting deception. *Journal of Investigative Psychology and Offender Profiling, 4*(3), 167–180.

Dando, C., Wilcock, R., & Milne, R. (2009). The Cognitive Interview: The efficacy of a modified mental reinstatement of context procedure for frontline police investigators. *Applied Cognitive Psychology, 23*(1), 138–147.

Debey, E., Verschuere, B., & Crombez, G. (2012). Lying and executive control: An experimental investigation using ego depletion and goal neglect. *Acta Psychologica, 140*(2), 133–141.

DePaulo, B. M., & Friedman, H. S. (1998). Nonverbal communication. In D. T. Gilbert, S. T. Fiske & G. Lindzey (Eds.), *The handbook of social psychology* (pp. 3–40). Boston, MA: McGraw-Hill.

DePaulo, B. M., Lindsay, J. L., Malone, B. E., Muhlenbruck, L., Charlton, K., & Cooper, H. (2003). Cues to deception. *Psychological Bulletin, 129*(1), 74–118.

Ekman, P. (1985). *Telling lies: Clues to deceit in the marketplace, politics and marriage.* New York, NY: W. W. Norton. (Reprinted in 1992, 2001 and 2009).

Evans, J. R., Michael, S. W., Meissner, C. A., & Brandon, S. E. (2013). Validating a new assessment method for deception detection: Introducing a psychologically based credibility assessment tool. *Journal of Applied Research in Memory and Cognition, 2*(1), 33–41.

Ewens, S., Vrij, A., Leal, S., Mann, S., Jo, E., Shaboltas, A., … Houston, K. (2016). Using the model statement to elicit information and cues to deceit from native speakers, non-native speakers and those talking through an interpreter. *Applied Cognitive Psychology, 30*(6), 854–862.

Fisher, R. P. (2010). Interviewing cooperative witnesses. *Legal and Criminological Psychology, 15*(1), 25–38.

Fisher, R. P., & Geiselman, R. E. (1992). *Memory enhancing techniques for investigative interviewing: The cognitive interview.* Springfield, IL: Charles C. Thomas.

Geiselman, R. E., & Callot, R. (1990). Reverse and forward order recall of script based text. *Applied Cognitive Psychology, 4*(2), 141–144.

Gilbert, J. A. E., & Fisher, R. P. (2006). The effects of varied retrieval cues on reminiscence in eyewitness memory. *Applied Cognitive Psychology, 20*(6), 723–739.

Granhag, P. A., & Hartwig, M. (2008). A new theoretical perspective on deception detection: On the psychology of instrumental mind-reading. *Psychology, Crime and Law, 14*(3), 189–200.

Hartwig, M., Granhag, P. A., & Luke, T. (2014). Strategic use of evidence during investigative interviews: The state of the science. In D. C. Raskin, C. R. Honts & J. C. Kircher (Eds.), *Credibility assessment: Scientific research and applications* (pp. 1–36). Cambridge: Academic Press.

Hartwig, M., Granhag, P. A., & Strömwall, L. (2007). Guilty and innocent suspects' strategies during police interrogations. *Psychology, Crime, and Law, 13*(2), 213–227.

Harvey, A., Vrij, A., Nahari, G., & Ludwig, K. (2017). Applying the verifiability approach to insurance claims settings: Exploring the effect of the information protocol. *Legal and Criminological Psychology, 22*(1), 47–59.

Henig, R. M. (2006, February 5). Looking for the lie. *New York Times.* Retrieved from www.nytimes.com.

Heuer, F., & Reisberg, D. (1990). Vivid memories of emotional events: The accuracy of remembered minutiae. *Memory and Cognition, 18*(5), 496–506.

Horvath, F., Jayne, B., & Buckley, J. (1994). Differentiation of truthful and deceptive criminal suspects in behavioral analysis interviews. *Journal of Forensic Sciences, 39*(3), 793–807.

Inbau, F. E., Reid, J. E., Buckley, J. P., & Jayne, B. C. (2013). *Criminal interrogation and confessions* (5th ed.). Burlington, MA: Jones & Bartlett Learning.

Kahana, M. J. (1996). Associate retrieval processes in free recall. *Memory and Cognition, 24*(1), 103–109.

Kassin, S. M., Goldstein, C. J., & Savitsky, K. (2003). Behavioral confirmation in the interrogation room: On the dangers of presuming guilt. *Law and Human Behavior, 27*(2), 187–203.

Lamb, M. E., Hershkowitz, I., Orbach, Y., & Esplin, P. W. (2008). *Tell me what happened: Structured investigative interviews of child victims and witnesses.* Chichester, UK and Hoboken, NJ: Wiley.

Lancaster, G. L. J., Vrij, A., Hope, L., & Waller, B. (2012). Sorting the liars from the truth tellers: The benefits of asking unanticipated questions. *Applied Cognitive Psychology, 27*, 107–114.

Leal, S., Vrij, A., Deeb, H., & Jupe, L. (2018). Using the model statement to elicit verbal differences between truth tellers and liars: The benefit of examining core and peripheral details. *Journal of Applied Research in Memory and Cognition, 7*(4), 610–617.

Leal, S., Vrij, A., Warmelink, L., Vernham, Z., & Fisher, R. (2015). You cannot hide your telephone lies: Providing a model statement as an aid to detect deception in insurance telephone calls. *Legal and Criminological Psychology, 20*(1), 129–146.

Leins, D., Fisher, R. P., Pludwinsky, L., Robertson, B., & Mueller, D. H. (2014). Interview protocols to facilitate human intelligence sources' recollections of meetings. *Applied Cognitive Psychology, 28*(6), 926–935.

Leins, D., Fisher, R., & Vrij, A. (2012). Drawing on liars' lack of cognitive flexibility: Detecting deception through varying report modes. *Applied Cognitive Psychology, 26*(4), 601–607.

Loftus, E. F. (2011). Intelligence gathering post-9/11. *American Psychologist, 66*(6), 532–541.

Mattison, M. C. L., Dando, C. J., & Ormerod, T. C. (2015). Sketching to remember: Episodic free recall task support for child witnesses and victims with autism spectrum disorder. *Journal of Autism and Developmental Disorders, 45*(6), 1751–1765.

Meissner, C. A., Surmon-Böhr, F., Oleszkiewicz, S., & Alison, L. J. (2017). Developing an evidence-based perspective on interrogation: A review of the U.S. Government's High-Value Detainee Interrogation Group Research Program. *Psychology, Public Policy, and Law, 23*(4), 438–457.

Nahari, G., Vrij, A., & Fisher, R. P. (2012). Does the truth come out in the writing? SCAN as a lie detection tool. *Law and Human Behavior, 36*(1), 68–76.

Nahari, G., Vrij, A., & Fisher, R. P. (2014a). Exploiting liars' verbal strategies by examining unverifiable details. *Legal and Criminological Psychology, 19*(2), 227–239.

Nahari, G., Vrij, A., & Fisher, R. P. (2014b). The verifiability approach: Countermeasures facilitate its ability to discriminate between truths and lies. *Applied Cognitive Psychology, 28*(1), 122–128.

Porter, S., & ten Brinke, L. (2008). Reading between the lies: Identifying concealed and falsified emotions in universal facial expressions. *Psychological Science, 19*(5), 508–514.

Roos af Hjelmsäter, E., Öhman, L., Granhag, P. A., & Vrij, A. (2014). Mapping deception in adolescents: Eliciting cues to deceit through an unanticipated spatial drawing task. *Legal and Criminological Psychology, 19*(1), 179–188.

Schubert, S. (2006, October). A look tells all. *Scientific American Mind*. Retrieved from www.sciamind.com.

Shaw, D., Vrij, A., Leal, S., Mann, S., Hillman, J., Granhag, P. A., & Fisher, R. P. (2014). 'We'll take it from here': The effect of changing interviewers in information gathering interviews. *Applied Cognitive Psychology, 28*(6), 908–916.

Thomson, D. M., & Tulving, E. (1970). Associative encoding and retrieval: Weak and strong cues. *Journal of Experimental Psychology, 86*(2), 255–262.

Tulving, E., & Thomson, D. M. (1973). Encoding specificity and retrieval processes in episodic memory. *Psychological Review, 80*(5), 352–373.

Vernham, Z., Vrij, A., Mann, S., Leal, S., & Hillman, J. (2014). Collective interviewing: Eliciting cues to deceit using a turn-taking approach. *Psychology, Public Policy and Law, 20*(3), 309–324.

Vrij, A. (2008). *Detecting lies and deceit: Pitfalls and opportunities* (2nd ed.). Chichester: John Wiley and Sons.

Vrij, A. (2016). Baselining as a lie detection method. *Applied Cognitive Psychology, 30*(6), 1112–1119.

Vrij, A. (2018). Verbal lie detection tools from an applied perspective. In J. P. Rosenfeld (Ed.), *Detecting concealed information and deception: Recent developments* (pp. 297–321). San Diego, CA: Elsevier, Academic Press.

Vrij, A. (2019). Deception and truth detection when analysing (non)verbal cues. *Applied Cognitive Psychology, 33*(2), 160–167.

Vrij, A., & Fisher, R. P. (2016). Which lie detection tools are ready for use in the criminal justice system? *Journal of Applied Research in Memory and Cognition, 5*(3), 302–307.

Vrij, A., Fisher, R., & Blank, H. (2017). A cognitive approach to lie detection: A meta-analysis. *Legal and Criminological Psychology, 22*(1), 1–21.

Vrij, A., Fisher, R., Blank, H., Leal, S., & Mann, S. (2016). A cognitive approach to elicit nonverbal and verbal cues of deceit. In J. W. van Prooijen & P. A. M. van Lange (Eds.), *Cheating, corruption, and concealment: The roots of dishonest behavior* (pp. 284–310). Cambridge, England: Cambridge University Press.

Vrij, A., & Granhag, P. A. (2012). Eliciting cues to deception and truth: What matters are the questions asked. *Journal of Applied Research in Memory and Cognition, 1*(2), 110–117.

Vrij, A., Hartwig, M., & Granhag, P. A. (2018). Reading lies: Nonverbal communication and deception. *Annual Review of Psychology, 70*, 295–317.

Vrij, A., Hope, L., & Fisher, R. P. (2014). Eliciting reliable information in investigative interviews. *Policy Insights from Behavioral and Brain Sciences, 1*(1), 129–136.

Vrij, A., Leal, S., & Fisher, R. P. (2018). Verbal deception and the Model Statement as a lie detection tool. *Frontiers in Psychiatry, section Forensic Psychiatry, 9*, 492. Doi: 10.3389/fpsyt.2018.00492

Vrij, A., Leal, S., Fisher, R. P., Mann, S., Dalton, G., Jo, E., … Houston, K. (2018a). Sketching as a technique to elicit information and cues to deceit in interpreter-based interviews. *Journal of Applied Research in Memory and Cognition*, 7(2), 303–313.

Vrij, A., Leal, S., Fisher, R. P., Mann, S., Deeb, H., Jo, E., … Hamzeh, S. (2020). The efficacy of using countermeasures in a Model Statement interview. *European Journal of Psychology Applied to Legal Context, 12*, 23–34.

Vrij, A., Leal, S., Granhag, P. A., Mann, S., Fisher, R. P., Hillman, J., & Sperry, K. (2009). Outsmarting the liars: The benefit of asking unanticipated questions. *Law and Human Behavior, 33*(2), 159–166.

Vrij, A., Leal, S., Jupe, L., & Harvey, A. (2018b). Within-subjects verbal lie detection measures: A comparison between total detail and proportion of complications. *Legal and Criminological Psychology, 23*, 265–279.

Vrij, A., Leal, S., Mann, S., Dalton, G., Jo, E., Shaboltas, A., … Houston, K. (2017). Using the Model Statement to elicit information and cues to deceit in interpreter-based interviews. *Acta Psychologica, 177*, 44–53.

Vrij, A., Leal, S., Mann, S., & Fisher, R. (2012). Imposing cognitive load to elicit cues to deceit: Inducing the reverse order technique naturally. *Psychology, Crime, and Law, 18*(6), 579–594.

Vrij, A., Leal, S., Mann, S., Vernham, Z., & Brankaert, F. (2015). Translating theory into practice: Evaluating a cognitive lie detection training workshop. *Journal of Applied Research in Memory and Cognition, 4*(2), 110–120.

Vrij, A., Mann, S., & Fisher, R. (2006). An empirical test of the Behaviour Analysis Interview. *Law and Human Behavior, 30*(3), 329–345.

Vrij, A., Mann, S., Kristen, S., & Fisher, R. (2007). Cues to deception and ability to detect lies as a function of police interview styles. *Law and Human Behavior, 31*(5), 499–518.

Vrij, A., Mann, S., Leal, S., & Fisher, R. (2012). Is anyone there? Drawings as a tool to detect deception in occupations interviews. *Psychology, Crime, and Law, 18*(4), 377–388.

Vrij, A., Meissner, C. A., Fisher, R. P., Kassin, S. M., Morgan III, A., & Kleinman, S. (2017). Psychological perspectives on interrogation. *Perspectives on Psychological Science, 12*(6), 927–955.

Warmelink, L., Vrij, A., Mann, S., Jundi, S., & Granhag, P. A. (2012). Have you been there before? The effect of experience and question expectedness on lying about intentions. *Acta Psychologica, 141*(2), 178–183.

5

POLITICAL VIOLENCE

Neil Ferguson

The context of the research

Since working towards my PhD in the early 1990s my research has focused on studying the mainly unconscious psychological forces behind political violence in Northern Ireland. I was born in 1970 in Northern Ireland and was a child of the 'Troubles'. By the time I was aged two, Northern Ireland had suffered both Bloody Sunday (British Paratroopers shot 27 people, killing 13, with 1 man later dying from his wounds) and Bloody Friday (22 bombs exploded over a period of about 1 hour, killing 9 people and injuring approximately 130) and had come to the brink of civil war. Thankfully, I had the opportunity to study psychology under Ed Cairns at the University of Ulster, and I was able to begin to apply psychological theories to understand more deeply the conflict I had lived through and, indeed, challenge many of the 'truths' I had grown up to believe.

Initially, my research came from a very quantitative, social developmentalist perspective, and focused on the impact political violence had on the identity, reasoning, attitudes, stress and the coping mechanisms used by children to understand and deal with the impact of the conflict taking place in Northern Ireland (for example, Ferguson, 2000; Ferguson & Cairns, 1996). However, during the mid-1990s, while researching the impact of the Northern Ireland loyalist and republican paramilitary ceasefires on how children understood war, peace and peacebuilding (McLernon, Ferguson & Cairns, 1997), I began to alter course.

While analysing the data for that study (McLernon et al. 1997) we noticed that the adolescents' understanding of how to build the conditions for peace in Northern Ireland were simple reflections of the current developments taking place in Northern Ireland at that time. Just months before the autumn ceasefires in the January of 1994, the adolescents could not articulate a strategy to bring peace; then, after the ceasefires in the days of the peace process in late 1994, their ideas simply regurgitated those being discussed in the media at the time. At this juncture I realised that in order to understand the peace process in Northern Ireland I needed to move away from researching children, adolescents and adults who were the passive recipients of a peace being designed and constructed by the politicians, policymakers and paramilitaries who were currently on the political stage, or in the shadows. Instead, I would need to focus on these peace process architects in order to have a deeper understanding of what peace in Northern Ireland would become.

To enable this change required some paradigm shifts and for me to explore different approaches to psychological research. This led to a move towards qualitative research and a shift from a more positivist worldview to a social constructionist interpretivist perspective of knowledge and the world. From this perspective, reality is fluid and changing, and knowledge creation happens through interaction between the researcher and the participant, jointly through consensus. Thus, knowledge is subjective and constructed, and there is no singular 'reality'. Instead, multiple realities exist depending on different people experiencing the same events differently and interpreting them distinctly. A fundamental aspect of this approach involves the dynamic process of the researcher playing an active role in a two-way interpretation of the participant's account, commonly referred to as the 'double hermeneutic'. This involves the researcher engaging in a critical interpretation of the participants' interpretations of their own experiences and involves digging below the surface meaning of their accounts. For more detail on my researcher stance and approach to conducting interpretative phenomenological analysis (IPA) see Ferguson (2016a) and Ferguson, Burgess and Hollywood (2010).

Initially, this research involved interviewing politicians, community representatives, paramilitaries, victims of violence and their advocates in order to get further insight into how they experienced and made sense of peace, conflict and peace-making in Northern Ireland. The initial analysis of interviews, and chiefly the interviews with paramilitaries and former combatants, led to attempts to understand how they made sense of their transition from being a Northern Irish civilian to joining armed paramilitary groups (Burgess, Ferguson & Hollywood, 2005a, 2005b; Ferguson & Burgess, 2009; Ferguson, Burgess & Hollywood, 2008). In part, this refocusing on the antecedent factors that 'pushed' or 'pulled' the participants towards engagement in politically motivated violence reflected the growing interest in radicalisation and engagement in terrorism fuelled by the events of 9/11 and the 'war on terrorism' within the wider academic community, and the developing area of 'terrorism studies' (see Horgan, 2005).

The unfortunately titled multi-disciplinary area of 'terrorism studies' endures some well-known conceptual and methodological problems (Silke, 2001) and, in particular, suffers from a shortage of primary research with real violent extremists conducted in a systematic way (Horgan, 2014; Schuurman, 2018). Thus, research conducted in post-agreement Northern Ireland with former and current paramilitaries offered an opportunity to test theory, and develop robust research based on primary data, actually collected from 'real' violent extremists, which should enhance research in terrorism studies.

Terrorism and political violence are one of the most significant threats facing contemporary society (Kruglanski et al., 2014) and in order to counter violent extremism, efforts must be made to stem the tide of new recruits and promote disengagement within militant groups. To do this effectively more needs to be known about the processes involved in people altering their ideology and/or moving towards engagement in violent extremism or terrorism and how they sustain this engagement (Borum, 2011). Therefore, as research in the area of terrorism studies is driven by governmental desires to counter terrorism and violent extremism, this field offers opportunities for the application of research to the real-world problems violent extremism, terrorism and terrorists pose to contemporary society.

Underpinning research

The research underpinning this case study explores the 'arc of terrorism', or the 'terrorist lifecycle' (Horgan & Taylor, 2011). It focused on the push-and-pull factors that help or hinder the transition from civilian life into and back out of terrorist activity. In particular, the research aimed to explore three keys aspects of this cycle: (i) how individuals initiate contact with paramilitary groups and begin to 'radicalise' or learn the ideology and techniques necessary to engage in politically motivated violence; (ii) once engaged in politically motivated violence and terrorism, how they sustain this activity and develop to become key 'players' in the conflict over the lifespan of their paramilitary careers, and (iii) how former combatants disengage from using political violence, transition back into their communities and engage in new non-violent careers in the post-conflict space.

The research focusing on the first stage of the arc of terrorism explores how people become involved with armed groups and begin to engage in criminality or politically motivated violence on behalf of these armed extremist groups. In the early research (Burgess et al., 2005a, 2005b, 2006; Ferguson & Burgess, 2008, 2009; Ferguson et al., 2008, Ferguson & Binks, 2015) the focus was on the antecedent factors involved in pushing or pulling people towards involvement with the extremist armed groups. This research integrates themes raised from the narrative accounts provided by the Northern Irish paramilitaries we interviewed, with research findings taken from studies utilising primary sources from armed militant or terrorist groups from across the globe.

The most widely cited paper from this body of work (Ferguson et al., 2008) aims, first, to move the psychological literature explaining terrorism and terrorist actions away from reductionist intra-individual explanations of terrorism that focus on abnormal psychological traits, personality disorders or the search for a terrorist personality; second, to promote the incorporation of wider social factors, and to assess those within the context of the conflict where the acts of violence are situated; third, to outline important reoccurring antecedent risk factors that could have an important influence on promoting engagement with armed extremist groups. Antecedent factors such as feelings of grievance or perceived injustice amongst a subgroup of the population, friendship and/or kinship ties to the group, community support for the armed group, being young and male, or group membership providing rewards (financial, status, sexual etc.) were frequently reported from dissimilar armed groups operating in different geopolitical contexts.

Additionally, the article also explores how people who became involved tended to narrate their initial involvement by pointing to specific or clusters of 'critical' incidents that prompted a period of reflection prior to involvement. The analysis of this process illustrated how some of the antecedent risk factors (e.g., being a young male who is subject to injustice) were mediated by the context, the individual's appraisal of the situation they found themselves in, and the alternative futures they could envision for themselves. The article demonstrates how the individual consciously and actively decides what course of action they take. Illustrating how psychological dispositions combine with prior experiences, socialisation and interpretations of the context, and potential futures intersect when individuals consider their potential engagement.

Recent research on this stage of becoming involved in extremism (Ferguson & McAuley, 2020) draws on a reanalysis of over 100 interviews with Northern Irish paramilitaries and builds on earlier studies and recent advances in the field, such as the various models of radicalisation that have been developed since 9/11 to explore narratives of engagement in political violence. This study indicated how much of the initial violence the paramilitaries engaged in looked political but was primarily a violent reaction to local events. The accounts also demonstrated how the interviewees were both politically and ideologically naive when they joined. Consequently, ideological radicalisation did not push or pull them into involvement with these armed groups. Instead, bonds of kinship, identity and empathy with their community, mixed with feelings of fear, pushed them into engagement with their respective extremist group. Ideological radicalisation came much later in their paramilitary careers, and was used to rationalise their violence and sustain it. The findings also illustrated the importance of collective identity, small group dynamics and the view that violence is the only solution to the problems faced by the ingroup in promoting involvement with paramilitary groups.

The second stage of the arc of terrorism, or the stage that focuses on engagement and the impact of engagement on the extremist, is the most under-researched aspect of the terrorist lifecycle (Horgan, 2017). The research focusing on this stage of terrorist involvement (Burgess, Ferguson & Hollywood, 2007; Ferguson et al., 2010; Ferguson & McAuley, 2020a) explores what impact taking this route into violent and non-violent activism has for the protagonist and illustrates the positive and negative psychological and physical impact of this activity.

This research illustrates how the former combatants interpret their violence, generally viewing it as an effective way to bring societal change in Northern Ireland. However, the violence brought more than socio-political change; it changed the perpetrators of violence and their families and brought them trauma and loss. The Burgess et al. (2007) study demonstrated how engagement increased feelings of efficacy and agency amongst the paramilitaries. The most recent study builds on this research (2020a) and is the most comprehensive of the three articles focusing on this stage of the arc of involvement. The findings show how engaging in political violence can have a dramatic impact on the former combatants.

Their accounts provide insights into the pressure and hardships associated with this lifestyle, with the paramilitaries describing how the struggle to survive and evade the security forces placed them and their families under intense pressure. Their membership of the organisations became an all-encompassing aspect of their identity, and led to a loss of their sense of conscience and their moral compass in order to fuse with organisational goals and participate in violence and killing.

Many of these findings mirror research conducted with combat veterans, illustrating how engagement in organised killing can lead to problematic mental health, alcohol and substance use, relationship health, readjustment problems and increased anger and aggression (Cabrera, Adler & Bliese, 2016; Cigrang et al., 2014; McNair, 2002; Russell et al., 2014). The findings also show how imprisonment can have positive as well as negative consequences, with many of the participants viewing prison as a transformational experience, similar to experiences of post-traumatic growth (Tedeschi & Calhoun, 2004). Finally, as with the research on getting involved in political violence, this study of sustaining involvement further demonstrates the important role of identity and small-group processes in sustaining engagement in political violence over years or decades of militant activism.

The final stage of the arc of involvement in violent extremism focuses on disengagement, deradicalisation and desistance from political violence. This stage has received less research attention than the initial involvement stage or research on radicalisation processes (Horgan, 2014). However, this lack of focus seems counterintuitive given the importance of this phase to counterterrorism or counter-extremism agencies who set the funding agendas for this research. Nonetheless, over the last ten years there has been a growth in interest, with some models beginning to be proposed and studied (Altier, Thoroughgood & Horgan, 2014). Likewise, this growth of research has been matched by a growth in the number of radicalisation programmes and interventions being delivered across the globe. However, it must be noted that the research evidence assessing the quality and success of these programmes is generally absent or limited at best (Horgan & Taylor, 2011).

Research exploring this critical phase in the lifecycle (Ferguson, 2010, 2011, 2014, 2016b; Ferguson, Burgess & Hollywood, 2015; Ferguson, McDaid & McAuley, 2018, Flack & Ferguson, in press) has fed into the debate around the conceptual distinction between disengagement and deradicalisation. Disengagement is conceptualised as behavioural change, while deradicalisation involves both behavioural and cognitive change. Thus, deradicalisation is understood as a desistance from political violence coupled with a moderation of the extremist attitudes and beliefs that supposedly buttress the political violence. While I acknowledge this simplifies the debate somewhat, the key aspect for this debate for stakeholders interested in stopping extremists continuing their violence is whether deradicalisation is essential for desistance, or could the same result (no violence) be achieved through disengagement alone.

As with research on radicalisation and getting involved in violent extremism, research on deradicalisation and disengagement tends to focus on factors that push or pull individuals or groups out of involvement in political violence. As with the research on initial involvement and sustaining involvement, it is clear that identity is important, with extremist identity, strength of identity and identity change as an individual or group member being crucial to these processes of engagement and disengagement (Ferguson, 2016b; Ferguson & McAuley, 2020; Flack & Ferguson in press). Likewise, as many violent extremists experience incarceration during their careers, the role of imprisonment is vitally important both for sustaining engagement with an extremist group and in pushing people and groups towards disengagement (Ferguson, 2016b; Ferguson & McAuley, 2020a).

This research pointed to a number of push-and-pull factors involved in disengagement, such as ageing and burnout, having children and changes in relationships, and organisational pressures, that have been reported elsewhere in research exploring right-wing or Islamist groups (Barelle, 2015; Bjorgo, 2009; Dalgaard-Nielsen, 2013; Sukabdi, 2015). However, some of the findings challenged commonly held assumptions, for example around radicalisation processes in prison, and instead of viewing prison radicalisation as a wholly negative process, the findings pointed to the potential for positive impact from prison radicalisation (Ferguson et al., 2015; Ferguson, 2016b).

Counterintuitively, this research indicated that ideological radicalisation in prison could have a positive impact on moving the armed groups towards the consideration of more peaceful strategies focused on longer-term goals, rather than the short-term cycles of 'tit-for-tat' violence that was fuelling conflict outside the prison gates. The research illustrated that if prison allowed a safe space to think about the conflict and challenged opinions, then moves towards non-violent futures were possible. These transformational openings were created through discussion, engagement in education, and interaction with other extremist groups. These transformational openings allowed the prisoners, and through them the wider organisation, opportunities to consider shifts away from the groups' reliance on political violence to achieve organisational goals. The research also pointed to the importance of moving away from viewing disengagement from extremism primarily through a policing, justice or counterterrorism lens. Instead, viewing desistance as a process of organisational change would potentially have a greater impact on moving individuals and groups away from political violence. Thus, these findings challenged many of the commonly held assumptions in the literature and amongst counterterrorism practitioners about achieving desistance.

This body of research also demonstrated how the former paramilitaries were damaged physically, psychology and economically through their engagement in political violence. These problems, created in the most part through the combatant's own choice to participate in violence, were still lingering on even 20 years after the signing of the 1998 peace agreement and affected both former combatants and their families. The stigma faced by the former combatants, coupled with the health problems they suffered, made it difficult for them to fully reintegrate back into society, and equally the violence they had created made it difficult for Northern Ireland to leave the past behind.

The research (Ferguson, 2011; Ferguson et al., 2015; Ferguson, 2016b; Flack & Ferguson, in press) also provided evidence that seeking to deradicalise violent extremists who were disengaging from political violence could be unnecessary or even counter-productive. Indeed, it seems that having developed a radicalised activist identity through their sustained engagement in political violence and during imprisonment, it could not realistically be switched off. Instead, it was this commitment and 'duty of care' to the community they saw themselves as serving through their extremism that was instrumental in their nonviolent political or community engagements after the organisations had gone on ceasefire, decommissioned and/or assumed civilian roles as part of the peace process.

This body of research on involvement, sustaining engagement and promoting disengagement for politically motivated violence has challenged some of the core assumptions around radicalisation and deradicalisation. It challenges the assumptions that terrorists are 'evil' or 'abnormal', it questions whether political or ideological violence actually is driven by political or ideological beliefs, and counterintuitively the findings suggest that radicalisation may actually be important in supporting moves towards desistance from political violence.

Concurrently, the research also replicates many of the push-and-pull factors for engagement and disengagement from violent extremism witnessed within other armed groups located in different geopolitical contexts that hold very different ideological and political motivations. The research also provides some conceptual clarity on how push-and-pull risk factors can dynamically interact in particular social contexts to promote or hinder potential engagement or disengagement. These findings assist in enhancing understanding of these different cycles in the violent extremist's lifecycle, while also illustrating continuity across the phases and the importance of considering a person's internal dispositions, the social context, their past and their imagined futures when trying to understand these processes.

The transition from pure research to application

As suggested earlier, research in the area of terrorism studies has been weak, much maligned (Horgan, 2017; Ranstorp, 2006; Schuurman, 2018; Silke, 2001) and even pronounced as stagnant (Sageman, 2014). The reasons for these weaknesses are multiple, and many of them are a result of a misalignment between the governmental stakeholders, funders and the academic community. Before reflecting on my experiences of making this transition from pure to applied research, I will outline some of these long-standing problems.

The primary failing is the lack of research based on primary data; most research is based on literature reviews, relies on anecdotes or is based on secondary data. Silke (2001) discovered over 80% of all research was based on data gathered from books, journals, the media reports, or datasets constructed from media reports or other secondary sources, with 65% of articles being little more than literature reviews (Silke, 2004). Schurrman's (2018) update on the state of the field demonstrated some improvement, with 55% of articles published between 2007 and 2016 using some primary data; however, the most popular approach (39% of all publications) was still the desk literature review.

Perhaps unsurprising, given the difficulty of accessing samples to study, there was very little quantitative research employing inferential statistics (5.8%, Schuurman, 2018). Silke (2001) also demonstrated that less than 1% of the research was based on systematic interviews with violent extremists, suggesting that 'the terrorist', who should be the main target of the discipline's focus, is almost completely absent from the research.

While the volume of work in this area has been expanding rapidly since the 9/11 attacks (Silke, 2004) most of the research is published by single-author (90%) and one-time (83%) contributors, something that endures until today (75% one-time contributors; Schurrman, 2018). Thus, there is restricted theory development and collaboration in a research field populated by interlopers who publish once and then return to their natural disciplinary home. In addition to these problems, the field has been dogged by definitional problems around the meaning of terrorism, radicalisation and deradicalisation that have hindered development to a greater or lesser extent, depending on whose assessment you believe (Schmid, 2011; Schurrman, 2018; Weinberg, Pedahzur & Hirsch-Hoefler, 2010).

Most pertinent for research impact are the problems created by funding being closely tied to the security agendas of Western nations, mainly that of the United States (Gearon, 2018). Marc Sageman's (2014) article in *Terrorism and Political Violence* is possibly the best account of the inherent problems in funding streams and the security-driven focus of the research agenda. In summary, these issues include: (a) lay people control the funding and their lay understanding pushes the research into areas that reflect their biases and misconceptions; (b) the lack of academic access to reliable data; (c) unwillingness of governments and security agencies to share data; (d) funding became focused on computing, modelling or technological solutions. However, without reliable data to feed into these models they lacked insight. Or, as Sageman (2014, p. 576) succinctly sums up, 'we have a system of terrorism research in which intelligence analysts know everything but understand nothing, while academics understand everything but know nothing'.

Within my own research I have encountered the problems created in an area that is driven by governmental understandings of terrorism and counterterrorism; for example, when the UK government's confused attempt to conceptualise terrorism led to the creation of an expedient distinction between 'international' terrorism and 'domestic' terrorism. This distinction was created in part to allow policymakers to discriminate between 'bad' international terrorists (e.g., Al Qaida) who could be punished, and 'good' domestic terrorists who could be bargained with and treated as humans (e.g., the on-ceasefire PIRA). As Sageman (2014) and Gearon (2018) discuss at length, these poorly conceptualised distinctions, designed for political expediency rather than grounded in evidence, are then eagerly taken up in academia and reified until they become accepted as 'truth'. Then, as I found out, research that challenges these assumptions, or does not fit into this worldview is difficult to publish. While events such as the London transport attacks of 7/7 falsified the conception that international terrorism and 'home-grown' terrorism were independent and easy to distinguish within the UK, this distinction still lingers on.

In my experience, the main challenge for researchers is methodological and involves the ability to collect reliable data. While there are some exceptions (Whitehouse, McQuinn, Bahrmester & Swann, 2014), getting access to large samples of 'real' violent extremists in order to collect suitable data for a detailed and robust quantitative analysis that would allow for generalisation is very difficult without access to governmental or security agency data or datasets. Therefore, if you are collecting primary data from violent extremists or terrorists you will probably need to rely on qualitative methodologies. Within the discipline of psychology, quantitative is the predominant paradigm. Therefore, qualitative research is less likely to be accepted into the more prestigious mainstream journals. As qualitative research relies on a posteriori interpretations based on the participant's own interpretation of their experiences, it can be difficult to persuade people of the importance or accuracy of the testimony. For example, in my own work this makes it difficult to untangle the initiation of the psychological trauma a participant is currently discussing. When did they really become traumatised, was the trauma self-induced through their perpetration of political violence, or was it caused beforehand and played a role in their initial engagement? This then limits a fully accurate assessment of the role of traumatic experiences in pushing people into extremism.

Other problems with collecting data from violent extremists are obvious, and ethical and safety concerns are clearly issues that need to be negotiated carefully and successfully. In particular, it is critical to maintain confidentiality and anonymity of the participants. Thankfully, post-agreement Northern Ireland is now a more benign research environment and former combatants can be accessed relatively safely and straightforwardly. Nonetheless, due to the negative impact some research projects such as the Boston College tapes and the Liverpool project have had on paramilitaries and former combatants in Northern Ireland, it has become more difficult to collect data on involvement with paramilitary groups and individual accounts of engagement in political violence.

Boston College conducted an oral history project recording interviews with republican and loyalist paramilitaries on the understanding that the interview material would not be released until after their deaths. However, the Police Service of Northern Ireland (PSNI) had other ideas, requisitioning the interview tapes and arresting a number of high profile 'players' from the conflict, including Gerry Adams, in an attempt to charge them in relation to historic crimes. Naturally, these arrests made many paramilitaries and former combatants nervous and reluctant to talk to academics about their past.

What has become known as the 'Liverpool Project' was an ESRC-funded research project on dissident Irish republicanism (see Hayes & McIntyre, 2014). When the project impact plan was posted online, it became clear that the research team had offered to share their findings with the UK security services, PSNI and the Irish police force, An Garda Siochana. This led the republican groups linked to the project to withdraw co-operation. Obviously, this made the opportunity for primary data collection in Northern Ireland with paramilitaries and former paramilitaries yet more difficult for researchers, as they now feared potential arrest, and suspiciously viewed researchers as potential agents of the state posing as academics.

These two examples illustrate some of the problems in researching an area where policing and politics are heavily entwined with the research area. They also demonstrate some of the ethical dilemmas that researchers need to carefully consider when researching these topics. Dilemmas that are not just played out in university ethics boards, but can have very real implications for the freedom, safety and security of both the participants and research teams.

After negotiating the challenges with ethics, data collection and publication, to make 'impact' as defined by the UK research councils or Research Excellence Framework (REF), the research must be communicated effectively and positively received beyond academia and have evidence of reach and demonstrate significant benefit to policy, society, etc. It is clear that while NGO organisations are interested in understanding and reducing violent extremism, the groups primarily tasked to reduce extremism are governmental and involved in policing, security, defence and intelligence gathering. Therefore, many of the issues and challenges discussed earlier, regarding data collection and the inherent problems with the field of terrorism studies, remain hurdles in the process of creating research impact. Indeed, over the last few years, I have had to adapt and refocus my research away from exploring the 'darker' aspects of how and why people engaged in violence, as this avenue of inquiry can create tensions within the participants and between the researcher and participant. Instead, my research has developed to focus more on conflict transformation, examining the former combatants in the present or exploring their imaginings of the future for Northern Ireland rather than focusing on past political violence.

As with the Boston tapes and the Liverpool project moral tales, interviewing participants who to some degree are also 'persons of interest' to policing and security agencies creates dilemmas. Then creating research aimed at influencing how the government and their policing and security agencies understand these individuals and the organisations they represent, can also be challenging. In my experience, while former combatants and state agents can be hostile, suspicious and antagonistic of each other, and while they can have very different political goals and understandings of what peace and security in Northern Ireland should look like, the vast majority on all sides do not want to see any more deaths or more young people in prison for terrorism-related offences. Consequently, while there are ethical and moral considerations about who is receiving the research and how they are using the research, everyone is better equipped to reduce engagement in future political violence with access to the best knowledge available, and in a small way, that is the potential impact this work can have.

The impact and legacy of the research

As expected for a researcher working in this area, most of the stakeholders concerned with reducing political and extremist violence are based in governmental departments and intelligence, military or policing agencies, along with charities and NGO groups. Being a British academic, most of my engagement with stakeholders comes from UK Government departments, police forces, military or security agencies. These engagements usually involve contribution to consultative reports, or providing research-based presentations, briefing policymakers and civil servants or offering advice on particular topics on a one-to-one basis or as part of advisory teams. In addition to UK-based stakeholders the research has had international reach, and reports, briefings and presentations have been presented to intelligence agencies, militaries, NGOs and police forces based in other countries such as the Netherlands, United States, NATO and Pakistan. I'll now move on to select some examples of this impact and provide more detail.

On the 24 February 2004 the then Secretary of State (David Blunkett) presented 'Counter Terrorism Powers: Reconciling Security and Liberty in an Open Society' to Parliament for discussion. This paper was intended to stimulate debate and begin a period of consultation arranged within Parliament and beyond on counterterrorism powers, and how to balance national security without 'overly' restricting freedoms. In particular, Part 4 of the Anti-Terrorism, Crime and Security Act (2001) included a sunset clause and the Home Office wanted something in place before November 2006 when the clause was enacted. I was consulted as part of a group of social scientists on these counterterrorism measures to explore potential solutions that could be fed into the creation of the Prevention of Terrorism Act (2005). My reflection on the consultation was that it was cordial, but I did not feel that the Home Office civil servants were taking the critical concerns raised by a group of social science academics particularly seriously at the time. However, when the Prevention of Terrorism Act (2005) was enacted I was surprised by how many of the changes reflected outcomes of the discussion that had taken place in that meeting, and no doubt in many other meetings as part of the wider consultation. This experience demonstrated that positive outcomes were possible through engagement with government departments. However, it also taught me not to expect to receive feedback or acknowledgement on how the consultation had influenced thinking within the Home Office.

In January 2009 the Consultative Group on the Past, commonly called the Eames–Bradley Report after the esteemed co-chairs of the consultative group, produced its report. The British Government had established the group in June 2007 to deal with the legacy of the Troubles. The Eames–Bradley report was a result of almost two years of consultations with hundreds of groups and individuals from across both communities in Northern Ireland and invited participants from Great Britain and the Republic of Ireland. The final report made 31 main recommendations, dealing with the legacy of the conflict, victims and survivors, societal issues, justice procedures and remembrance. However, the report and the co-chairs were ruthlessly attacked from all sides of Northern Ireland's political spectrum (see Belfast Telegraph, 2009, for an example). This hostility led to proposals being universally rejected by all Northern Ireland political parties and subsequently shelved by the British Government. In particular, the recommendation that the families of *all* victims of the conflict should each receive a payment of £12,000 received the most ire. This truly was a historic report, probably a historic failure, but historic nonetheless, and the report was informed by research I had published (Ferguson et al., 2007). Thus, while the recommendations of this report were rejected in the media spotlight, it did demonstrate that academic research could make an impact in these consultations, and that psychologists could have a role to play in contributing to the policy outcomes they create.

Working with the British Council in Pakistan in 2013–2014 was some of the most interesting and rewarding impact work I have been involved in. The British Council Pakistan convened a task force to create a research series titled 'Next Generation Voices'. I was involved with part of the research project focused on political violence, which aimed to highlight the negative impact of violence and how cultures of violence could change. As part of this project the British Council sent a diverse group of representatives from charity and community groups, politicians, activists, journalists etc. from countries that had suffered political conflict from across the globe (Bosnia, Iraq, South Sudan, Afghanistan, Myanmar, etc.) to spend time in Pakistan, meet and brief politicians and hold a series of meetings and conferences to promote the 'New Generation: Insecure Lives, Untold Stories' report (2014).

The British Council report wanted to highlight the health crisis that violence, and the trauma it created, was having on the Pakistani youth in order to persuade the Pakistan Government to challenge the violence that had gripped the country since 2001 and to invest in health, education and infrastructure in order to provide young people with productive employment opportunities. The assembled group of international representatives travelled to try to influence the Pakistani Government and key stakeholders, and illustrate how even countries fractured by political violence could have alternative non-violent futures.

Interacting with this diverse group and engaging with a variety of influential political figures within Pakistan was stimulating, inspirational and thought-provoking. The powerful report we were promoting drew on the testimonies of over 1,800 young people from Pakistan and provided harrowing accounts of violence and the trauma it created for individuals and communities across the country. This engagement with the British Council provided a fascinating lesson in the use of soft power in international relations, and hopefully the research, keynote speeches, briefings, media interviews, newspaper coverage, discussions and panels influenced governmental thinking, activists, educators and the wider public to the extent that the British Council had planned.

Much of the impact activity I normally engage in revolves around providing critical guidance or presenting research. Most of these engagements are short, over a day or a couple of consecutive days, perhaps meeting stakeholders every year or a couple of times per year. Over the years I have regularly engaged in this activity with a variety of bodies in the UK and beyond. These types of engagements usually involve trying to communicate how aspects of the research I have been involved in can challenge some of the more commonly held assumptions about violent extremism and especially biased thinking about violent extremists.

The aim of these presentations and discussions is to create some critical reflection that may challenge thinking among policymakers, practitioners and analysts, who otherwise can be drip-fed distilled biased information that tends to be alarmist and one-sided (see Sageman, 2014). Hopefully, this approach can create some cognitive dissonance while stimulating thinking and challenge misperceptions, stereotypes, biases and other barriers to critical thinking that can lead to defective decision-making and risky shifts in choices of action towards more amoral strategies (Stoner, 1961) – strategies that have the potential to create more violence, rather than lessen it.

Over the years I have worked in this manner with numerous governmental branches within the UK and overseas, including the Home Office, the Foreign and Commonwealth Office and the Northern Ireland Office. I have worked with non-governmental organisations such as the UK Sri Lanka Trauma Group on post-conflict reconstruction, Peace Direct and the Tim Parry and Jonathan Ball Foundation for Peace. I have also presented research to UK and United States military and intelligence branches, such as United States Africa Command (AFRICOM) and to other NATO partners. Finally, I have been consulted by different police agencies, such as INTERPOL, EUROPOL and the Police Service of Northern Ireland.

These research impact engagements offer opportunities to alter perspectives and, through the qualitative richness of the material presented, lend depth to understandings of why and how people engage in terrorism and politically motivated violence, and to break down commonly held assumptions about them being 'mad' or 'bad'. Challenging these stereotypes should help in deconstructing prototypes of 'terrorists' or 'men of violence' and improve understanding of how antecedent factors, such as socialisation, supportive community contexts, feeling under threat or in crisis can combine to create the conditions when people make decisions and take routes that can lead them to engagement in seemingly ideological or politically motivated violence. These stakeholder engagements should also help to expand practitioner and policymaker awareness of the role that psychological approaches can bring to these multifaceted and dynamic problems. They also help me develop a better understanding of the pressures and challenges faced by stakeholders within these communities.

Lessons learnt

Being an academic requires the ability to spin many plates. You have to concentrate on the teaching and your obligations to the students; you have your day job and the duties towards, and demands from, your home university; you have your own research interests and goals; you have the demands of the REF, and the need to bring in research income, etc. Then, on top of all those tasks, if you are contributing to an impact case study, you have the additional demands of being out in society, applying your research and making it appealing to stakeholders in governments, NGOs, business, etc.

The first lesson is learning how to manage this diverse range of activities and keeping detailed enough records of impact activities to support any future return. In a perfect world, you would have time and resources to allow you to collect evidence and prepare for the return. However, life in university is rarely perfect, and the problem I faced in the REF 2014 return was the timeframe within which I had to create an impact case study. I was asked to coordinate an impact case study based on my research, only a matter of weeks before the submission date. Consequently, my advice is – be prepared to join a case study at shorter notice than you would like, so keep evidence and records of impact reach and significance as up to date as possible just in case you are called on to do so.

Be patient – in this area when you are dealing with government departments, or organisations such as intelligence agencies, where being opaque is a natural state; you may find it difficult to get meaningful feedback on your input. If you have the time and energy you can chase this up, but how much success you have with the chasing is variable, to say the least. As I mentioned in one of the cases earlier, in time, reports or working papers may be produced and with some luck your thoughts and ideas may be visible through these documents. Otherwise, you will have to become accustomed to spending time presenting work or in consultation, with very limited evidence as to how your engagement has made impact in return, or chasing down stakeholders for fragmented evidence of impact.

A stakeholder's demands from the research can be very different from those of an academic audience; the reasons for researching the topic and the application of the findings are probably driven by very different agendas. There are also issues about how much time and detail a policymaker has the capacity for, for example, it is unlikely they will read your 40-page report. Accordingly, how do you condense the essence of years of research endeavour into one or two sentences, and how do you drive the importance of those sentences to the right people in the department or agency so that it is actually incorporated in an assessment that can affect policy? I have found that using quotes from interviewees can make the research more personalised and relevant, which helps stakeholders understand the experiences of combatants from a new angle, which can alter their mindset and approach to problems of political violence. Thus, while qualitative data lacks the statistical solidity of quantitative research, it can create impact by allowing people to relate personally to the problem in focus.

Further challenges are created when the different communities use language differently or the concepts and definitions used do not have the same core meaning to all the people sitting around the same table. Often stakeholders want a simple solution to a complex problem, so in the counter-extremism arena stakeholders constantly want to find quick technological solutions or models to simplify and counter possible threats. On the other hand, academics want to problematise issues, and often research does not find a simple solution but opens the problem up and makes the issue more complex and multi-layered than initially thought. This can be frustrating for a time-short stakeholder who needs a solution today. These differences are inherent in the fundamental nature of what each group is expected to achieve in their role, and consequently can be difficult to surmount.

In order to build sustainable collaboration between academic researchers and governmental stakeholders, there needs to be a better understanding of the pressures each work under, the different working practices involved, and how and what each party wants the research to achieve. I believe, where possible, it would be beneficial for academics to have the opportunity for secondments with the stakeholder agencies and departments to focus on the problem from a practitioner point of view for a consolidated period. Likewise, having more opportunities for government analysts and counterterrorist practitioners to work alongside academics in research centres would bring benefits to both communities.

In a post-GDPR world, data-sharing between governmental departments who are hoarding data they do not have the time to process and academics who need the data to try and understand the problems they are researching more clearly, is going to be tricky. However, given the necessary effort, these problems could be overcome and collaboration between data-rich governments and academics could increase. As discussed earlier, finding a way to clear barriers to this collaboration could be the key to unlocking real developments in the field of terrorism studies.

A final problem that causes difficulty in maintaining relationships between academics and partners in the government is the frequent changes of personnel within government offices. People rotate in and out of departments frequently, and with new personnel come new ideas and approaches, which can make working on a particular problem in a consistent way difficult. Similarly, changes in government and the removal or rotation of Ministers can affect internal agendas as political will ebbs and flows, further impeding collaboration over the long term. Better communication chains between academia and departments or agencies would resolve this issue. This pragmatic look at lessons learnt should offer routes for better collaboration between academics and practitioners and policymakers in these areas, while alerting those about to embark on this journey to some of the problems they may face.

References

Altier, M.-B., Thoroughgood, C. N., & Horgan, J. G. (2014). Turning away from terrorism: Lessons from psychology, sociology and criminology. *Journal of Peace Research, 51*(5), 647–661.

Barelle, K. (2015). Pro-integration: Disengagement from and life after extremism. *Behavioral Sciences of Terrorism and Political Aggression*, 7(2), 129–142.

Belfast Telegraph. (2009). Why no one wants the Eames/Bradley report to open up a new can of worms. Retrieved from http://www.belfasttelegraph.co.uk/opinion/columnists/laurence-white/why-no-one-wants-the-eamesbradley-report-to-open-up-a-new-can-of-worms-28496526.html.

Bjorgo, T. (2009). Processes of disengagement from violent groups of the extreme right. In T. Bjorgo & J. Horgan (Eds.), *Leaving terrorism behind: Individual and collective disengagement* (pp. 30–48). London: Routledge.

Borum, R. (2011). Radicalization into violent extremism I: A review of social science theories. *Journal of Strategic Security, 4*(4), 7–36.

Burgess, M., Ferguson, N., & Hollywood, I. (2005a). A social psychology of defiance: From discontent to action. In M. Sönser-Breen (Ed.), *Minding evil: Explorations of human iniquity* (pp. 19–38). New York, NY & Amsterdam: Rodophi.

Burgess, M., Ferguson, N., & Hollywood, I. (2005b). Violence begets violence: Drawing ordinary civilians into the cycle of military intervention and violent resistance. *Australasian Journal of Human Security, 1*(1), 41–52.

Burgess, M., Ferguson, N., & Hollywood, I. (2006). From individual discontent to collective armed struggle: Personal accounts of the impetus for membership or non-membership in paramilitary groups. In W. A. Myers (Ed.), *The range of evil: Multidisciplinary studies of human wickedness* (pp. 29–40). Oxford: Inter-Disciplinary Press.

Burgess, M., Ferguson, N., & Hollywood, I. (2007). Rebels' perspectives of the legacy of past violence and of the current peace in post-agreement Northern Ireland: An interpretative phenomenological analysis. *Political Psychology, 28*(1), 69–88.

Cabera, O. A., Adler, A. B., & Bliese, P. D. (2016). Growth mixture modelling of post-combat aggression: Application to soldiers deployed to Iraq. *Psychiatry Research, 246*, 539–544.

Cigrang, J. A., Talcott, G. W., Tatum, J.-L., Baker, M., Cassidy, D., Sonnek, S., ... Smith Slep, A. M. (2014). Impact of combat deployment on psychological and relationship health: A longitudinal study. *Journal of Traumatic Stress, 27*(1), 58–65.

Dalgaard-Nielsen, A. (2013). Promoting exit from violent extremism: Themes and approaches. *Studies in Conflict and Terrorism, 36*(2), 99–115.

Ferguson, N. (2000). The impact of sectarian injustice and the paramilitary ceasefires on adolescent just world beliefs in Northern Ireland. *Irish Journal of Psychology, 21*(1–2), 70–77.

Ferguson, N. (2010). Disarmament, demobilization, reinsertion and reintegration: The Northern Ireland experience. In N. Ferguson (Ed.), *Post conflict reconstruction* (pp. 151–164). Newcastle: Cambridge Scholars Press.

Ferguson, N. (2011). Disengaging from terrorism. In A. Silke (Ed.), *The psychology of counter-terrorism* (pp. 111–123). London: Routledge.

Ferguson, N. (2014). Northern Irish ex-prisoners: The impact of imprisonment on prisoners and the peace process in Northern Ireland. In A. Silke (Ed.), *Prisons, terrorism and extremism: Critical issues in management, radicalisation and reform* (pp. 270–282). London: Routledge.

Ferguson, N. (2016a). Researching proscribed armed groups: Interviewing Loyalist and Republican paramilitaries in Northern Ireland. In A. J. Williams, K. N. Jenkings, M. F. Rech & R. Woodward (Eds.), *The Routledge companion to military research methods* (pp. 153–166). Abingdon, Oxon: Routledge.

Ferguson, N. (2016b). Disengaging from terrorism: A Northern Irish experience. *Journal for Deradicalization, 6*, 1–23.

Ferguson, N., & Binks, E. (2015). Understanding radicalization and engagement in terrorism through religious conversion motifs. *Journal of Strategic Security, 8*(1), 16–26.

Ferguson, N., Binks, E., Roe, M. D., Brown, J. N., Adams, T., Cruise, S. M., & Lewis, C. A. (2007). The IRA apology of 2002 and forgiveness in Northern Ireland's Troubles: A cross-national study of printed media. *Peace and Conflict: Journal of Peace Psychology, 13*(1), 93–113.

Ferguson, N., & Burgess, M. (2008). The road to insurgency: Drawing ordinary civilians into the cycle of military intervention and violent resistance. In M. D. Ulusoy (Ed.), *Political violence, organized crime, terrorism and youth* (pp. 63–71). Amsterdam: IOS.

Ferguson, N., & Burgess, M. (2009). From naivety to insurgency: The causes and consequences of joining a Northern Irish paramilitary group. In D. Canter (Ed.), *Faces of terrorism: Cross-disciplinary explorations* (pp. 19–33). Chichester, England: Wiley.

Ferguson, N., Burgess, M., & Hollywood, I. (2008). Crossing the Rubicon: Deciding to become a paramilitary in Northern Ireland. *International Journal of Conflict and Violence, 2*(1), 130–137.

Ferguson, N., Burgess, M., & Hollywood, I. (2010). Who are the victims? Victimhood experiences in post agreement Northern Ireland. *Political Psychology, 31*(6), 857–886.

Ferguson, N., Burgess, M., & Hollywood, I. (2015). Leaving violence behind: Disengaging from politically motivated violence in Northern Ireland. *Political Psychology, 36*(2), 199–214.

Ferguson, N., & Cairns, E. (1996). Political violence and moral maturity in Northern Ireland. *Political Psychology, 17*(4), 713–725.

Ferguson, N., & McAuley, J.W. (2020). Radicalization or Reaction: Understanding Engagement in Violent Extremism in Northern Ireland. *Political Psychology, 41*(2), 215–230. doi:10.1111/pops.12618.

Ferguson, N., & McAuley, J. W. (2020a). Staying Engaged in Terrorism: Narrative Accounts of Sustaining Participation in Violent Extremism. *Frontiers in Psychology, 11*, 1338. doi: 10.3389/fpsyg.2020.01338

Ferguson, N., McDaid, S., & McAuley, J. W. (2018). Social movements, structural violence and conflict transformation: The case of Northern Irish loyalist paramilitaries. *Peace and Conflict: Journal of Peace Psychology, 24*(1), 19–26.

Flack, P., & Ferguson, N. (in press). Conflict transformation: Relinquishing or maintaining social identity among former loyalist combatants. *Political Psychology*.

Gearon, L. (2018). Terrorism and counter-terrorism policy and research in UK universities (1997–2017): An analytic-structural review of the literature and related sources. *Reviews in Higher Education, 21*, 32–60.

Hayes, M., & McIntyre, A. (2014). The Liverpool University project on "dissident" Irish republicanism – Working for the British state. Retrieved from http://www.thepensivequill.com/2014/10/the-liverpool-university-research.html.

Horgan, J. (2005). *The psychology of terrorism*. London: Routledge.

Horgan, J. (2014). *The psychology of terrorism*. London: Routledge.

Horgan, J. (2017). Psychology of terrorism: Introduction to the special issue. *American Psychologist, 72*(3), 199–204.

Horgan, J., & Taylor, M. (2011). Disengagement, de-radicalization and the arc of terrorism: Future directions for research. In R. Coosaet (Ed.), *Jihadi terrorism and the radicalization challenge: European and American experiences* (pp. 173–186). London: Ashgate.

Kruglanski, A. W., Gelfand, M. J., Belanger, J. J., Sheveland, A., Hetiarachchi, M., & Gunaratna, R. (2014). The psychology of radicalization and deradicalization: How significance quest impacts violent extremism. *Advances in Political Psychology, 1*, 69–93.

McLernon, F., Ferguson, N., & Cairns, E. (1997). Comparison of Northern Irish children's attitudes to war and peace before and after the paramilitary ceasefires. *International Journal of Behavioural Development, 20*(4), 715–730.

McNair, R. M. (2002). Brief reports: Perpetration-induced traumatic stress in combat veterans. *Peace and Conflict: Journal of Peace Psychology, 8*(1), 63–72.

New generation: Insecure lives, untold stories report. (2014). Retrieved from https://www.britishcouncil.pk/programmes/society/next-generation.

Ranstorp, M. (2006). *Mapping terrorism research*. Oxford: Routledge.

Russell, D., Russell, C. A., Riviere, L. A., Thomas, J. L., Wilk, J. E., & Bliese, P. D. (2014). Changes in alcohol use after traumatic experiences: The impact of combat on Army National Guardsmen. *Drug and Alcohol Dependence, 139*, 47–52.

Sageman, M. (2014). The stagnation in terrorism research. *Terrorism and Political Violence, 26*(4), 565–580.

Schmid, A. P. (2011). *The Routledge handbook of terrorism research*. New York, NY: Routledge.

Schuurman, B. W. (2018). Research on terrorism, 2007-2016: A review of data, methods, and authorship. *Terrorism and Political Violence, 30*, 1–16.

Silke, A. (2001). The Devil you know: Continuing problems with research on terrorism. *Terrorism and Political Violence, 13*(4), 1–14.

Silke, A. (2004). The road less travelled: Trends in terrorism research. In A. Silke (Ed.), *Research on terrorism: Trends, achievements and failures* (pp. 186–213). London: Frank Cass.

Stoner, J. A. F. (1961). *A comparison of individual and group decisions involving risk* (Unpublished Master's Thesis). Cambridge, MA : Massachusetts Institute of Technology, School of Industrial Management

Sukabdi, Z. A. (2015). Terrorism in Indonesia: A review on rehabilitation and deradicalization. *Journal of Terrorism Research, 6*(2), 36–56.

Tedeschi, R. G., & Calhoun, L. G. (2004). Posttraumatic growth: Conceptual foundations and empirical evidence. *Psychological Inquiry, 15*(1), 1–18.

Weinberg, L., Pedahzur, A., & Hirsh-Hoefler, S. (2010). The challenges of conceptualizing terrorism. *Terrorism and Political Violence, 16*(4), 777–794.

Whitehouse, H., McQuinn, B., Buhrmester, M., & Swann, W. B. (2014). Brothers in arms: Libyan revolutionaries bond like family. *Proceedings of the National Academy of Sciences, 111*(50), 17783–17785.

6

SPORT AND PHYSICAL ACTIVITY IN PRISONS

Rosie Meek

Context of the research

There are currently over 83,000 people in prison in England and Wales, nearly 4,000 of whom are women (Ministry of Justice, 2019). Our prisons and other places of youth detention also currently hold over 800 children aged 17 and under (Youth Custody Service, 2019). Although by their very nature, prisons are *closed* institutions, what takes place in our prisons is a public concern: not only because they are funded from the public purse and represent the state's decision to deprive an individual of their liberty, but because the way our prisons are resourced, organised and managed has an impact on reoffending and the safety of our communities. Almost a half of adults and over 70% of children released from prison will reoffend within a year (Ministry of Justice & National Statistics, 2019) and the total annual economic and social cost of reoffending has been estimated by the Ministry of Justice to be £18.1 billion (Newton, May, Eames & Ahmad, 2019). Now more than ever our discipline of psychology needs to lend itself to this issue of enormous social and political concern.

One such way in which research and theory can contribute is by building upon our established understanding of mental and physical health. As well as the fact that those in prison are much more likely to have poor physical and mental health, there is a direct link between an individual's health and the likelihood of them reoffending (Social Exclusion Unit, 2002). The physical and psychological wellbeing of our incarcerated population also remains a public health issue since most people held in prison custody will be released, and those who return to their communities after serving a prison sentence will bring with them their experiences of custody, both negative and positive. An often overlooked element of the custodial experience relates to exercise and physical activity, and this chapter will attempt to summarise why I have directed so much research attention to this area, the political and practical impact that it has generated, and the challenges that have arisen in carrying out interdisciplinary research in this domain.

A body of international literature has made the case for the primary benefits of prison-based sport and physical activity in terms of improved physical health (Amtmann & Kukay, 2016; Elger, 2009) as well as mental health (Buckaloo, Krug & Nelson, 2009; Woods, Breslin & Hassan, 2017). There is also a growing awareness of wider psychological – as well as social – benefits, where sport can offer an alternative means of excitement and risk-taking to that gained through engaging in offending behaviour (Zuckerman, 1991). It can also provide access to a pro-social network and positive role models, and offer the opportunity to gain new experiences and achievements. It can simply be a positive, cost-effective and healthy leisure activity, and even a distraction from anti-social behaviour. Participating in sport can represent an alternative to offending which not only has intrinsic value but also provides a relatively easy way to establish a more positive self-identity (Meek, 2014). Also of relevance here is the abundant psychological and educational evidence of the importance of *play* in healthy child development (see for example, Frost, Wortham & Reifel, 2007), particularly when working with those who have experienced trauma and neglect, as we know that so many of the people we detain in custody have.

Prison-based sport and physical activity may be classified in different jurisdictions as a health, recreation or education issue or requirement, but provision and access are considered part of the basic principles of prison laws and policies of many countries (van Zyl & Snacken, 2002). Having served 27 years in prison, Nelson Mandela drew attention to the transformative potential of sport, opening an award acceptance speech with the words:

> Sport has the power to change the world. It has the power to inspire, it has the power to unite people in a way that little else does. It speaks to youth in a language they understand. Sport can create hope, where once there was only despair.
>
> *(Mandela, 2000)*

In England and Wales, as well as official directives (referred to as Prison Service Orders and Instructions), legislation which the UK has signed up to includes that from the United Nations, where the standard minimum rules for the treatment of prisoners prescribe that:

> Every prisoner who is not employed in outdoor work shall have at least one hour of suitable exercise in the open air daily if weather permits. Young prisoners, and others of suitable age and physique, shall receive physical and recreational training during the period of exercise. To this end space, installations and equipment should be provided.
>
> *(United Nations, 2015, Article 21.1-2)*

The UK has also adopted the European Prison Rules, legislation recognising the importance of exercise and recreation for those residing in prisons, by stating that:

> Recreational opportunities, which include sport, games, cultural activities, hobbies and other leisure pursuits, shall be provided and, as far as possible, prisoners shall be allowed to organise them.
>
> *(European Committee for the Prevention of Torture and Inhuman or Degrading Treatment, 2006)*

Despite an expectation that those held in custodial care should have the opportunity to be physically active, prisoners consistently report highly sedentary lifestyles, and repeated HM Inspectorate reports confirm that many establishments fail to meet policy expectations in this domain. It remains the case that incarcerated men, women and children are less likely than those in the community to participate in sufficient physical activity. Sedentary behaviour in prisons has consequently been identified as a high-risk health behaviour which, as well as the implications for psychological ill health, contributes to an increased risk of obesity, hypertension, diabetes, cardiovascular disease and mortality (Battaglia et al., 2013). This not only places a considerable cost burden on health-care providers both in custody and the community, but also acts as a barrier to efforts to rehabilitate. A strong body of evidence confirms that the provision of physical activity represents a simple intervention which can ameliorate the negative health effects of a sedentary lifestyle in prison (Jebb & Moore, 1999).

This chapter explores the role and impact of a particular feature of prison life, that relating to sport, exercise and physical activity (terms that although distinct, tend to be used interchangeably in the context of this research). But in particular, this chapter explores the rehabilitative potential of sport and physical activity as a crime prevention technique, drawing predominantly on my most recent research in this area, work undertaken on behalf of the Ministry of Justice (Meek, 2018a) and the impact this work had on shaping government policy and practice.

Having originally trained as a social psychologist, I have always had an interest in how psychology can be applied in real-world settings and to contemporary issues, and I was able to apply this in a forensic context with my doctoral research, which I carried out through the lens of identity theory with young men in prisons, having developed an interest in this population through a number of voluntary roles with criminal justice charities. I knew I wanted to direct my professional efforts to prison settings but did not want to pursue what I saw as the rigidity of the Prison Service psychologist role (see Warr, 2012, for a damning critique of prison psychologists based on his lived experiences of serving a long prison sentence). However, I recognised that psychologists could have a positive impact in prisons and other criminal justice settings through, amongst other things, the application of our wide-ranging theoretical understanding of human behaviour. I have found it rewarding to explore the application of social psychological concepts to prisoner populations in ways that have not been explored before (for example, the better-than-average effect: Sedikides, Meek, Alicke & Taylor, 2014). My research trajectory has centred predominantly on intervention evaluations and a determination to create more sensitive, inclusive research methodologies with prisoner populations, including co-created practices (for example, Mehay & Meek, 2016), and by expanding my theoretical approaches to encompass criminology, sociology and social policy. As someone who relished the use of both qualitative and quantitative methods, I also enjoyed the real-world nature of intervention evaluation. However, it was through being invited to evaluate a sports-based prison intervention for young men (and specifically the legacy of footballer Ian Wright's 2009 television programme for Sky TV, *Football Behind Bars*) that initially led me to focus on prison sport, and inspired me to develop a programme of research in this hitherto overlooked area.

Introducing *A Sporting Chance*: an independent review of sport and physical activity in youth and adult prisons

Having established a research profile in this field, in 2017 I was invited by the office of Dr Phillip Lee MP, then the Under Secretary for Justice, to meet with the Minister in order to talk about the body of work I have produced over the last decade on the role of sport in prison settings, which has encompassed a number of prison sports evaluations as well as my *Sport in Prison* monograph (Meek, 2014), and engagement with a wide range of voluntary and community organisations in the sports for development sector. As a GP with an interest in sport, Dr Lee was aware of the health and wider benefits of physical activity, and as a Minister with responsibility for, amongst other things, youth prisons, women in prison and prison healthcare, he wanted to get a sense of the research evidence for the role of physical activity within his remit, as well as a better idea of current practice and future opportunities in this area. I was subsequently asked to carry out an independent review, which as an academic was an exciting opportunity not only to undertake a substantial piece of work in the area to which I have devoted my research career, but also to have a direct impact on policy and practice developments and wider prison reforms.

I commenced my review in September 2017, and was given the opportunity to visit adult prisons, young offender institutions, secure children's homes and secure training centres throughout England and Wales. I was given access to a wide range of data and had the opportunity to meet staff and residents across these facilities. To supplement my visits across the secure estate I collated written consultations from nearly 300 young people in prison and other stakeholders (the latter through an online public consultation). As well as collecting primary data and scrutinising secondary data sources, I was able to draw on my knowledge of existing theory and prior research. The resulting report represented the application of a decade of my interdisciplinary research in the area, while giving me the valuable opportunity to occupy a social policy role.

Although I submitted my review to the Ministry of Justice on time in February 2018, it was not published until August 2018, by which point the Minister who had commissioned my review had resigned, and so it was his successor Edward Argar MP (since moved on to another ministerial role, at the time of writing as a Health Minister) who was responsible for launching *A Sporting Chance* (Meek, 2018a) and publishing the government's official response to my review (Ministry of Justice, 2018).

The gap between submission and publication of the review was a frustrating one because it included uncertainty about whether the report would be published at all under a new Minister (it was), or whether I would be asked to modify the contents (I was not). During these six months between submission and publication there was some media coverage of my findings, in particular the 'leaked' controversial recommendation concerning boxing and martial arts (The Observer, 2018; The Sun, 2018), and I was asked to give evidence to the Department for Culture, Media and Sport (DCMS) select committee inquiry into the social impact of participation in culture and sport (House of Commons, 2018a). However, eventually the report was published at short notice on a Saturday in August, 2018. Although there had originally been plans to have a launch event to coincide with the publication of the review, I was told by ministerial staff that this was no longer happening. But I was relieved that it was in the public domain and the report received a good deal of coverage on national television, radio and in print media. Although as academics we are used to navigating the peer review process, managing negotiations with publishers and resigning ourselves to lengthy waits between submission and seeing one's work in print, this was a different kind of frustration. It highlighted not only the precarious nature of an academic's relationship with government (even an academic who had been directly instructed by a Minister to carry out an independent review) but also the relative impotence of a large government department (in this case, the Ministry of Justice) and the numerous and slow-moving cogs that drive parliamentary business.

The report culminated in a dozen recommendations (see Box 6.1), largely targeted at prison staff and senior managers, HM Prison and Probation Service and the Ministry of Justice. I also asked for my findings and recommendations to be understood and applied in the context of other government campaigns, thus encouraging the Ministry of Justice to work with, amongst others, the Department for Digital, Culture, Media and Sport, the Department of Health and Social Care, the Department for Education and the Home Office, many of whom are progressing with their own related strategies,[1] in order to develop coordinated efforts to promote physical activity.

BOX 6.1 SUMMARY OF RECOMMENDATIONS FROM *A SPORTING CHANCE: AN INDEPENDENT REVIEW OF SPORT IN YOUTH AND ADULT PRISONS* (MEEK, 2018A)

Recommendation 1: Every prison, young offender institution, secure training centre and secure children's home should devise and implement an integrated physical activity and wellbeing strategy.

Recommendation 2: Commissioners and education providers should develop a flexible approach to delivery which enables collaborations and creative delivery.

Recommendation 3: Prisons should offer nutritional advice as part of their physical activity and wellbeing provision, and promote a readily available range of healthy eating options.

Recommendation 4: Bringing prisoners together for sport can resolve conflict. Governors should revise 'keep apart' list policies and establishments should include gym staff in 'keep apart' decision-making.

Recommendation 5: Sport provision needs to be responsive to individual needs, with a focus on health, wellbeing and rehabilitation at the heart of practice.

Recommendation 6: The Ministry of Justice should develop a physical activity strategy for women and girls in prison.

Recommendation 7: The Ministry of Justice should reconsider the national martial arts/boxing policy and pilot the introduction of targeted programmes which draw on boxing exercises, qualifications and associated activities.

Recommendation 8: Senior managers and the Ministry of Justice need to monitor physical activity participation and outcomes according to ethnicity, and ensure that any disproportionality is addressed.

Recommendation 9: Senior managers need to encourage partnerships between prisons, communities, sporting groups and bodies.

Recommendation 10: The Ministry of Justice should review Release on Temporary Licence, Mobility and related policies to facilitate meaningful sports-based learning, team-building activities, placements and training.

Recommendation 11: The Ministry of Justice, HM Prison and Probation Service and senior managers need to provide the leadership, staffing, training and facilities required to support a wide-reaching and high-quality sport and physical activity provision.

Recommendation 12: HM Prison and Probation Service should create and implement a dedicated physical activity monitoring and evaluation strategy which supplements existing Ofsted and HM Inspectorate of Prisons monitoring.

My work on behalf of the Ministry of Justice, and some of my subsequent media work (see Meek, 2018b), also served as a 'call to arms' to the wider criminal justice and sport and fitness sectors, including the thriving body of voluntary sector organisations occupying this space. I wanted my findings to culminate in a set of distinct recommendations because I feel that, as academics, we do have a responsibility to challenge outdated and ineffective policies and practices. I want my research efforts to help instil in our prisons cultures of learning, of physical and psychological wellbeing and of hope, all fundamental in promoting a wider rehabilitative culture. I also wanted the Ministry of Justice to be held accountable on my review findings, and so I was pleased that a document responding to my recommendations was published alongside my review (see Ministry of Justice, 2018) and that the Minister also agreed to co-host an event with me six months after publication of my review (see later).

Where several of these 12 recommendations – those relating to the relationship between physical activity and the promotion of education, collaborative working in promoting wellbeing in prisons, the importance of offering diverse sporting programmes in prisons, and food and nutrition – have been discussed in more detail in another publication (see Meek, 2020), in this chapter I will focus more specifically on four different recommendations relating to the use of physical activity in our prisons: the need for a physical activity strategy for women and girls; the staffing and resource of physical activity in prisons; using sport to resolve conflict; and the use of martial arts and boxing-related programmes in custodial settings. In concluding, I will also reflect on developments in influencing policy and practice in the first six months since the Ministry of Justice published my review.

Underpinning research and the transition to real-world application

1. *The need for a physical activity strategy for women and girls in prison*

Official data verifies that women in prison are significantly less likely to participate in sport and physical activity than their male counterparts, and that participation among female prisoners is not only lower than that of male prisoners (Meek, 2014), but also lower than that of non-incarcerated females (Herbert, Plugge, Foster & Doll, 2012; Plugge, Foster, Yudkin & Douglas, 2009). In community settings, in spite of the proliferation of national (Sport England, 2012, 2015) and international (International Working Group on Women and Sport, 1994) campaigns and initiatives that have aimed to increase women's participation in sport, a longstanding gender disparity in sports participation has remained, a disparity which is amplified in our custodial settings, where the majority of women in British prisons are insufficiently active to benefit their health (Plugge et al., 2009). Participation figures within the female estate reflect the well documented lower levels of sports participation among females more generally, particularly those from lower socio-economic groups (Jones, Millward & Buraimo, 2011), but a cursory read of HM Inspectorate of Prisons reports from the women's estate also indicate that establishments holding female prisoners are less likely to have outdoor sporting facilities, so participation may also be limited by provision.

The visits I carried out as part of my review to the Secure Children's Homes and Secure Training Centres included those holding the small number of girls under 18 in custody: in January 2019 there were 26 girls in custody in England and Wales (Youth Custody Service, 2019) and unlike the rest of the prison population, girls in custody tend to be held in establishments that also hold boys. My review concluded that provision for girls in custody is not routinely meeting their needs, and for the small but often overlooked numbers of girls in custody, participating in PE and recreation activities alongside boys can be a barrier to engagement. I suggested that the Secure Children's Homes and Secure Training Centres which hold girls and boys together should consider offering separate gym sessions for girls, dedicated fitness space and PE provision, as well as tailored extra-curricular activities where appropriate. Reiterating my emphasis on making physical activity accessible throughout the secure estate, I reminded the

Ministry of Justice that provision for women and girls should be part of a programme of diverse offerings, promoting physical activity for all.

Reflecting my own observations concerning levels of physical activity for girls in custody, a recent Ofsted's inspection of Rainsbrook Secure Training Centre raised serious concerns regarding physical activity and enrichment provision for the girls, stating that 'there is an urgent need to ensure that the girls have their aspirations raised and undertake adequate physical exercise as well as benefiting from more sedentary activities' (Ofsted, 2017, p. 11).

I also reminded the Ministry of Justice that, as suggested by others (Dymond-White & Finnegan, 2016), there is a need to revisit standard-issue gym clothing, particularly for women and girls, who are entitled to wear their own clothes and shoes but will not necessarily have access to – or funds to purchase – exercise gear, in which case they are provided with standard issue clothes and trainers for boys and men. It is evident that this is a significant barrier to participation, mirroring community findings that clothing can have a considerable impact on a woman's motivation to exercise in prison (see also Meek & Lewis, 2014).

Taking these various gendered factors into account, together with the interviews with women and girls in prison – and the staff working with them – that I carried out as part of my review, Recommendation 6 urged the Ministry of Justice to develop a physical activity strategy for women and girls in prison. I pointed out that for a number of reasons women and girls in custody do not engage in physical activity to the same extent as men and boys and as a result they are not benefiting from the social, physical and psychological benefits of doing so. I concluded that a dedicated women and girls strategy was required to guide practice and target resource: there is a need to continue to develop a female-centred approach which reflects an understanding of gendered barriers to participation and exercise. As part of this understanding, I suggested that establishments should be guided by a policy which takes into account the high levels of trauma that women entering custody are likely to have experienced and that staff should be trained to deliver a practice which is informed by an understanding of, and responsiveness to, the impact of trauma.

In response to my recommendation on a physical activity strategy for women and girls in prison, the Ministry of Justice (2018) simply stated:

> HMPPS (HM Prison and Probation Service) is developing a detailed framework for delivery of PE in the women's estate which will include the specific clothing, equipment and interests of women.
>
> *(p. 7)*

2. *The need to invest in Physical Education staff and associate resource*

As a result of a staff restructuring process which commenced in 2013, the management of individuals with responsibility for physical activity was moved to Custodial Managers (those middle managers between a prison's Senior Management Team and frontline staff) who would not necessarily have training in or direct experience of delivering physical activity in prisons. As a result, despite representing a much-valued group of professionals with a unique skill set (and typically a uniquely positive relationship with those in their care), Physical Education (PE) staff have since been in a position of particular vulnerability in terms of job security and role, the allocation of resources and leadership support, leading to evidence of disengagement and poor staff morale:

> We need someone on the Senior Management Team fighting our corner.
>
> There's no pride, no leadership, no autonomy.
>
> *(PE Instructors in an adult male prison and a Young Offender Institution, cited in Meek, 2018a, pp. 72–73)*

I recommended to the government that in order to boost morale, support retention and enhance delivery, prison gym staff need to be able to take ownership of (and be held accountable for) their initiatives and to feel supported and empowered in offering effective provision. As with the workforce in other prison departments, PE staff need to see and be supported to work towards a clear career progression pathway.

I also suggested to the Ministry of Justice that in order to support more effective partnership working with external organisations and sporting bodies, prisons and secure settings should have a designated and supported member of the PE team with responsibility for external liaison. Such a role would include developing and enhancing external links, sourcing education and employment placements, identifying and promoting post-release opportunities and overseeing liaison with sports clubs and key figures (e.g., in order to schedule guest coaching sessions, matches with external teams and motivational talks[2]). An individual in a liaison role of this kind would be especially valuable in providing those living in prisons with post-release employment guidance on DBS checks and offence-specific restrictions and in contributing to post-release monitoring and contact.

Recognising the value of ex-offenders in the workforce, and the unique perspective they can bring to a role, more can be done in order to promote employment in the sports and fitness sectors for those who have previously been incarcerated, by developing a suitably qualified and supported workforce and by ensuring that skills and qualifications are appropriate to the sector's needs. I would suggest that prisons should also consider the recruitment of ex-offenders in delivering sports programmes. The community sports sector has set a strong example in this domain, and although there is not a widespread ban on people with criminal records working within prisons, more could be done to incorporate the 'user voice' in both the design and the delivery of prison initiatives.

At present, a number of community sporting organisations employ or provide volunteering opportunities to individuals who have progressed through their programmes, but only a small number of these operate in prisons, thus enabling only a few ex-offenders who have successfully navigated the transition from custody to community to return to prison to support those in the positions they used to occupy. And of further relevance to the topic of developing better partnership working with the voluntary sector, I have suggested that prisons should be encouraged to develop a sports volunteer framework in order to make better use of community volunteers as a supplement to, rather than a replacement of, existing staff (such an approach is already successfully used in other prison departments, such as the Chaplaincy).

The final element of this recommendation refers to a prison's infrastructure and facilities, necessary to enable staff to carry out their duties fully. Prison design and layout varies considerably, so that although some establishments cover large rural sites with ample outdoor spaces, others occupy relatively small urban premises. Just as prison establishments themselves vary dramatically in their physical size, the facilities available to PE departments can range from a small general-purpose gym to a variety of indoor and outdoor facilities.

In the course of my visits I was struck by some examples of poor physical infrastructure which would undermine any efforts to provide a decent and safe environment and pose a real barrier to an establishment's physical activity provision. I received dozens of complaints about poorly maintained facilities, with many of the establishments I visited affected by the Carillion maintenance crisis which was exposed while this review was under way.

To give an example of how such poor facilities have a direct impact on participation in physical activity, one particular barrier to activity for those living in prisons is where there is a lack of in-cell showers, requiring prisoners either to shower using gym facilities and during gym allocated time (which lack privacy and are often not fit for purpose) or to face a long delay – perhaps of several days – before being able to shower at all. This was cited to me by both prisoners and staff as a strong disincentive to participate in physical activity. For staff, having to oversee showering prevents them from carrying out their primary duties, impacts on staffing (for example a female PEI is not able to supervise males) and is not a good use of PEI staff time. For prisoners, there are clear concerns about bullying and intimidation in communal showers which often lead them to self-exclude. These concerns are supported by data I reviewed from the Prisons Inspectorate which found that young people who have been victimised are significantly more likely to say they 'don't want to go to the gym' (39%) than those who haven't been victimised (22%).[3]

Although Secure Children's Homes, Secure Training Centres, newly built and women's prisons do have in-cell showers, most of the rest of the secure estate, including juvenile Young Offender Institutions, still does not. And while I recognise that this may be difficult to implement, my review recommended that there should at the very least be a clear aspiration to move all young people into establishments with showers within rooms.

As with other aspects of the prison regime, the governor/director of each establishment has a certain amount of autonomy regarding the allocation of resources (financial and staffing) to sport and physical activity. However, previous findings have confirmed that attitudes towards, support for, and the resourcing of sport and physical activity varies dramatically between institutions, even those of the same security status holding comparable populations (Meek, 2014). This extends to the resourcing of suitably qualified staff since, as reported in Meek (2018a), the number of PE Instructors in our prisons is lower now (the last confirmed figures were 643 in 2017) than the service had 30 years ago (714), despite the fact that the prison population has more than doubled in that period.

As a result of my review I proposed that in order to develop an integrated culture of promoting physical activity and wellbeing in our prisons, a number of structural and organisational changes would need to be made. I suggested that prison PE staff should be directly accountable to, and supported by, a suitably qualified gym manager, wellbeing coordinator or equivalent, who would be able to offer expertise in the sports sector, provide a direct link to the prison's governor and the rest of the Senior

Management Team and support partnership working in implementing the establishment's physical activity and wellbeing strategy. I also recommended that HM Prison and Probation Service and the Ministry of Justice invest in developing a sport and PE staff training and development strategy which can better respond to the diverse and changing needs of the sector's workforce and the youth and adult prison population.

In response to my recommendations on staffing, the Ministry of Justice (2018) stated that:

> HMPPS are reviewing the management of Physical Education at national and local levels. We will develop and grow the capability and the skills of PE staff to enable provision of activities beyond the mandatory activities envisaged by the current education contract, through access to specialist training for working with young people or teaching qualifications. Introducing flexibility into the core day will enable young people to access a greater range of activities and qualifications and enable more partner organisations to come in and deliver programmes to young people. Local PE staff should be empowered to deliver training or alongside external providers that will provide offenders with support 'Through the Gate' so they can benefit after their release.
>
> *(p. 8)*

3. *Revisiting the ban on the use of martial arts and boxing-related programmes in custodial settings*

The current official position is that prisons in England and Wales are not authorised to offer boxing-related programmes, despite the fact that such initiatives were recognised and approved by a previous Justice Secretary as a way of engaging non-violent offenders:

> Mr Gerry Sutcliffe (Bradford South) (Lab): One of the busiest places in prison is the gym. I hope that the Secretary of State will look at how sports can help to reduce reoffending. Will he look at the boxing project in Doncaster prison? It teaches offenders to get involved in boxing and uses boxing coaches. Unfortunately, it has had to be stopped because of a change in the guidelines on boxing in prisons. I understand some of the problems, but the scheme is great and people get jobs at the end of the course.

> Chris Grayling: I can give an assurance to the hon. Gentleman. I am aware of the project to which he refers. I have seen a number of projects around the country in which boxing is used as a way of engaging young people. I have no problem with that happening in our prisons. My hon. Friend the Under-Secretary of State for Justice, the hon. Member for Kenilworth and Southam is writing to the hon. Gentleman to say that we are happy for the project to go ahead; our only caveat relates to violent offenders. We are happy to see the project continue as a way of engaging non-violent offenders.
>
> *(House of Commons, 2013)*

Despite this exchange within a Commons debate, there remains a blanket ban on any boxing- or martial-art-related activity in prisons in England and Wales, which includes boxercise exercise classes and non-contact martial arts such as Tai Chi. However, while some concerns remain about managing boxing and martial arts activities safely, there was a widespread frustration from many of the professional staff I spoke to (as well as most young people and adults, including women, in custody) that boxing-related programmes are not considered in any prisons. Where they are (in some Secure Children's Homes and Secure Training Centres where the Prison Service directive has not been implemented), they are well received and highly valued, both as a behaviour management tool and as a vehicle through which to facilitate education, discipline and communication.

On occasions where boxing initiatives have in the past been offered in the private sector, they have also led to positive outcomes. For example, in 2016 the gym staff at HMP/YOI Parc were commended by the Butler Trust for their work, including the healthy living programme which incorporated non-contact boxing as an effective way to instil discipline and promote positive health behaviours. And when it operated as a juvenile establishment, YOI Ashfield (which has held only adults since 2013) operated a highly successful 'boxing academy' which drew on external partners to deliver a 12-week holistic education and wellbeing programme, combining theoretical and practical sessions with coaching and sport leadership awards and multi-agency support and resulting in fewer incidences of violence and better educational outcomes for the children held in that prison.

Recognising an opportunity to draw on the successes of previous and existing prison-based programmes[4] as well as the numerous community initiatives that use boxing to engage offenders or with those at-risk of offending (Wright, 2006), particularly those which combine boxing activities with therapeutic treatment (Draper, Errington, Omar & Makhita, 2013), I wanted to draw attention to some of the positive ways in which boxing programmes could be developed in our custodial settings.

First, although competitive boxing may involve competing individually, the ethos of boxing training is team-based and often non-contact, and community initiatives highlight the unique way in which, because it is physically demanding, it offers a credible alternative to anti-social behaviour for the most disengaged groups (England Boxing, 2016). Indeed, in her foreword to the All-Party Parliamentary Group's report into boxing, Olympic medallist Nicola Adams claimed that her sport:

> has an almost unmatched capability to engage some of the most disaffected young people and help to combat a massive range of social problems, covering crime, educational underachievement, health and fitness and community cohesion.
>
> *(All-Party Parliamentary Group for Boxing, 2015)*

Although limited research evidence can be drawn from custodial settings due to the government's current ban on any such programmes, evidence from community settings is strong. The charity Fight for Peace is an international organisation that combines boxing and martial arts with mentoring, education and personal development, to great effect. In a 2015 evaluation of their London-based project, ex-offender participants reported being not only less likely to engage in crime (substantiated with follow-up reconviction data), but also less likely to engage in gang-related activities or carry a weapon (Sampson, 2015).

Also of relevance to the previous recommendation to develop a dedicated physical activity strategy for women and girls, it is striking that a number of women and girls across different establishments spontaneously mentioned kickboxing and boxercise when I enquired about which activities would motivate them to be more active (bearing in mind that women and girls are the least active population in our prisons). It is also noteworthy that boxing-related initiatives have proven to be an effective tool in engaging with Gypsy and Traveller communities, groups over-represented in prisons, particularly in youth custody, where the Prisons Inspectorate identified that as many as 22% of children in one Secure Training Centre considered themselves to be Gypsy, Romany or Traveller (HM Inspectorate of Prisons, 2014).

In my review, instead of suggesting that all prisons change their policy in order to offer boxing sessions, I suggested that – where prison governors and directors thought it appropriate – the development and delivery of appropriate martial art or boxing exercises, qualifications and associated activities should be introduced as a pilot targeted intervention, and evaluated to assess the impact of such a scheme. However, this was my only recommendation that was not accepted by the government, bizarrely justified as being due to 'limited evidence' for the impact of such activities in prison settings (despite the fact that I had recommended that a pilot programme be implemented and evaluated in order to explore the potential of such a scheme).

In response to my recommendation to reconsider the ban on any boxing or martial arts programmes in prisons, the Ministry of Justice (2018) stated:

> We acknowledge that there is a great deal of evidence about the way in which participation in boxing and martial arts programmes in the community can have positive outcomes for individuals, however there is currently limited evidence about how that translates into the custodial environment. In reconsidering any policy our priority must be the safety and security of the custodial environment and the wellbeing of staff, participants and other prisoners. We have no plans to make boxing or martial arts based activities permissible.
>
> *(p. 7)*

Despite slow progress in the England and Wales context, the Northern Ireland prison service *have* supported a new non-contact boxing initiative, initially through the delivery of a pilot project in Hydebank College, a prison holding young men aged between 18 and 21 years. Northern Ireland Justice Minister Naomi Long has supported such a development: 'This course has not only helped these individuals build their physical strength, but it has made them feel mentally stronger, which in turn helps them to deal with the challenges life will bring them' (BBC, 2020).

4. *Using sport to reduce and resolve conflict in our prisons*

Although it is recognised that there may be occasions where a young person's safety requires separation from another young person, my review raised a concern that 'keep apart' lists (where lists are kept of 'non-associate' children within the prison who should not interact with each other) are being overused. Rather than managing risk dynamically, there appears to be a focus on keeping young people apart for longer than is necessary instead of challenging and changing their behaviour in more constructive ways. Of course, where a child's daily regime while in custody is determined by a restriction to remain in the same small group of learners (who may be of very different abilities), educational and recreational provision can be severely compromised, but also children are not practising realistic or meaningful forms of conflict resolution.

As an alternative to a default position of keeping individuals who have been in conflict – or at risk of conflict – apart from one another on non-associate or 'keep apart' lists, I suggest that sport can be better used as a useful mechanism by which to bring together groups or individuals in conflict, either directly or by promoting non-violent communication. In Meek (2014) I give examples of where sports-based programmes have the opportunity to encourage participants to develop and practise their thinking skills, which for many could have important implications in preventing impulsive behaviours and developing better communication strategies ('I've learnt to think more before I act': Young adult male, cited in Meek, 2014). Participants described how they had learnt to react to frustrations in an adaptive and responsive way, rather than by resorting to aggression, thus lending support to the notion that sport can be an effective way to promote conflict resolution skills (Ravizza & Motonak, 2011). The development of such techniques is of course reliant on a facilitator skilled in the principles of emotional regulation.

The positive impact of sport throughout the prison and most specifically its use as a tool in promoting compliance appears to be especially valued by staff, thus echoing early rationales for the use of physical exercise in prison as a way of *managing* behaviour. As well as being recognised as fulfilling an important function in terms of proving a meaningful way to pass time, another recognised way in which sport contributes to the social control of a prison is by providing an incentive for positive behaviour:

> Sport is a massive part of prison, if it wasn't here I don't know what I would do with myself. The gym was a real coping mechanism for me when I came to prison.
>
> The gym is good for control. If I get in a fight I'm banned from here and the last thing I'm going to do is jeopardise my gym time.
>
> *(Residents in two different adult male prisons, cited in Meek, 2014, p. 141)*

As well as playing an important role in improving physical and psychological wellbeing, sports initiatives can contribute to fewer instances of violence and conflict in prison (Martos-Garcia, Devis-Devis & Sparkes, 2009; Murtaza & Uddin, 2011; Wagner, McBride & Crouse, 1999).

An interactionist approach to prison violence (Bottoms, 1999) – the need to consider the dynamic interaction between prisoners, prison staff and the social and physical context in which they are placed – recognises the various processes at play in escalations of prison violence. Psychology has an important role to play here, in understanding the causes of prison violence but also in developing violence reduction techniques.

Politicians, social commentators and academics have long proclaimed the social benefits of sport: leadership, teamwork and self-sacrifice are words and concepts which are commonly used in association with sporting endeavour (Collins, 2009) and sport is recognised as an important way of promoting social cohesion and interaction. Given the isolating aspect of incarceration it is not therefore surprising that sport can be seen as having an especially important role to play in promoting relational interaction and the development of social skills in prison settings:

> (Sport) improves social skills and breaks down barriers within rival gangs.
>
> It brings a togetherness amongst offenders.
>
> *(Members of staff from youth and adult prisons, cited in Meek, 2014, p. 144)*

As well as recognising the unique role that sport can play in reducing violence and bringing together disparate groups, I wanted to draw attention to the overuse of the dominant approach to managing conflict in youth prisons, that of 'keep apart' lists. My investigations revealed that in the three public sector prisons holding children under the age of 18 in England, between 72% and 88% of all children are impacted by being included on 'keep apart' lists and thus deemed necessary to be kept separate from at least one other individual, demonstrating that most children held in these prisons are restricted by which other children in the same establishment they interact with. I argue that the use of 'keep apart' lists dramatically undermines the regime of establishments and act as a direct barrier to promoting inclusion and conflict resolution. Furthermore, these lists, rather than individual ability, determine a young person's access to appropriate education. They are therefore a major barrier to sport and physical activity provision, and fail to reflect a real-world or sustainable response to conflict. Therefore, Recommendation 4 of my review was that establishments should invest resources in the regular reassessment of 'keep apart' lists, favouring mediation and resolution over sustained separation, and making better use of sport to bring together individuals who have been in conflict with one another, rather than resorting to separation.

In response to my recommendation on 'keep apart' lists and alternative forms of conflict resolution, the Ministry of Justice (2018) confirmed:

> We will ensure that establishments develop approaches to the management of non-associates in the population of young people in their care which are joined-up and multidisciplinary and reflect the experience and insight of a range of teams including PE, residential staff, education, security and conflict resolution. PE Teams will be invited to participate in weekly allocation meetings and receive lists of young people who are taking part in Outreach programmes so that the insight of PE Teams is available for consideration in the risk management process and ensure that those children who are subject to enhanced supervision have access to physical activity. We will encourage PE Teams to become a partner in conflict resolution, so that those involved in conflict resolution activities are not denied access to sports, and physical activity can be used in innovative ways to end disputes.
>
> *(p. 6)*

The impact and legacy of the research: policy and practice developments or empty promises?

It was both rewarding and positive that the Ministry of Justice published their reaction to my review findings at the same time as publishing my 100-page report, and the Minister's foreword to that reaction reiterated the general theme of my research, that physical activity can be used as a vehicle for supporting positive change for those in the justice system:

> When we are inspired to get involved in organised sport, it brings people from all walks of life together – I am determined to incorporate that into our approach to rehabilitation … Taking part in sport

> has obvious benefits for our physical health and wellbeing, but it also has an impact on our mental health and self-discipline.
>
> *(Ministry of Justice, 2018, p. 3)*

Although the Ministry of Justice accepted all but one of my recommendations, this was of course no guarantee that my proposals would be implemented, or an indication of how.

It was, then, encouraging when the Ministry of Justice agreed to co-host with me an event to mark six months since publication of my review. This wasn't an academic event, but the audience of over 100 (the maximum capacity for the Ministry of Justice's meeting space) contained academics, practitioners, civil servants, prison managers and staff, and representatives from community sports groups and sporting bodies. Ultimately the guest list had to be approved by a senior civil servant in HM Prison and Probation Service, which I found frustrating when PE staff from the adult men's and women's prison estate were omitted. The media was also excluded. However, I had the opportunity to talk about my research process and share further details of the findings, and senior prison staff outlined some of the progress made in meeting my recommendations.

Minister Edward Argar opened the event with a speech that reiterated the potential impact of these types of interventions:

> in sport we have a marvellous tool at our disposal. A tool that improves health – both physical and mental; a tool that develops social skills – cooperation, communication and confidence; a tool that can engage children with education and encourage them to think positively about their future; a tool that, ultimately, can help prevent crime and reduce recidivism.
>
> *(Argar, 2019)*

The Minister closed his speech with a message which I found positive, particularly in thinking about the continued role of academics and academic research in developing a better evidence base:

> If we are to guarantee the sustainability of such programmes, however, we need to ensure that there is a strong, validated and widely-recognised body of evidence for their efficacy. Not only to address the scepticism that, unfortunately, the use of these programmes

> continues to attract, but also to improve our understanding of how we can tailor these programmes to meet the needs of those in custody.
>
> *(Argar, 2019)*

Although the event served as a good opportunity for the minister and senior civil servants to reiterate their support for this work (Edward Argar and I also did pieces to camera at the event which were published by the Ministry of Justice on their Twitter feed) it did not include a comprehensive analysis of the implementation of the recommendations, and official lines were, although positive, lacking in detail and at risk of being empty rhetoric. What was detailed, however, was the scrutiny that the minister faced from the Digital, Culture, Media and Sport Committee when he was called to give evidence to the same inquiry into the social impact of sport that I had spoken to five months earlier, where he came under repeated criticism for rejecting (or upon taking up his role, inheriting a rejection of) one of my recommendations, the one concerning boxing. This example serves as a reminder of the way political decisions may be taken in spite of, not because of, academic evidence:

> Her report is quite evidence based. I think she impressed that upon the Committee when she gave evidence to us and that was one of the key recommendations. She cites numerous examples of why she believes it has a role within the secure environment. The Government's response seemed to be relatively dismissive, half a sentence in a very relatively short document saying, 'We are not going to do it. We don't believe the evidence is there'.
>
> *(DCMS chair, cited in House of Commons, 2018b, Q329)*

Aside from ministerial and parliamentarian influence, the responsibility for improving sports-based initiatives in our prisons, especially those based on community and prison partnerships, also of course partly lies with the voluntary sector. I have particularly enjoyed acting as a mediator between prisons and the voluntary sector and acting as an advisor in establishing new sports-based interventions in our prisons. I'm now supporting a whole host of local and national sporting groups and bodies and voluntary sector organisations who haven't previously taken their work into prisons (from parkrun to Table Tennis England), and it is really rewarding to know that my research has had a direct impact on these new initiatives and partnerships. These new partnerships also provide me with an opportunity to continue to develop the evidence base around the impact of sport and physical activity in promoting wellbeing and reducing reoffending.

In summing up, and reflecting back at the time of writing on the 18 months since I was asked to commence my review on behalf of the government, I would largely see this research experience as a positive one. At a time when academic research is increasingly judged on its non-academic impact (and rightly so), this felt like a valuable opportunity to go deeper into my subject area, to gain more insight into the organisational and political landscape surrounding this topic, and to have a unique opportunity to help shape policy and practice. I originally started carrying out research in criminal justice and prisons because I felt that psychology had so much to offer in responding to the real-world issues being played out in our prisons, and I do still feel that. But I also recognise that translating research into policy and practice brings with it some particular challenges and lessons. In this chapter I hope to have relayed some of those experiences and lessons, in terms of making research findings accessible to a range of stakeholders, embracing opportunities to work with public and voluntary sector partners and, of course, holding those with the power to influence policy and practice to account.

I have learnt that it is important to be clear in setting out research outcomes in the form of clear priorities, and to tailor recommendations to specific stakeholders, be they a particular government department, someone in a given role, or the wider sector – in my case the sport and fitness sector as well as the criminal justice and voluntary sectors. But I have also learnt the importance of holding those stakeholders – and their successors – accountable in taking necessary action; and that other bodies can be valuable in this process. And lastly, as I noted above, the same DCMS committee that I was invited to give evidence to while we awaited publication of my review subsequently took evidence from the Minister on its publication and implementation (House of Commons, 2018b), and the committee reiterated a number of my recommendations in the publication of their own inquiry (Digital, Culture, Media and Sport Committee, 2019). I have realised that internal mechanisms such as these are critical in maintaining momentum in bringing about the policy changes we seek through our research.

Notes

1 For example, HM Government (2015). *Sporting Future: A New Strategy for an Active Nation*. London: Cabinet Office.

2 For example, prison pilot schemes have been delivered by State of Mind Sport, a mental health initiative which aims to raise awareness and tackle stigma, in partnership with ex-professional rugby players who have themselves experienced mental health problems: see Woods, Leavey, Meek, & Breslin (in press)
3 Analysis of HM Inspectorate of Prisons raw data from the year 2016–2017, reported in Meek (2018a).
4 While it was still operating, the now closed women's prison HMP Peterhead piloted a successful ten-week boxing fundamentals programme with the aim of promoting confidence and wellbeing among the women residing in the prison.

References

All-Party Parliamentary Group for Boxing. (2015). *Boxing: The right hook*. London: APPG Boxing.

Amtmann, J., & Kukay, J. (2016). Fitness changes after an 8-week fitness coaching program at a regional youth detention facility. *Journal of Correctional Health Care, 22*(1), 75–83.

Argar, E. (2019). *Opening speech: Six months on from publication of the Meek Review*. London: Ministry of Justice.

Battaglia, C., Di Cagno, A., Fiorilli, G., Giombini, A., Fagnani, F., Borrione, P., … Pigozzi, F. (2013). Benefits of selected physical exercise programs in detention: A randomized controlled study. *International Journal of Environmental Research and Public Health, 10*(11), 5683–5696.

BBC. (2020). Frampton and Barnes inspire young prisoners to change path. *BBC News*. Retrieved from https://www.bbc.co.uk/news/uk-northern-ireland-51666908.

Bottoms, A. (1999). Interpersonal violence and social order in prison. In M. Tonry & J. Petersilia (Eds.), *Crime and justice: A review of research* (pp. 205–282). Chicago, IL: University of Chicago.

Buckaloo, B., Krug, K., & Nelson, K. (2009). Exercise and the low-security inmate: Changes in depression, stress and anxiety. *The Prison Journal, 89*(3), 328–343.

Collins, M. (2009). *Examining sports development*. Abingdon: Routledge.

Digital, Culture, Media and Sport Committee. (2019). *Changing lives: The social impact of participation in culture and sport*. London: House of Commons.

Draper, C., Errington, S., Omar, S., & Makhita, S. (2013). The therapeutic benefits of sport in the rehabilitation of young sexual offenders: A qualitative evaluation of the Fight with Insight programme. *Psychology of Sport and Exercise, 14*(4), 519–530.

Dymond-White, S., & Finnegan, B. (2016). *Health and wellbeing in women's prisons: A thematic review*. London: HMPPS.

Elger, B. (2009). Prison life, television, sports, work, stress and insomnia in a remand prison. *International Journal of Law and Psychiatry, 32*(2), 74–83.

England Boxing. (2016). *The role of boxing in development: A social marketing perspective*. Sheffield: England Boxing/Walker Research Group.
European Committee for the Prevention of Torture and Inhuman or Degrading Treatment. (2006). *European prison rules*. Strasbourg: Council of Europe.
Frost, J., Wortham, S., & Reifel, S. (2007). *Play and child development*. Upper Saddle River, NJ: Pearson.
Herbert, K., Plugge, E., Foster, C., & Doll, H. (2012). Prevalence and risk factors for non-communicable diseases in prison populations worldwide. *Lancet, 397*(9830), 1975–1982.
HM Inspectorate of Prisons. (2014). *People in prison: Gypsies, Romany and Travellers*. London: HMIP.
House of Commons. (2013). Extract from House of Commons debate, Hansard: 9 January 2013: Column 326.
House of Commons. (2018a, July 3). *Digital, culture, media and sport committee oral evidence: Social impact of participation in culture and sport*, HC 734. Retrieved from http://data.parliament.uk/writtenevidence/committeeevidence.svc/evidencedocument/digital-culture-media-and-sport-committee/the-social-impact-of-participation-in-culture-and-sport/oral/86436.pdf.
House of Commons. (2018b, December 12). *Digital, culture, media and sport committee oral evidence: Social impact of participation in culture and sport*, HC 734. Retrieved from http://data.parliament.uk/writtenevidence/committeeevidence.svc/evidencedocument/digital-culture-media-and-sport-committee/the-social-impact-of-participation-in-culture-and-sport/oral/93899.pdf.
International Working Group on Women and Sport. (1994). *The Brighton declaration on women and sport*. Helsinki, Finland: IWG.
Jebb, S., & Moore, M. (1999). Contribution of a sedentary lifestyle and inactivity to the etiology of overweight and obesity: Current evidence and research issues. *Medicine and Science in Sports and Exercise, 31*(11), S534–S541.
Jones, H., Millward, P., & Buraimo, B. (2011). *Adult participation in sport: Analysis of the taking part survey*. London: DCMS.
Mandela, N. (2000). *Acceptance speech, Laureus Lifetime Achievement Award*. Monaco, France: Laureus.
Martos-Garcia, D., Devis-Devis, J., & Sparkes, A. (2009). Sport and physical activity in a high security Spanish prison: An ethnographic study of multiple meanings. *Sport, Education and Society, 14*(1), 77–96.
Meek, R. (2014). *Sport in prison: Exploring the role of physical activity in correctional settings*. Abingdon: Routledge.
Meek, R. (2018a). *A sporting chance: An independent review of sport in youth and adult prisons*. London: Ministry of Justice.
Meek, R. (2018b, September 11). How sport in prison could stop reoffending. *The Guardian*.
Meek, R. (2020). The use of sport to promote employment, education, and desistance from crime: Lessons from a review of English and Welsh prisons. In P. Ugwudike, H. Graham, F. McNeill, P. Raynor, F. Taxman & C. Trotter

(Eds.), *The Routledge companion to rehabilitative work in criminal justice* (pp. 409–418). Abingdon: Routledge.

Meek, R., & Lewis, G. (2014). Promoting well-being and desistance through sport and physical activity: The opportunities and barriers experienced by women in prison. *Women and Criminal Justice, 24*(2), 151–172.

Mehay, A., & Meek, R. (2016). The development of a peer-based approach for promoting prisoner health in an English male Young Offender Institution. In L. Abrams, E. Hughes, M. Inderbitzin & R. Meek (Eds.), *The voluntary sector in prisons: Encouraging personal and institutional change* (pp. 143–170). New York, NY: Palgrave Macmillan.

Ministry of Justice. (2018). *Government response to a sporting chance: An independent review of sport in youth and adult prisons*. London: Ministry of Justice.

Ministry of Justice. (2019). *Prison population statistics. Population Bulletin: Weekly 2 August 2019*. London: Ministry of Justice.

Ministry of Justice & National Statistics. (2019). *Proven reoffending statistics Quarterly Bulletin, July 2017 to September 2017*. London: Ministry of Justice.

Murtaza, T., & Uddin, R. (2011). Probing study on facilities of competitive sport in District Jail, Lucknow (India). *European Journal of Business and Management, 3*(8), 69–79.

Newton, A., May, X., Eames, S., & Ahmad, M. (2019). *Economic and social costs of reoffending: Analytical report*. London: Ministry of Justice.

Ofsted. (2017). *Inspections of secure training centres: Inspection of Rainsbrook*. London: Care Quality Commission / HM Inspectorate of Prisons / Ofsted.

Plugge, E., Foster, C., Yudkin, P., & Douglas, N. (2009). Cardiovascular disease risk factors and women prisoners in the UK: The impact of imprisonment. *Health Promotion International, 24*(4), 334–343.

Ravizza, D., & Motonak, E. (2011). *Peaceful play: Guidelines for conflict in sport and strategies for resolution*. Salisbury, Maryland: Centre for Conflict Resolution: Salisbury University.

Sampson, A. (2015). *An evaluation of the longer-term outcomes of the pathways programme at Fight for Peace*. London: University of East London.

Sedikides, C., Meek, R., Alicke, M., & Taylor, S. (2014). Behind bars but above the bar: Prisoners consider themselves more prosocial than non-prisoners. *British Journal of Social Psychology, 53*(2), 396–403.

Social Exclusion Unit. (2002). *Reducing re-offending by ex-prisoners*. London: Office of the Deputy Prime Minister. Social Exclusion Unit.

Sport England. (2012). *Sport participation factsheet: Summary of results for England*. London: Sport England.

Sport England. (2015). *This girl can*. London: Sport England.

The Observer. (2018, July 7). *Government rejects proposal to teach boxing in prisons: Ex-justice minister Phillip Lee hits out at 'culture of cowardice' after report he commissioned is shelved*.

The Sun. (2018, June 28). Taekwon-NO! *Ex-minister's radical plans to teach lags deadly martial arts such as kickboxing gets rejected with public humiliation*.

United Nations. (2015). *Standard minimum rules for the treatment of prisoners (the Nelson Mandela Rules).*

van Zyl, D., & Snacken, S. (2002). *Principals of European prison law and policy: Penology and human rights.* Oxford: OUP.

Wagner, M., McBride, R., & Crouse, S. (1999). The effects of weight-training exercise on aggression variables in adult male inmates. *Prison Journal, 79*(1), 72–89.

Warr, J. (2012). Personal reflections on prison staff. In J. Bennett, B. Crewe & A. Wahidin (Eds.), *Understanding prison staff* (pp. 39–51). Abingdon: Routledge.

Woods, D., Breslin, G., & Hassan, D. (2017). Positive collateral damage or purposeful design: How sport-based interventions impact the psychological well-being of people in prison. *Mental Health and Physical Activity, 13*, 152–162.

Woods, D., Leavey, G., Meek, R., & Breslin, G. (in press). Developing mental health awareness and help seeking in prison: A feasibility study of the State of Mind Sport programme. *International Journal of Prisoner Health.*

Wright, W. (2006). Keep it in the ring: Using boxing in social group work with high-risk and offender youth to reduce violence. *Social Work with Groups, 29*(2–3), 149–174.

Youth Custody Service. (2019). *Monthly youth custody report January 2019: England and Wales.* London: Youth Custody Service.

Zuckerman, M. (1991). Sensation seeking: The balance between risk and reward. In L. Lipsitt & L. Mitnick (Eds.), *Self regulatory behavior and risk taking: Causes and consequences* (pp. 143–152). Norwood, NJ: Ablex.

7

PROCEDURAL JUSTICE – THE IMPACT OF A THEORY

Ben Bradford

Introduction

The idea that a positive relationship with the public is vital for the successful functioning of the police stretches back to the foundation of the modern British police in the early nineteenth century. 'Peel's principles', with their emphasis on policing by consent, may be apocryphal. But there is no doubt that a central goal during the foundation and establishment of the London Metropolitan Police Service (MPS) was securing and maintaining public support for an organisation many initially considered to be, literally and metaphorically, a foreign imposition. An important part of the legitimating 'myth' of the MPS was that it was unlike continental police systems in operation at the time (Reiner, 2010). Central to this claim was the idea that the police governed with the consent of the policed, and, at least in theory, that the police were to be drawn from communities they served. Nor was concern about the police–public relationship limited to those directly involved in setting up and managing the new police organisation: there was a widespread feeling that public trust and legitimacy were important. This concern has persisted to the present day, right across the United Kingdom, as witnessed by the almost ever-present debate over public 'trust and confidence' in the police and criminal justice system.

Concern about public opinion among interested parties – politicians, policymakers, senior police, academics – has of course waxed and waned over the years. But starting in the late 1990s a significant set of concerns began to emerge which proved to be extremely 'sticky', and which have since had almost continuous resonance. There was evidence of a significant decline in public trust since the late 1970s (Fitzgerald, Hough, Joseph, & Qureshi, 2002; Hough, 2007), which may indeed have started even earlier, in the 1960s (Jackson, Bradford, Stanko, & Hohl, 2013). While it is important not to overstate the extent of this decline (Bradford, 2016), it is nonetheless true that over this period the police seem to have slipped from being one of the most trusted societal institutions to being simply one example of a range of more or less controversial and contested state bodies or agencies (Reiner, 2010). More important for current purposes, though, is that by the late 1990s policymakers and others 'felt' and believed in this decline. And when it continued into the new millennium, despite the fact that crime had been falling since the middle of the previous decade, this caused significant consternation. There was a widespread assumption that if crime was down, public trust should be up.

Answers to this apparent puzzle tended at the time to revolve around the so-called reassurance gap (Millie & Herrington, 2005). On this account, crime may have been going down, but people did not feel this to be the case, and they blamed the police for an ongoing sense of insecurity. To be sure, there is likely to be some truth in this account. Public opinion of the police did eventually start to move in a more positive direction, and at least some of the reason for this may have been that the crime decline began to make itself felt in terms of people's sense of safety and security (Sindall, Sturgis, & Jennings, 2012). But in this chapter I want to describe the impact a quite different account of public trust began to have around the same time, which has since become arguably *the* dominant understanding of police–public relations – procedural justice theory (PJT) (Lind & Tyler, 1988; Tyler, 2006; Tyler & Huo, 2002). As the ground-breaking work of Tyler and colleagues in the US began to be taken up by policing scholars in the UK, the idea that policing was not only, or even primarily, about crime – long a mainstay of the sociological literature on policing as an activity – was properly integrated into understandings of trust, legitimacy and the wider arena of police–public relations. Other values and outcomes were, and are, at stake in the judgements people make of police, and this explains the apparent disjuncture between levels of crime and levels of trust.

This chapter is therefore unlike most of the others in this volume, in that it charts not the impact of a particular research project, or a specific theoretical, empirical or methodological innovation, but rather the effect of a theoretical paradigm. The chapter sets out to do three things. First, I describe PJT and some of the concepts most closely associated with it, notably trust and legitimacy. Second, I sketch out the effects PJT has had on police policy and practice in the UK. Third, and by way of contrast, I outline some of the barriers to impact that persist and which, it might be argued, have stymied transformative change.[1]

Procedural justice theory

Procedural justice theory is fundamentally concerned with understanding the way people experience power and authority in group settings. The core idea is simple and supported by a mass of empirical evidence. When interacting with powerholders such as police officers, teachers and employers, people attend closely to the quality of the process through which that interaction takes place, most particularly in relation to dimensions of process fairness: dignity, respect, voice, openness, honesty and neutrality. A sense of 'procedural justice' during encounters with police motivates trust in the officer(s) concerned, acceptance of and satisfaction with their decisions, institutional trust (i.e., that spills beyond the specific encounter in question) and legitimacy. A more generalised sense or perception that police behave in such a manner – and perhaps in particular *would* behave that way if they were to be encountered – is also associated with cooperation, compliance and other outcomes.

Procedural justice thus refers to the quality of interactions between power-holders and those over whom they have power, and the neutrality of the processes through which the former make decisions relating to the latter. While this may seem to be primarily a characteristic of interpersonal, face-to-face interactions, it is important to recognise that the experience of procedural justice strengthens the social bonds between individuals and *institutions*. People tend to feel a stronger affiliation with an institution when its human representatives – with whom they actually interact – make fair and neutral decisions, treat them respectfully and legally, and do not act in ways based on bias and stereotypes. Procedural justice, or injustice, provides people with information about where they stand in relation not just to 'this police officer' but also 'the police'.

Viewed from some perspectives this account seems simple, and almost simplistic. Who doesn't want to be treated with respect, and to interact with trustworthy others? It seems obvious that trust and legitimacy are heavily bound up with notions of fairness. We might note that even this observation appeared until recently to elude many policymakers, police and academics, who remained fixed on more instrumentally inflected elements of public opinion and concerns about crime, safety and fear. Yet from this fundamental observation PJT develops in ways that have had significant impacts both within academia and, increasingly, in the 'real world' of policing. Work conducted within and around the PJT paradigm has placed conceptually and empirically rich social science concepts of trust and legitimacy centre stage in policing debates, and, crucially, opened up a much clearer view of the wider implications of police–public relations. Before moving on to consider the ways that PJT has been used in research and practice, and the extent to which it has become embedded in policing debates, it will be useful therefore to sketch out these concepts and ideas, the meanings they have within PJT research, and the ways they link to the 'downstream' implications of police activity.

Trust and legitimacy

While public opinion of policing has been considered important for many years, what 'public opinion' actually means in this context was usually unstated, taken for granted or glossed (to be clear, the issue here is 'opinions in the public', and not, of course, a unified, singular view of police among the policed). But before the arrival of PJT only rarely was any kind of conceptual underpinning of public opinion even provided, let alone rigorously discussed or defined. By the mid-2000s, academics, policymakers and others were most commonly using phrases like 'public confidence' and 'trust and confidence' as kinds of catch-all labels (Jackson & Bradford, 2010), with a more or less implicit understanding that confidence meant much the same thing as trust (and perhaps also legitimacy). But it was often unclear what, precisely, was at stake.

Work within the PJT paradigm has addressed this theoretical lacuna. Drawing not only on concepts developed within the 'core' PJT literature but also ideas in the wider fields of social psychology, sociology and political science, better defined and more robust concepts of trust and legitimacy have been inserted into the debate, alleviating some, although by no means all, of the previous conceptual confusion, and focussing attention on the underlying mechanics of police–public relations and the kinds of outcomes at stake in these relationships.

Turning first to trust, academic research has recently coalesced around the idea that trust is a 'willingness to be vulnerable' to another that is founded in beliefs about that other person's current and likely future behaviours (Bradford, Jackson, & Hough, 2018). We can say that an individual trusts a person or institution when they willingly place valued outcomes

– for example their security and freedom – in the hands of that actor or institution *on the basis of a belief* that they have the right intentions and are competent to perform relevant actions. The emphasis on assessments of the intentions of the trustee accords with the 'motive-based' concept of trust often referred to in the PJT literature (Tyler, 2006). Trust in the police is thus *premised* in beliefs that officers and institution are effective in the tasks set them, are well intentioned and will continue to be so in the future; and *instantiated* in a willing acceptance of the police role in securing outcomes such as security, safety, justice and freedom.

Trust thus emerges from direct and indirect experience of the behaviour of police officers – in relation both to the self and others. These are important moments in which the beliefs that constitute trust are formed (Bradford, Jackson, & Stanko, 2009; Mazerolle, Antrobus, Bennett, & Tyler, 2013; Mazerolle, Bennett, Antrobus, & Eggins, 2012; Skogan, 2006; Tyler & Fagan, 2008). But it is also based on generalised motivations *to* trust. In particular, people will be motivated to trust when they feel they share group membership with police (Tyler & Blader, 2000), and when police are located within appropriate 'value-bearing narratives': social and cultural stories about the values officers and institution represent, enact and embody (Earle & Cvetkovich, 1999; Earle & Cvetkovich, 1995). In other words, what police do has significant implications for trust but, equally, wider and perhaps deeper factors are also in play.

Turning to legitimacy, recent work within the PJT paradigm in the UK, US and elsewhere has developed what is becoming a relatively widely accepted definition, at least within criminology (Jackson, 2018); it is also worth noting, though, that this process has also been marked by a lively debate about the meaning of legitimacy, and there remain a variety of positions on this question – see for example Bottoms and Tankebe (2012) and Tankebe (2013). At stake in all these accounts is an 'empirical' concept of legitimacy. As developed within the procedural justice literature, legitimacy concerns the judgements people make about police and the reasons for those judgements; not, in any direct sense, the appropriateness of the rules that govern police work or the extent to which police adhere to these rules (which would define a normative account of legitimacy). This empirical notion of legitimacy relates to both the justification of power (do we believe that the ability of the police to issue orders, to direct and to command, is valid, appropriate and proper?), and recognition of the right to wield power (do we believe that the police have the right to issue orders to us *and that we have a corresponding duty to obey*?).

Two constituent components of legitimacy judgements have thus been identified. The first is normative appropriateness. People make judgements about whether the actions of the organisation and its representatives are in line with commonly accepted expectations, norms, and values (Suchman, 1995). Legitimacy is premised on a 'fundamental accord' (Pardo, 2000) between institutions and those they govern that is founded in shared ideas of what is the 'right thing to do' in a given circumstance. It is established via 'rightful behaviour', or the 'moral performance of power' (Liebling, 2004), and can be identified as present when people believe relevant actors do, indeed, behave in such a way.

The second component of legitimacy is an internalised sense of consent to authority structures. Here, legitimacy can be said to be present when people feel they have a moral *duty to obey* the instructions of an authority (Tyler & Jackson, 2014). On this account the power of the police to issue commands can be considered legitimate when the individual or group commanded feels a normatively grounded obligation to follow those instructions. To put it another way, one might argue that when considering the relationship individuals have with police, legitimacy is an unobservable psychological construct, an attitude-orientation people have towards this particular authority. The extent to which an individual holds police legitimate can be inferred, in part, from the extent to which they report feeling a moral imperative to abide by police instructions. Implicit here is the idea that institutional behaviour in line with widely accepted norms grants the right to dictate appropriate behaviour in certain prescribed circumstances: the former provides the basis for the latter, such that normative alignment motivates a sense of duty to obey (Huq, Jackson, & Trinkner, 2017; Van Damme, 2017).

Why do people care (so much) about procedural justice?

Trust and legitimacy are therefore embedded in a set of norms and values concerning intentions, abilities and moral appropriateness. PJT suggests that in many social contexts and situations the most salient norm is fairness, and particularly process fairness. People believe that officers *should* make decisions in an objective and neutral fashion, treat people with dignity, respect and be open and honest in their decision-making processes, and they make judgements about the moral rectitude of the police largely on the basis of such behaviours (or their absence). Acting in a procedurally just manner indicates that police have the right intentions, that they have in mind the interests of those they police, that they are trustworthy and that they operate according to an appropriate moral framework. Procedural *in*justice, of course, communicates precisely the opposite.

One of the reasons why people believe police should behave in a procedurally fair manner is legal socialisation (Tyler & Trinker, 2017). In many countries across the world, children are brought up to expect that legal actors should adhere to values of justice, equality and liberty. Although the actual content of such behaviours – what constitutes 'justice' – may of course be highly culturally dependent, in the UK and in many other contexts questions of dignity, respect, transparency and neutral decision-making are central: whatever outcomes people may want from justice processes, they seem to consistently value a particular set of qualities in decision-making and interactional processes. Nor is this process restricted to legal authorities. As Trinkner and Tyler (2016, p. 424) argue:

> people are constantly exposed to rule-creation and enforcement throughout their daily lives, all of which provides them with information about their relationship with authority and rules as general social concepts ... the internalization of law-related values, formation of legal attitudes, and development of reasoning capacities are facilitated by experiences in non-legal contexts as well as legal contexts.

In other words, our socialisation into the multiple institutional frameworks that structure our lives involves: learning about rules, those who make them, and their justification; internalising (but also making judgements about) the values upon which those rules are based; and holding the behaviour of authorities up against the values we have learnt. On this account, people look for procedural justice during encounters with police in part because they have been brought up to expect that the police and other power-holders should behave in this manner.

But there are likely to be other reasons for the importance of procedural justice concerns in evaluations of police. One is the concept of respect, which research within a wide variety of paradigms has shown to be of fundamental importance to social relationships (e.g., Honneth, 2007; Sennett, 2004). Most people wish to be treated as rights-bearing subjects worthy of a sense of dignity and status by all those with whom they interact, and procedural fairness is an important vector for such respect.

Naturally, other norms and values are likely to be at stake in people's judgements of police. These include: effectiveness (an ineffective, inefficient police force seems unlikely to live up to normative expectations about how police *should* behave); the idea that the actions of authorities should be restrained within certain limits (that the police should respect the boundaries of their rightful authority) (Huq et al., 2017); and a wider set of concerns about the nature of order in society and the types of behaviours needed to assert it, from people's psychological preferences (e.g., for order and hierarchy) to their social, cultural and economic position within a particular context (Bradford & Jackson, 2018). It is a significant 'impact' of the PJT, however, that attention has become closely focussed on the links between everyday officer behaviour, on the one hand, and trust and legitimacy on the other.

Social identity and procedural justice

Another reason why fairness tends to be important to people is that it indicates and carries value in inter- and intra-group relationships. Fair procedure indicates value-congruence, and therefore commonality, a sense of inclusion and/or shared endeavour. There are two contrasting, although not necessarily conflicting, accounts of this basic underlying idea. On the first, the moral performance of power (Liebling, 2004) is central to the process through which the police demonstrate, through their actions, that they share group membership with those they are policing, or are at least valid partners within a properly constituted intergroup relationship (Gorringe, Stott, & Rosie, 2012; Stott, Hoggett, & Pearson, 2012). Most obviously pertinent in situations where police are interacting with people as members of (possibly diverse) social groups that are situationally salient to the actors involved, for example at football matches, demonstrations or in settings marked by strong ethno-cultural distinctions, the feeling that one has a legitimate relationship *with* police is motivated by the experience of procedural justice in interactions with officers. In turn, a sense that this relationship is legitimate – properly constituted and embedded in appropriate norms and values – serves to persuade that this is the appropriate authority to deal with relevant issues, whether these be crimes, disorder and/or the maintenance of order, accidents or disasters.

According to the second account (arguably still the dominant one within PJT), in many circumstances, and particularly those that comprise the bulk of quotidian police–public interaction, such as routine patrol, enquiries or traffic stops, some level of shared group membership between police and policed can be taken as a given. In many social and political contexts police represent social identities shared by many of those with whom they interact, to which these individuals feel at least some affiliation, and within which they recognise the figure of the police officer as an important group representative. Candidate groups include but are not limited to those defined by nation, state and/or community (Bradford, 2014; Loader & Mulcahy, 2003; Reiner, 2010): fundamentally polysemic, police can socially, culturally and symbolically represent all these and more. This makes many people with whom police interact highly attuned to the identity-relevant aspects of officer behaviour – to their ability to say 'you belong' or 'you do not belong'. The experience of procedurally *just* policing strengthens the bonds between individual and this superordinate group, while procedural injustice denigrates, marginalises and excludes. By and through the ways in which they treat people officers can generate, encourage and/or enhance a sense of inclusion and value within the group, and promote identification with police as a source of authority and with the values the institution of police is intended to represent. The strengthening of bonds with the group, and with police as its representatives, in turn enhances trust, legitimacy, and, as discussed below, cooperation and compliance.

Trust and legitimacy promote 'pro-social' behaviour

As well as advancing debate on the meaning of trust and legitimacy, and their empirical underpinnings, PJT has also generated insight into the downstream effects of the relationship between the public and criminal justice agencies. This is neatly summarised by the titles of two seminal books within the field: *Why People Obey the Law* (Tyler, 2006); and *Trust in the Law: Encouraging Public Cooperation with the Police and the Courts* (Tyler & Huo, 2002). In these and other works, Tyler and colleagues advance a normative theory of legal compliance and of cooperation with legal authorities. In short, they argue that one important reason why people comply with the law, and with the instructions of legal authorities, is the legitimacy those authorities command: those who grant legitimacy are more likely to obey the law and legal authorities because they have internalised the idea that it is right in and of itself to follow the dictates of legitimate authorities. To this core insight can be added the importance of group membership as a factor shaping people's behaviour – we are more likely, for example, to follow the rules of groups to which we feel we belong (Tyler & Jackson, 2014). Similarly, trust and legitimacy promote cooperative behaviour, first because we are more likely to summon and work with police if we trust them, second because legitimate authorities command cooperation from those they govern, and third because both trust and legitimacy are linked with forms of in-group solidarity and a sense of shared social endeavour (Tyler, 2013).

What emerges here is a model of social regulation – of the contribution police might make to social order – quite different to that commonly envisaged by many actors in this field (e.g., policymakers, media and police themselves). Policing is usually considered to be about 'catching the bad guys' and 'controlling the streets' – presenting a deterrent threat that demonstrates a credible risk of sanction to potential offenders and convinces the general population that legal/state authorities are in control of public space and those who use it. Few would argue that these are not roles police can and should fulfil, at least in certain times and spaces. But as Tyler (2009, p. 309) notes, such an approach to crime control and order maintenance is, overall, minimally effective, since it relies on extrinsic motivations for behaviour that are by definition short-lived. If one complies with the law simply because of the presence or possible presence of police, then absent such presence the motivation for compliance is gone. PJT, however, holds the promise of generating or at least enhancing an internal locus of control. Trust, legitimacy and a sense of shared group membership encourage intrinsic motivations for legal compliance and cooperative behaviours that are not reliant on extrinsic factors but rather flow from the individuals place in and relationship with legitimate – normatively appropriate, justified – institutional structures.

It should be noted that evidence for the associations between trust and legitimacy and compliance behaviour is somewhat less conclusive than in relation to the associations between procedural justice, trust, and legitimacy (see Nagin & Telep, 2017 for a critique of this aspect of the literature). But there is evidence to support the core proposition that procedural justice promotes cooperation and compliance behaviour via the intervening mechanisms of trust, legitimacy and identity (Tyler, 2017). Considering the policy arena and ever-present debates about the nature and import of police–public relations, the implications of this research are striking. The way we think about 'trust and confidence' has shifted from being something important primarily for the *policed* – in terms, for example, of reassurance – to something that is just as important for the *police*. PJT has given theoretically robust and empirically supported teeth to the long-standing claim that the police rely on the support of the public to function effectively. In doing so, it has also shifted attention to the importance of process in generating cooperation and compliance. And it highlights the idea that trust and legitimacy are granted to the police by the public and are thus contested and subject to change (albeit also, in all likelihood, quite stable within and across individuals over time).

The 'impacts' of PJT

To summarise the story so far, by the middle of the first decade of the new millennium police and policymakers across the UK had been concerned for some time about declining 'trust and confidence' in the police. While public opinion has been slowly improving since then, concerns remain, with the focus shifting from the general population to particular groups and communities thought to have 'difficult' relationships with the police. However, this discussion was until recently rooted in some essentially mistaken views about what people, in a general sense, want from police. An important impact of work within the PJT paradigm has been to shift, in an ongoing and still partial way, the terms of the debate; and it has done so in a number of ways. This section sketches these out; many of the points raised are revisited and elaborated in the case studies that follow.

First, it bears repeating that research on procedural justice has highlighted the value most people place on, precisely, *process*. By contrast, police leaders, politicians, and stake-holders of various stripes previously placed an almost exclusive emphasis on the *outcomes* produced – or thought to be produced – by police. This shift has, naturally, been incremental in nature. In the early 2000s, for example, there was a move away from crime figures as the primary measure of 'success' (upon which public confidence was thought to be founded) towards a wider focus on fear of crime and antisocial behaviour:

> The current over-focus on crime figures as a substitute measure for police performance will not lead to greater public confidence. The public is convinced that the UK is a high-crime society. A reassurance strategy will provide an opportunity to shift people's perception and begin to change the embedded culture of fear of crime.
>
> *(ACPO 2001, para.5.3, quoted in Millie and Herrington 2005, p. 41)*

Despite such shifts, and as the quote attests, the emphasis on outcomes persisted, culminating in England and Wales in the National Reassurance

Policing Programme, which was specifically aimed at 'tackling criminality in all its forms' (APA, 2001), perhaps particularly in relation to low-level 'local' crime, reducing fear of crime, and closing the 'reassurance gap'. Yet as Adam Crawford has argued, this aim was premised on essentially impossible goals, the management of public anxieties about crime and the satisfaction of 'unattainable expectations of police performance' (2007, p. 144). The outcomes intended to be produced by police were no longer 'simply' (lower) crime rates but – as, or more, importantly – worry about crime and disorder, a necessarily nebulous mass of diverse, contradictory and sometimes competing perceptions, emotions and motivations. Surely police were being asked to do too much?

The idea of reassurance policing did however open up the idea that when deciding on how policing should be conducted, police and policy-makers should attend closely to the opinions and concerns of the public. Into this space stepped academics such as Mike Hough, Jonathan Jackson, Tony Bottoms, Justice Tankebe and myself, as well as policy researchers, most notably Betsy Stanko at the MPS, and Paul Quinton and Andy Myhill at the (then) National Policing Improvement Agency. Frequently working together – in various combinations and on various projects – this group of researchers and others began to inject core social science ideas and methods into discussions of police–public relations. 'Public confidence' research had hitherto been dominated largely by political categories and priorities, and responses to these by policy researchers were sometimes rather detached from wider social science literatures (Fitzgerald et al., 2002; Salisbury, 2004; Singer & Cooper, 2008). As Tyler (2017) has recently noted, albeit in a rather different context, the types of claims made about public trust and police legitimacy in the PJT-related papers that began to appear in the mid-2000s (Bradford et al., 2009; Jackson & Sunshine, 2006; Viki, Culmer, Eller, & Abrams, 2006; Wells, 2008) were supported by the much larger social psychological literature, significantly adding to the plausibility of the findings that related specifically to the police.

The integration of PJT into debates on 'trust and confidence' introduced, then, some conceptual rigour (Stanko et al., 2012). For example, development and application of more precise definitions opened up insight into the extent to which public opinion surrounding the police is not a static 'thing' but rather a dynamic process, constituted by different attitudes and experiences that feed into and shape one another (see, for example, Bottoms & Tankebe, 2012; Harkin, 2015b; Jackson & Sunshine, 2006; Jackson et al., 2013). Moreover, understanding what legitimacy 'is' helps in understanding the range of effects police activity might have on the behaviour of the policed – most obviously, that when police act in ways that enhance legitimacy this may promote normative compliance with the law.

Indeed, the turn towards PJT as a way of understanding people's relationships with the police also marked what Tankebe (2013) has called the 'legitimacy turn' in criminology (which had also previously been heralded by the work of Richard Sparks, Alison Liebling and others in prison research). While legitimacy, construed broadly as described earlier, was certainly present in prior debates, this presence was obscured. The very importance of legitimacy may in fact have been part of the reason for this. To suggest that police were losing *confidence* may have been politically more palatable than saying they were losing *legitimacy* – an altogether more challenging idea. No such constraints are apparent today, as several of the following case studies illustrate, and the popular legitimacy of the police is now a common way of framing and understanding public opinions of the police and, in particular, the implications that arise from the ways people understand and react to policing (e.g., cooperation, compliance, sense of value and self-worth, etc.).

Case studies

Having sketched out some broad claims about the impact of PJT (primarily in relation to the way it shifted the terms of debate), in this section I turn to some specific examples: four 'case studies' that illustrate in more concrete terms the impact PJT has had on police organisations in the UK. Note at the outset that there is a certain narrative flow here, a definite sense in which later projects built on the earlier ones, producing an iterative process as the core ideas of PJT began to diffuse across the policing landscape.

MPS confidence model

By the second half of the 2000s the emphasis on 'reassurance', and dealing with fear, as ways of increasing public confidence in police seemed to have somewhat run out of steam (notwithstanding some of the positive outcomes of the National Reassurance Policing Programme – Tuffin, Morris, & Poole, 2006). Yet police, policy and academic attention was focussed on public opinion of policing as never before. Public confidence had been included in the then Labour government's first Police Performance

Assessment Framework (2003), with trust and confidence as a performance measure based on a question fielded in national and local public attitudes surveys: 'How good a job do you think the police are doing?'; later changed to 'How well do you think the police and local council are dealing with issues of crime and anti-social behaviour in your area?'. By the time of the publication of the 2008–2011 Public Service Agreements, public confidence, as measured by this second survey item, was the overarching performance target for police across England and Wales.

Within this policy context a team of researchers from the London School of Economics and the MPS research unit began developing a model of 'public confidence' in the MPS that went some way beyond a restricted focus on 'how good a job' the police were doing (Bradford, Stanko, & Jackson, 2009). Drawing on PJT and wider social-psychological and sociological literatures relating to the importance of 'neighbourhood concerns' in shaping trust in police (Jackson & Sunshine, 2006; Sampson & Bartusch, 1998; Stoutland, 2001) the MPS confidence model contained four key 'drivers' of trust and confidence: perceptions of fairness (do police manage interpersonal interactions in a procedurally fair manner?); community engagement (do police seek, listen and respond to community needs and desires?); effectiveness; and perceptions of low-level disorder/anti-social behaviour (ASB). A diverse range of variables were implicit in the model as factors affecting opinions across the four drivers – most obviously, while perceptions of crime and/or victimisation were not included as drivers, it was recognised that experiences of crime would shape both perceptions of police and of the local area.

The MPS confidence model was based on and evidenced by its Public Attitudes Survey (PAS), a large-scale, long-running population survey conducted across the capital (Bradford et al., 2009; Stanko, Jackson, Bradford, & Hohl, 2012). Not only did the survey data and its analysis add significant empirical meat to the bones of the model, but, once the MPS had taken it on as a key performance indicator in 2008, the PAS provided a tool for tracking and evaluating MPS performance. A reporting regime was developed which produced London-wide and Borough-level estimates of public opinion across the four drivers, allowing change over time as well as across borough comparisons – including, inevitably and problematically, 'league tables' (see later). A central contribution of work on the PAS was the empirical finding that when it came to overall trust and confidence, as measured by 'how good a job' type questions, police fairness and community engagement were by some margin the most important – exactly as

PJT would predict but, it is probably fair to say, contrary to the beliefs of many senior officers at the time.

While the performance management regime(s) within policing have changed since 2008 – not least due to the advent of Police and Crime Commissioners and the accompanying shift away from central targets – a version of it is still in use today, and regular updates are posted on the website of the Mayor's Office for Policing and Crime (MOPAC). While the language of targets has been largely dropped, it is clear that the MPS is still being held to account against measures of fairness, community engagement and effectiveness – and 'public confidence' remains centre-stage in discussion of successful policing.

National Policing Improvement Agency/College of Policing

The MPS was not the only organisation working with procedural justice concepts around this time. Within the National Policing Improvement Agency (NPIA) and its 'successor', the College of Policing (CoP), Andy Myhill, Paul Quinton and others were in parallel and often collaboration with the MPS researchers developing ideas and guidance for much wider dissemination across British policing.

This process led to the production of two important and influential reports. 'It's a fair cop? Police legitimacy, public cooperation, and crime reduction' was published by the NPIA in 2011. It was specifically aimed at 'injecting' ideas of procedural justice and legitimacy into the wider body of policing. Key components of the document, for example, were the claims that fairness is a more important predictor of legitimacy than effectiveness, and that legitimacy is a stronger predictor of public cooperation and compliance than instrumental concerns and the risk of sanction. Significant emphasis was also placed on the idea that, at a time of austerity and forthcoming cuts to police budgets, enhancing legitimacy is a more cost-effective and more durable way of securing public cooperation and compliance.

The NPIA report was followed in 2015 by 'Fair cop 2: Organisational justice, behaviour and ethical policing' (Quinton, Myhill, Bradford, Fildes, & Porter, 2015). This time, the aim was to focus attention on the kind of organisational structures and processes best placed to motivate officer behaviour congruent with procedural justice theory. Drawing explicitly on organisational justice theory and its extensions into criminology (see Bradford, Quinton, Myhill, & Porter, 2013; Bradford & Quinton, 2014; Colquitt, Conlon, Wesson, Porter, & Ng, 2001; Trinkner, Tyler, & Goff,

2016), this report aimed, for a police audience, to link 'the "internal" organisational justice and "external" procedural justice models together' to show 'how fairness and respect inside the police could … improve the public's perceptions of, and their voluntary cooperation with, the police' (p. 2). The central argument here is if police managers desire police officers and staff to treat the public in as procedurally fair a manner as possible, then they need to ensure that those officers and staff feel fairly treated by their immediate supervisors and the organisation they work for.

These policy documents and the collaborations behind them proved pivotal, not least in the way that they triggered dialogue and change at the national level (see later). This is also a good example of the way in which non-academic publications, outside the traditional format of the journal article, can generate significant impact – indeed, possibly the most important impact of the story so far.

HMICFRS inspections

'Fair cop' and Fair cop 2' fed directly into a change in HMIC/HMICFRS inspection regimes from 2014 onwards. The Police Effectiveness, Efficiency and Legitimacy Assessment (PEEL) specifically sets out to examine, under its legitimacy 'pillar', whether police forces operate fairly, ethically and within the law. Tellingly, the 2014 report argued that 'it is not enough to look only at what the police do, it is also important to consider how they do it' (HMIC, 2014, p. 74), tapping directly into the outcome/process distinction outlined above. It is furthermore striking to see reports include quotes such as the following, from a young person participating in HMICFRS research, which aptly summarises the meaning of legitimacy as it is generally construed in the procedural justice literature:

> The police are meant to be the fair ones, they're meant to be the moral compass, so when they're not acting right or protecting people that makes me want to not have any contact with them at all.
>
> *(HMICFRS, 2017, p. 10)*

For its 2018/19 inspections HMICFRS provides the definition of and criteria for assessing legitimacy shown in Box 7.1 (HMICFRS, 2018). Note the centrality of notions of 'fairness' and 'respect', and how these are linked not only to sometimes controversial police practice such as stop and search and the use of force, but also to questions of ethics and the lawful use of power.

BOX 7.1 2018/19 HMICFRS DEFINITION OF, AND CRITERIA FOR, ASSESSING POLICE LEGITIMACY

Definition

A police force is legitimate if it has the consent of the public, and those working in the force consistently behave in a way that is fair, reasonable, effective and lawful, which generates the trust and cooperation of the public.

Headline question

How legitimately does the force treat the public and its workforce?

Core question	*Diagnostic*
How well does the force treat the people it serves with fairness and respect?	How well does the force understand the importance of engaging with people it serves and treating them with fairness and respect? How well does the force understand and improve the way it uses force? How well does the force understand and improve the way it uses stop and search powers?
How well does the force ensure that its workforce behaves ethically and lawfully?	How well does the force develop and maintain an ethical culture? How well does the force tackle potential corruption?
How well does the force treat its workforce with fairness and respect?	How well does the force identify and improve potential unfairness at work? How well does the force support the wellbeing of its workforce? How fairly and effectively does the force manage and develop individual performance of its officers and staff and its selection process?

PEEL represents perhaps the most fundamental and important 'impact' of PJT discussed in this chapter. Police forces across England and Wales are now held directly to account for the extent to which they: treat all the people they serve with fairness and respect; ensure their workforce behaves ethically and lawfully; and whether they treat their workforces with fairness and respect (HMICFRS, 2017, pp. 5–6). PEEL reports explicitly 'score' police forces against this criteria. The establishment of this novel regulatory framework built on a long period of engagement between HMIC and some of the key people listed; most notably Mike Hough, who worked with HMIC on various projects from the late 1990s. Crucially, academics working on PJT in the UK were not simply writing reports and papers and waiting for them to circulate, but actively engaging with policymakers and practitioners – taking a seat at the table, as it were, and actively engaging in policy development.

West Midlands Police 'Fairness in Policing' project

If PEEL is arguably the most *important* – or at least the widest – impact of PJT in the UK thus far, the *clearest* expression comes in the form of the West Midlands Police (WMP) 'Fairness in Policing' project (FiP). The overarching aim of the project, as expressed by the Chief Constable, is:

> To improve perception of legitimacy externally amongst the communities that WMP serves and also internally amongst our staff. The ambition is to integrate the principles of procedural justice and organisational justice into everything WMP do internally and externally.

FiP developed, again, out of active engagement between police practitioners and academics. Particularly important in this regard was the University of Cambridge MSt in Applied Criminology and Police Management, which drew in a number of WMP officers and exposed them to the work of leading PJT scholars such as Justice Tankebe. More links were drawn between police and academics at a series of meetings held at WMP during the inception and planning stages, which were attended by a range of researchers with interests in PJT and related fields. Finally, a number of academics have been directly involved in designing and/or assessing various parts of the project, including myself.

This project represents an extremely ambitious attempt by a major UK force to embed the idea, and practice, of procedural justice throughout the organisation. FiP is explicitly grounded in the academic research, not only on procedural justice but also legitimacy. Notably, the project has both 'internal' and 'external' elements – echoing 'Fair cop 2', it is premised on the idea that the way police organisations treat their staff is central in determining how those staff go on to treat the public. FiP therefore includes a whole range of internal change programmes, for example in relation to selection and promotion exercises, leadership development, structure and implementation of people policies, professional standards and HR. 'Outward'-facing efforts have at the time of writing focussed on neighbourhood policing, deployment and use of Taser, policing of sporting events, use of Body Worn Video as a training tool, victim satisfaction and use of the 101 number.

Always envisaged as a multi-year project, at the time of writing FiP is in its second year. This in itself is a noteworthy development. Many police change processes – often admittedly much more limited in scope and ambition – are marked by unrealistically short time scales, with transformative effects expected within periods of months, not years. The multi-year duration of FiP indicates both the importance placed on it by senior management in WMP *and* a realistic set of assumptions about how difficult it is, given the complexity of the processes shaping trust and legitimacy, to achieve meaningful shifts in police–public relations at a force-wide level through developing police practice in the ways defined by PJT.

Challenges

The accounts provided earlier demonstrate the impact PJT has had on policing at multiple levels, from performance targets to inspection regimes to training. Yet, it will come as little surprise to policing scholars and others that significant barriers to impact, and the wider process of changing police behaviour in line with PJT, persist. These challenges range from those of a more practical nature, for example how to translate academic findings into everyday language a politician might be comfortable using, or into policing modes that can be 'trained', through the extent to which core claims of the theory remain under-supported by empirical evidence, to much more fundamental issues with the ability of PJT 'reforms' to produce normatively desirable policing.

Translation issues

The first set of challenges is the most familiar. While the 'core message' of PJT is in many ways simple, it has proven rather difficult to translate into policy and, in particular, 'street-level' police practice. From one perspective, this merely reflects the well-known difficulties in changing police working practices in ways more fundamental than technical fixes. Police reform processes can indeed often seem doomed to fail (Skogan, 2008). Yet there may be something particular to PJT that sets it apart from this general pattern. This can perhaps be best summarised by noting the likely difficulty in *training* 'right behaviour'. While it should not be controversial to state most police officers try to do the right thing most of the time, gains from 'applying' PJT to police practice will only arise if, at the margins, officer behaviour is shifted in ways aligned to the theory. And this seems hard to do, at individual and organisational levels.

One reason for this may be the pull of the 'bad apple' thesis and a sense that individuals predisposed to procedurally unfair behaviour cannot be forced or cajoled to change their ways. If one believes that most of the 'bads' of policing are caused by a few rogue officers, then PJT may seem less relevant. Bad people cannot be trained to be good, so the emphasis should be on weeding them out, either at hiring, during training or later on. On this view, everyone else is basically doing fine and can be left to get on with the job.

The nature of day-to-day policing may also work against principles of procedural justice; and perhaps more so when those principles are most needed. Put bluntly, it may be easy to 'apply' procedural justice when dealing with people who are already complying, but much more difficult when they are refusing to do so. Faced with challenges to their authority officers can respond in several ways (Hough et al., 2017, p. 287): withdraw or cave in, making no further demands and thus squandering their authority; overwhelm the challenge with coercive force, most obviously through arrest, which is tempting in many ways and not least because it forestalls the threat of further escalation; or use procedural justice in a tactical sense to de-escalate the challenge and to secure consent. How often this last option is taken remains an open question – although it certainly does occur – but the problem facing police in many contexts may be that they find themselves in a 'hard power trap', wherein force is used to solve dilemmas, prompting greater resistance further down the line, reapplication of force, and so on.

Of course, the nature and quality of current police–public interactions are conditioned on the history of policing in an area, neighbourhood or community, a history that may trace back many years. Once coercive tactics have been overused, persuasive 'soft power' may be much less effective than might otherwise be the case (Hough, 2013). Moreover, when negative relations with police have become embedded in a particular context, procedural justice policing may be less 'effective' – less able to repair the damage done – because people have for a variety of reasons become predisposed to read police activity in a negative light. In such situations systematic and long-term change will likely be needed, a process that operates above and beyond the level of individual officers' practice (although this too will be important); and, to reiterate, this has often proved difficult to do.

A related issue is that while procedural justice – treating people with dignity and respect, making neutral and unbiased decisions, communicating clearly – is fundamental to good police-work, it may not look particularly like 'real' police-work. The dominance of classic 'cop culture' – an emphasis on action, apprehending offenders and constituting the thin blue line – in modern police organisations is probably over-stated. There are many 'police cultures' and indeed always have been. But there is no doubt that the cultural resonance of this vision of policing retains valence. From this viewpoint, while procedural justice might be 'nice to do', it is not 'essential', unlike the thief-taking and order-maintenance activity of police (Foster & Jones, 2010): the latter will always take precedence relative to the quality of interpersonal interaction. Such effects are likely to be all the more pertinent at a time when significant cuts to police budgets, a result of the austerity programme imposed by the coalition government in 2010 and largely continued since then, have resulted in a roll-back of neighbourhood policing resources and an increasing emphasis on 'core business'.

These and other factors seem to come together to produce significant resistance within police organisations to some of the core messages of PJT, or perhaps more specifically to policies aimed at embedding procedural justice in practice. For example, a recent experimental study based in Scotland (MacQueen & Bradford, 2015), which aimed to replicate QCET, the first randomised controlled trial (RCT) of procedural justice in policing (Mazerolle et al., 2013), seemed to identify a 'back-fire' effect. The intervention, designed to boost perceptions of procedural justice during road traffic encounters, actually diminished satisfaction with traffic stops and assessments of officer fairness among the drivers concerned. A follow-up study

(MacQueen & Bradford, 2017) identified both implementation failure and a wider effect of the intervention *on the officers asked to deliver it*, which may account for the apparently puzzling findings of the original trial. A significant factor in both cases seems to have been resistance among some of the officers delivering the intervention not so much to the core messages of PJT but to being asked to do 'more of it'. For example, many felt their professionalism was being impugned, that being too 'nicey-nicey' to people was not appropriate in many circumstances, and/or that they already knew how to behave in this way and didn't need to be told to do more.

Wider and deeper concerns

As well as some familiar concerns about the ability of academic research to truly penetrate into police practice, there are some arguably more significant barriers to impact in this area of work. One issue, already noted, is the argument that one of the core theoretical claims of PJT – that legitimacy promotes compliance – is less well evidenced than it could be. The basic correlations are well established, but the direction of causality has not been so clearly identified. Nagin and Telep (2017, p. 1) argue that it is uncertain whether the associations between perceptions of procedural justice, legitimacy and compliance 'reflect a causal connection whereby changes in policies that are effective in changing actual procedurally just treatment of citizens by police and others lead to changes in legal compliance and perceived legitimacy'. This view is, in part, premised on a rather narrow reading of the literature that focusses almost entirely on criminology and ignores work within the wider field of social psychology (Tyler, 2017). But it is certainly the case that more research in policing and criminal justice contexts is needed to properly ascertain whether police legitimacy really does generate compliance with the law in such a way that 'increasing' procedural justice motivates greater compliance. Without this research there is at a minimum room for doubt and confusion among 'consumers' of PJT research; it might also be argued that until such an important claim is better evidenced, PJT, despite the extent of existing research, remains provisional in important ways.

How PJT research is operationalised at the level of policy remains another important question. In particular, it has proved hard to track the outcomes of PJT-based reforms. Given the nature of many of the issues at hand, which essentially revolve around public opinion, and the dominance of survey research in the field (Harkin, 2015a), there seems to be a natural temptation to put in place performance targets, based on survey measurements, to motivate police behaviour and assess the extent of any progress. This is in part a legacy of the last Labour government's Public Service Agreements. But it also taps into the wider, and well-known, obsession with quantification and the definition of discrete outcomes that can be targeted and tracked, and against which police can be held to account (Muller, 2018). A significant issue here is that it is far from clear that 'public opinion', so construed, *should* be used to direct and assess police performance. The sources of public trust and legitimacy are many and varied, meaning it is difficult to be sure that changes in levels of trust (for example) recorded in general attitudes surveys can be attributed to shifts in police behaviour. Reforms based on PJT will almost inevitably focus on the quality of interaction between police and public, for example, yet only a minority of the latter have meaningful contact with police in any given time period. Views and understandings of police among the majority without contact will be based largely on factors other than actual officer behaviour.

Still more concerning, Diarmaid Harkin (2015b) and others have argued that some strands of public feeling in relation to policing are actively antithetical to the core normative underpinnings of PJT. In particular, while it seems fairly obvious that people would like procedural justice for themselves and 'people like them' it is far less clear they always want it for others (Radburn et al., 2018). Some at least might valorise *unfair* police behaviour in relation to denigrated outgroups, and police might gain boosts to trust and legitimacy among some sections of the population from procedurally unjust behaviour. There is thus an important sense in which 'public opinion' cannot be treated as a neutral arbiter of procedural justice in policing. Even a widespread belief among the public that police behave in a particular manner is not sufficient to claim this to be true.

All this raises significant questions over how progress on PJT-based reforms can be evidenced and tracked. The obvious, albeit partial, answer is to concentrate not on the 'general population' but rather on specific groups affected by a particular policy development or change in practice, such as victims of crime, residents of a certain area, or those who experience stop and search. Indeed, sample surveys of such 'special populations' *do* seem an appropriate tool, since the incidence of actual contact with police will be either 100% (e.g., among crime victims who report to, or people stop/searched by, police) or very high (e.g., among residents of a neighbourhood targeted for a community policing initiative). Gauging the opinions of particular 'publics' can reveal the success or otherwise of PJT-inspired reform.

But perhaps the most fundamental barrier to achieving 'transformational' PJT-based impact is that the theory has frustratingly little to say about some of the wider normative and ethical challenges facing policing. While PJT is very good at explaining how police should behave when they are interacting with people, it is largely silent on whether those interactions should be happening in the first place. To give just one example, training on how to conduct stop/searches can, should and sometimes does include material based on PJT (Giacomantonio et al., 2016). Conducting stop and search in a procedurally fair manner is both ethically the right thing to do and likely to make use of the power less 'difficult' (Bradford, 2017). It may even promote cooperation and compliance further down the line (or at least avoid undermining them). But how often should police conduct stop/searches? Is the practice appropriately distributed across social and geographic space? How should the success of use of this power be conceptualised and assessed? And how do all these questions interact with procedural justice in shaping trust and legitimacy? It can be more difficult to see what PJT as presently construed has to say about these types of questions.

Such concerns are tempered somewhat by the emphasis in PJT on neutral and unbiased decision-making. If police make decisions on such a basis they would be both true to the notion of procedural justice and likely to minimise the negative effects of stop and search and indeed many other powers (Tyler et al., 2015). But it is nevertheless the case that PJT is a mid-range theory that, on its own, cannot address the 'big issues' of policing, such as how much police activity, where and directed at whom, is appropriate. The answer here is likely to involve integrating PJT with other empirical and normative theories of policing that do address these questions. From the former perspective, integrating PJT with more expansive theories of crime causation such as Situational Action Theory (Wikström et al., 2012) would seem a fruitful avenue for future research (Morrell & Bradford, 2018). From the latter, one could argue with Loader and Sparks (2013) that procedural justice approaches should attend more closely to the *politics* of crime and crime control. One could focus, for example, on the arrangements and democratic structures in place 'for debating, deliberating, and deciding on what it is that (criminal) justice institutions are being called upon to do' (p. 113), thus adding to an understanding of how people experience policing as individuals and members of social groups with the wider question of *why* they experience the type of policing they do, and the extent to which they have a say in determining this.

Conclusion

There are two ways one could summarise the impact of PJT on policing in the UK. On the one hand, the account provided here suggests the theory, and its operationalisation into British policing, has had fundamental and long-lasting effects – on performance target regimes, organisational structures and learning activities, and on the way significant numbers of police officers think about their work. The accounts provided tell a compelling story about the way ideas originating from PJT have percolated through British policing and, in many respects, the extent to which things have changed as a result. On the other hand, though, one could point to a lack of evidence concerning impacts at (a) the street level (has the behaviour of frontline officers really changed as a result of the work presented above?) and (b) the institutional level (has evidence concerning the need to make decisions in a neutral, unbiased and transparent fashion produced discernible effects on the distribution and outcomes of policing?). If PJT had never been heard of in the UK, would policing have looked much different to the way it does now?

These apparently divergent interpretations have yet to be reconciled. In some senses it is too early to tell – the timescale proposed by WMP's Fairness in Policing project (five years) is probably at the lower end of what might be reasonable for producing persistent, discernible, change. More fundamentally, though, it may be that there is an irreconcilable tension between them, particularly at the level of institutional change. Whether work within the PJT paradigm is able, for example, to fundamentally alter the disproportionality evident in police activity such as stop and search – which has social, economic and political roots distinct from the behaviour of individual officers (whilst also implicating their behaviour, Bradford, 2017) – is far from clear. A central challenge for PJT researchers over the next decade will be to consider whether, how and to what extent their work can address such issues, and what other theories and understandings they need to draw upon in order to answer such questions.

Note

1 I am indebted to Mike Hough and Clifford Stott for their comments on earlier drafts of this chapter.

References

ACPO. (2001). *Reassurance – civility first. A proposal for police reform.* London: Association of Chief Police Officers of England, Wales and N. Ireland.

APA. (2001). Police reform programme: Strands on engaging criminality and reassurance – APA Policy Framework. London: Association of Police Authorities.

Bottoms, A., & Tankebe, J. (2012). Beyond procedural justice: A dialogic approach to legitimacy in criminal justice. *Journal of Criminal Law and Criminology, 102*(1), 119–170.

Bradford, B. (2014). Policing and social identity: Procedural justice, inclusion and cooperation between police and public. *Policing and Society, 24*(1), 22–43.

Bradford, B. (2016). The dog that never quite barked: Social identity and the persistence of police legitimacy. In M. Bosworth, C. Hoyle & L. Zedner (Eds.), *Changing contours of criminal justice* (pp. 29–41). Oxford: Oxford University Press.

Bradford, B. (2017). *Stop and search and police legitimacy.* Oxford: Routledge.

Bradford, B., & Jackson, J. (2018). Police legitimacy among immigrants in Europe: Institutional frames and group position. *European Journal of Criminology, 15*(5), 567–588.

Bradford, B., Jackson, J., & Hough, M. (2018). Trust in justice. In E. Uslaner (Ed.), *The Oxford handbook of social and political trust* (pp. 633–656). Oxford: Oxford University Press.

Bradford, B., Jackson, J., & Stanko, E. A. (2009). Contact and confidence: Revisiting the impact of public encounters with the police. *Policing and Society, 19*(1), 20–46.

Bradford, B., & Quinton, P. (2014). Self-legitimacy, police culture and support for democratic policing in an English constabulary. *British Journal of Criminology, 54*(6), 1023–1046.

Bradford, B., Quinton, P., Myhill, A., & Porter, G. (2013). Why do 'the law' comply? Procedural justice, group identification and officer motivation in police organizations. *European Journal of Criminology, 11*(1), 110–131.

Bradford, B., Stanko, E. A., & Jackson, J. (2009). Using research to inform policy: The role of public attitude surveys in understanding public confidence and police contact. *Policing, 3*(2), 139–148.

Colquitt, J. A., Conlon, D. E., Wesson, M. J., Porter, C. O. L. H., & Ng, K. Y. (2001). Justice at the millenium: A meta-analytic review of 25 years of organizational justice research. *Journal of Applied Psychology, 86*(3), 425–445.

Crawford, A. (2007). Reassurance policing: Feeling is believing. In A. Henry, & D. Smith (Eds.), *Transformations of policing* (pp. 143–168). Aldershot: Ashgate.

Earle, Timothy C., & Cvetkovich, G. (1995). *Social trust: Toward a cosmopolitan society.* Westport, CT: Praeger.

Earle, T. C., & Cvetkovich, G. (1999). Social trust and culture in risk management. In G. Cvetkovich & R. E. Löfstedt (Eds.), *Social trust and the management of risk* (pp. 9–21). London: Earthscan.

Fitzgerald, M., Hough, M., Joseph, I., & Qureshi, T. (2002). *Policing for London.* Cullompton, Devon, UK: Portland, or: Willan.

Foster, J., & Jones, C. (2010). 'Nice to do' and essential: Improving neighborhood policing in an English police force. *Policing: a Journal of Policy and Practice, 4*(4), 395–402.

Giacomantonio, G., Jonathan-Zamir, T., Litmanovitz, Y., Bradford, B., Davies, M., Strang, L., & Sutherland, A. (2016). *College of Policing stop and search training experiment: Process evaluation*. London: College of Policing.

Gorringe, H., Stott, C., & Rosie, M. (2012). Dialogue police, decision making, and the management of public order during protest crowd events. *Journal of Investigative Psychology and Offender Profiling, 9*(2), 111–125.

Harkin, D. M. (2015a). Police legitimacy, ideology and qualitative methods: A critique of procedural justice theory. *Criminology and Criminal Justice, 15*(5), 594–612.

Harkin, D. M. (2015b). The police and punishment: Understanding the pains of policing. *Theoretical Criminology, 19*(1), 43–58.

HMIC (2014). *State of Policing. The annual assessment of policing in England and Wales 2013/14.* Her Majesty's Chief Inspector of Constabulary.

HMICFRS (2017). *PEEL: Police legitimacy 2017. A national overview.* Her Majesty's Inspectorate of Constabulary, Fire and Rescue Services.

HMICFRS (2018). *PEEL: Police legitimacy 2018. A national overview.* Her Majesty's Inspectorate of Constabulary, Fire and Rescue Services.

Honneth, A. (2007). *Disrespect: The normative foundations of critical theory.* Cambridge: Polity Press.

Hough, M. (2007). Policing London, 20 years on. In A. Henry, & D. Smith (Eds.), *Transformations of policing* (pp. 191–212). Aldershot: Ashgate.

Hough, M. (2013). Procedural justice and professional policing in times of austerity. *Criminology and Criminal Justice, 13*(2), 181–197.

Hough, M., Jackson, J., & Bradford, B. (2017). Policing, procedural justice and prevention. In A. Sidebottom & N. Tilley (Eds.), *Routledge handbook of crime prevention and community safety* (pp. 275–293). Oxford: Routledge.

Huq, A. Z., Jackson, J., & Trinkner, R. (2017). Legitimating practices: Revisiting the predicates of police legitimacy. *British Journal of Criminology, 57*(5), 1101–1122.

Jackson, J. (2018). Norms, normativity, and the legitimacy of justice institutions: International perspectives. *Annual Review of Law and Social Science, 14*(1), 145–165.

Jackson, J., & Bradford, B. (2010). What is trust and confidence in the police? *Policing: an International Journal of Police Strategies and Management, 4*(3), 241–248.

Jackson, J., Bradford, B., Stanko, B., & Hohl, K. (2013). *Just authority?: Trust in the police in England and Wales.* Abingdon: Routledge.

Jackson, J., & Sunshine, J. (2006). Public confidence in policing: A Neo-Durkheimian perspective. *British Journal of Criminology, 47*(2), 214–233.

Liebling, A. (2004). *Prisons and their moral performance: A study of values, quality, and prison life* (Reprinted). Oxford, UK: Oxford University Press.

Lind, E. A., & Tyler, T. R. (1988). *The psychology of procedural justice.* New York, NY: Plenum Press.

Loader, I., & Mulcahy, A. (2003). *Policing and the condition of England: Memory, politics and culture.* Oxford, UK: Oxford University Press.

Loader, I., & Sparks, R. (2013). Unfinished business: Legitimacy, crime control and democratic politics. In J. Tankebe & A. Leibling (Eds.), *Legitimacy and criminal justice: An international exploration* (pp. 105–126). Oxford: Oxford University Press.

MacQueen, S., & Bradford, B. (2015). Enhancing public trust and police legitimacy during road traffic encounters: Results from a randomised controlled trial in Scotland. *Journal of Experimental Criminology, 11*(3), 419–443.

MacQueen, S., & Bradford, B. (2017). Where did it all go wrong? Implementation failure—And more—In a field experiment of procedural justice policing. *Journal of Experimental Criminology, 13*(3), 321–345.

Mazerolle, L., Antrobus, E., Bennett, S., & Tyler, T. R. (2013). Shaping citizen perceptions of police legitimacy: A randomized field trial of procedural justice. *Criminology, 51*(1), 33–63.

Mazerolle, L., Bennett, S., Antrobus, E., & Eggins, E. (2012). Procedural justice, routine encounters and citizen perceptions of police: Main findings from the Queensland Community Engagement Trial (QCET). *Journal of Experimental Criminology, 8*(4), 343–367.

Millie, A., & Herrington, V. (2005). Bridging the gap: Understanding reassurance policing. *The Howard Journal, 44*(1), 41–56.

Morrell, K. & Bradford, B. (2018). *Policing and public management.* Oxford: Routledge.

Muller, J. Z. (2018). *The tyranny of metrics.* Princeton, NJ: Princeton University Press.

Nagin, D. S., & Telep, C. W. (2017). Procedural justice and legal compliance. *Annual Review of Law and Social Science, 13*(1), 5–28.

Pardo, I. (2000). *Morals of legitimacy: Between agency and system.* New York, NY: Berghahn Books.

Quinton, P., Myhill, A., Bradford, B., Fildes, A., & Porter, G. (2015). *Fair cop 2: Organisational justice, behaviour and ethical policing.* Retrieved from http://whatworks.college.police.uk/Research/Pages/Published.aspx.

Radburn, M., Stott, C., Bradford, B., & Robinson, M. (2018). When is policing fair? Groups, identity and judgments of the procedural justice of coercive policing. *Policing and Society, 28*(6), 647–664.

Reiner, R. (2010). *The politics of the police* (4th ed.). Oxford, UK: Oxford University Press.

Salisbury, H. (2004). *Public attitudes to the criminal justice system: The impact of providing information to British Crime Survey respondents.* London: Home Office.

Sampson, R. J., & Bartusch, D. J. (1998). Legal cynicism and (subcultural?) tolerance of deviance: The neighborhood context of racial differences. *Law and Society Review, 32*(4), 777–804.

Sennett, R. (2004). *Respect: The formation of character in a world of inequality.* London: Penguin.

Sindall, K., Sturgis, P., & Jennings, W. (2012). Public confidence in the police: A time-series analysis. *British Journal of Criminology, 52*(4), 744–764.

Singer, L., & Cooper, S. (2008). *Inform, persuade and remind: An evaluation of a project to improve public confidence in the Criminal Justice System*. London: Ministry of Justice.

Skogan, W. G. (2006). Asymmetry in the impact of encounters with police. *Policing and Society, 16*(2), 99–126.

Skogan, W. G. (2008). Why reforms fail. *Policing and Society, 18*(1), 23–34.

Stanko, B., Jackson, J., Bradford, B., & Hohl, K. (2012). A golden thread, a presence amongst uniforms, and a good deal of data: Studying public confidence in the London Metropolitan Police. *Policing and Society, 22*(3), 317–331.

Stott, C., Hoggett, J., & Pearson, G. (2012). Keeping the peace: Social identity, procedural justice and the policing of football crowds. *British Journal of Criminology, 52*(2), 381–399.

Stoutland, S. E. (2001). The multiple dimensions of trust in resident/police relations in Boston. *Journal of Research in Crime and Delinquency, 38*(3), 226–256.

Suchman, M. C. (1995). Managing legitimacy: Strategic and institutional approaches. *Academy of Management Review, 20*(3), 571–610.

Tankebe, J. (2013). Viewing things differently: The dimensions of public perceptions of police legitimacy. *Criminology, 51*(1), 103–135.

Trinkner, R. & Tyler, T.R. (2016). Legal socialization: Coercion versus consent in an era of mistrust. *Annual Review of Law and Social Science, 12*(1), 417–439.

Trinkner, R., Tyler, T. R., & Goff, P. A. (2016). Justice from within: The relations between a procedurally just organizational climate and police organizational efficiency, endorsement of democratic policing, and officer well-being. *Psychology, Public Policy, and Law, 22*(2), 158–172.

Tuffin, R., Morris, J., & Poole, A. (2006). *An evaluation of the impact of the National Reassurance Policing Programme Research*. London: Home Office.

Tyler, T. (2017). Procedural justice and policing: A rush to judgment? *Annual Review of Law and Social Science, 13*(1), 29–53.

Tyler, T. R. (2006). *Why people obey the law*. Princeton, NJ: Princeton University Press.

Tyler, T. R. (2009). Legitimacy and criminal justice: The benefits of self-regulation. *Ohio State Journal of Criminal Law*, 7, 307–359.

Tyler, T. R. (2013). *Why people cooperate: The role of social motivations*. Princeton, NJ: Princeton University Press.

Tyler, T. R., & Blader, S. L. (2000). *Cooperation in groups: Procedural justice, social identity, and behavioral engagement*. Philadelphia, PA: Psychology Press.

Tyler, T. R., & Fagan, J. (2008). Legitimacy and cooperation: Why do people help the police fight crime in their communities. *Ohio State Journal of Criminal Law, 6*(1), 173–230.

Tyler, T. R., & Huo, Y. J. (2002). *Trust in the law: Encouraging public cooperation with the police and courts*. New York, NY: Russell Sage Foundation.

Tyler, T. R., & Jackson, J. (2014). Popular legitimacy and the exercise of legal authority: Motivating compliance, cooperation, and engagement. *Psychology, Public Policy, and Law, 20*(1), 78–95.

Tyler, T. R., Jackson, J. & Mentovich, A. (2015). The consequences of being an object of suspicion: Potential pitfalls of proactive police contact. *Journal of Empirical Legal Studies, 12*(4), 602–636.

Tyler, T. R., & Trinker, R. (2017). *Why children follow rules: Legal socialization and the development of legitimacy.* New York, NY: Oxford University Press.

Van Damme, A. (2017). The impact of police contact on trust and police legitimacy in Belgium. *Policing and Society, 27*(2), 205–228.

Viki, G. T., Culmer, M. J., Eller, A., & Abrams, D. (2006). Race and willingness to cooperate with the police: The roles of quality of contact, attitudes towards the behaviour and subjective norms. *British Journal of Social Psychology, 45*(45), 285–302.

Wells, H. (2008). The techno-fix versus the fair cop: Procedural (in)justice and automated speed limit enforcement. *British Journal of Criminology, 48*(6), 798–817.

Wikström, P. O., Oberwittler, D., Treiber, K., & Hardie, B. (2012). *Breaking rules: The social and situational dynamics of young people's urban crime.* Oxford: Oxford University Press.

8

POLICING CROWDS

Clifford Stott

The context

At around 8.30 pm on 6 August 2011 rioting began in Tottenham in North London following an otherwise peaceful protest about the fatal shooting by the police of a young mixed-heritage man, some two days earlier. Across the next few hours, what started as an anti-police riot spread through the surrounding Borough of Haringey and, as it did, transformed into widespread looting and arson. The following day the neighbouring North London Borough of Enfield experienced further widespread rioting, as did the South London Borough of Brixton. By the third day disturbances had spread throughout London and on to other regions in England such as the West Midlands and then afterwards to Greater Manchester and Merseyside. While rare in their occurrence, these major eruptions of crowd violence and criminality are profoundly important socially, politically and academically.

Despite their significance, we actually understand very little about the social psychological dynamics through which riots occur and spread or how academic theory can be utilised to understand, prevent and police them. Instead, media analysis and policy are often driven by political agendas and assumptions that bear scant relationship to the underlying evidence. For example, following these riots the UK Government invested upwards of £1.36 billion in its 'troubled families' programme, designed to tackle what the then Prime Minister David Cameron described as the underlying 'culture of disruption and irresponsibility' that he believed had led to the riots. A national evaluation of the programme concluded that there was little evidence of it achieving any meaningful impact (The Guardian, 2016) and more recent research highlights the complexity of the social and psychological dynamics through which the riots developed and spread (Drury et al., 2020). What seems apparent then is a disconnect between policy and research. How then can we advance the relationship between theory and practice in this important domain of public policy? This chapter addresses this question by providing an overview of the development of crowd theory in psychology and its impact on the policy and practice of policing of crowds. The chapter will conclude by discussing some of the lessons that this research can teach us about the underlying causes of riots and what the relationships between theory and practice in this domain can tell us about the wider impact agenda.

Underpinning research and theory

It is now widely known that 'scientific' forms of crowd psychology were born in the late nineteenth century in a context of unprecedented social change and were themselves developed with impact in mind, at least 'impact' in the form of social control (Stott & Drury, 2017). As industrialisation took hold there were unprecedented forms of migration from the countryside into rapidly expanding cities. In this milieu of urbanisation, there was a corresponding breakdown of historically embedded aristocratic modes of power and social regulation. The instability of the new urban social order was increasingly seen to be a problem of 'public disorder' and apparent moral breakdown among the urban working classes. Thus, the psychology of the 'masses', manifest most clearly in the form of the crowd, began to be an increasingly salient social, political and intellectual concern; particularly to the elite middle classes keen to protect their new-found wealth and opportunity (Carey, 1992).

The then embryonic social sciences pretended to offer both explanation and solution and did so, in part, in the form of classical crowd theory (Barrows, 1981; McClelland, 1989; Nye, 1975; Stott & Drury, 2017). Drawing upon some of the dominant intellectual and political trends of the late nineteenth century, several high-profile academics debated, over several years, the nature and origins of crimes committed by the crowd. These debates drew upon and developed specific suppositions about mass psychology that are important because they remain with us today (Stott, Radburn, & Savigar-Shaw, 2020). Drawing directly from Lombrosian criminology, the Italian jurist, sociologist, cultural and literary critic Scipio

Sighele argued that the 'criminal crowd' was the result of the *convergence* of those subclasses of humanity biologically, or racially, predisposed toward wrongdoing (Sighele, 2018). In contrast, the French magistrate and social theorist Gabriel Tarde saw the crimes of the crowd as the result of a powerful imitation process unlocked through the inherent irrationality of convergence – what is often referred to now as 'mob psychology' (McClelland, 1989). In each case, the crowd was depicted as a pathological and inherently criminal intrusion by the 'lower orders' of society into an otherwise civilised and naturally evolved hierarchical social order. These debates on crowd criminality, along with other important works (e.g., Taine, 1876), were distilled into a single and powerful piece of ideology published by Gustave Le Bon (1895); a book described by some as one of the most influential social psychology texts of all time (Reicher, 1987).

This body of work, referred to as 'classical crowd theory', is fundamental to our understanding of riots in at least two respects. First, it formed several key assumptions and the broad perspective of subsequent theoretical work on the psychology of crowds throughout the twentieth century. Perhaps the best example of this being 'deindividuation' theory, which made a key social psychological contribution to contemporary scientific understanding of crowds from the 1970s onwards (e.g., Festinger, Pepitone, & Newcomb, 1952; Zimbardo, 1970). Indeed, even today, those psychology textbooks that refer to crowds still largely defer to deindividuation theory as if this perspective is a valid explanation (cf., Brown & Pehrson, 2019; Postmes & Spears, 1998). Second, these classical theories formed the ideological basis of forms of social control that legitimised the repression of crowds and have embedded themselves deeply into everyday 'common sense' explanations of crowd action (Neville & Reicher, 2018; Stott & Drury, 2017).

From a scientific perspective, the central problem with these early classical forms of crowd psychology is their lack of explanatory power. Put simply, the theories are flawed because they cannot explain, nor can they predict, how crowds behave. Indeed, classical theory would not be considered 'scientific' in the contemporary sense of the term, since it was produced by 'arm-chair' theorists, who had little if any observational experience of or objective data relating to crowd actions (Reicher, 1987; Turner, Hogg, Oakes, Reicher, & Wetherell, 1987). In effect, the theorisation was without empirical foundation. It was also largely politically motivated (McClelland, 1970), as well as being informed through distorted historical representations of crowd actions. As a consequence, across the latter half of the twentieth century, historians (e.g., Reddy, 1977; Rude,

1964; Thompson, 1971; Tilly, Tilly, & Tilly, 1975) and sociologists (e.g., McPhail, 1991; Turner & Killian, 1957) began to reject these classical models and the search began for a psychological explanation of the normative dimensions of crowd action. Toward the end of the twentieth century, Reicher (1982, 1984, 1987) developed his highly influential Social Identity Model of crowd behaviour (SIM). Through a rich and powerful qualitative study, Reicher detailed the patterned nature of collective action witnessed during the St Paul's riot in Bristol, UK – the first of a series of so called 'race riots' that would spread across England in the summers of 1980 and 1981. His study accounted for the normative patterns within a crowd in terms of participants acting on the basis of a shared and socially determined identity.

The SIM drew heavily upon Self-Categorisation Theory (Turner et al., 1987), adapting and developing it to explain the social psychology and thus the normative patterning of the riot. Accordingly, collective action in the riot was made possible through participants defining themselves in terms of a St Paul's identity. This identity was made possible through a social and historically determined social context defining what it meant to be British, Bristolian and Black at that time. Through a series of precipitating incidents, such as a police raid on a local community café, a confrontation developed that rapidly escalated. Within that confrontation collective action was normative in that there was a clear pattern of target selectivity that related meaningfully to participants' sense of themselves as a community suffering from racist practices by agencies of the state. For example, in the first stages of the riot, it was the police that bore the brunt of collective attacks as they were understood to be the agent through which these forms of racism were most regularly exercised.

At the time it was written, Reicher's focus was primarily on the rejection of classical theory. As such, the SIM was primarily a theoretical explanation of rioting after it had developed, at the expense of a detailed consideration of how that riot came about in the first place or of how the norms within the riot changed over time. Thus, the next phase of theoretical and empirical development was around the question of how identities within crowds changed and how it was that peaceful crowds develop into riots (Reicher, 1996a, b). Accordingly, if collective action in crowds is driven by shared and salient identities, one can study the dynamics of change by directly observing transitions in normative behaviour during crowd events. Put slightly differently, our research questions called for an observational methodology, the difficulty being that riots are very challenging to predict and even harder to study. This led to two routes of research, both fundamentally qualitative and ethnographic in their orientation. The first was a programme of observations of the shifting patterns of crowd action in and among football crowds. Luckily, in the first year of this research England qualified for Italia '90, the football World Cup finals in Italy, enabling a programme of fieldwork at the tournament. The second was a series of observations at demonstrations in the UK, of which there were several at the time, given the impending implementation of a highly controversial new form of local taxation referred to by many as the 'Poll Tax'. Several of these protests had already developed from peaceful demonstrations into violence (Drury & Reicher, 1999).

A demonstration in London on 31 March 1990 provided an opportunity for me, both as a protestor and a researcher, to undertake an ethnographic observation, by participating in a national demonstration involving upwards of 200,000 people protesting against the tax. The event began peacefully, with participants united by a shared identity defined in terms of a common peaceful opposition to the tax and the Conservative government that was about to introduce it. Across the first phase of the demonstration there were no incidents of collective conflict but, following a peaceful sit-down protest in the roadway opposite Downing Street, the police decided to initiate a forceful dispersal of the crowd. It was following this initial intervention that the first collective conflict against the police emerged and then developed into one of the most serious riots witnessed in London since the 1980s.

This riot marked the shift in norms within the crowd that was of central theoretical interest. What became clear from our research on this riot (Stott & Drury, 2000) was that it was impossible to understand its emergence without reference to the impact of the actions of the police upon the social identity of protestors within the crowd. The majority in the vicinity of police interventions saw themselves and others around them as acting entirely legitimately, and as such they saw police actions as unwarranted. In addition, protestors could see no justification for the indiscriminate use of force by the police, crushing people as they drove the crowd away and apparently arresting protestors and striking out at them at random. This created a social context where large numbers of protestors came to see conflict with the police as a legitimate form of collective self-defence and to feel empowered through the psychological unity that police action created. Our research also suggested that the emerging conflict confirmed police perceptions of the crowd as a threat, which led to further deployments, pulling more protestors into the cycle of escalation. Put more theoretically, the development of the riot highlighted the centrality of intergroup interactions as one of the key factors driving the dynamics of identity change.

Around two months later the fieldwork took me to Caligari, the capital of the Italian island of Sardinia, conducting further ethnographic observations. England had been dispatched to the island for the first round of Italia '90 along with upwards of 7,000 Italian police to keep the notorious English 'hooligans' in check. With English club sides still banned from European competition, as a result of the Heysel stadium disaster, expectations of collective violence from England fans among the authorities were extremely high. However, while serious rioting did develop during the two weeks of England's residency on the island, it was evident its dynamics and form could not be understood merely in terms of the acting out of pre-existing dispositions on the part of English hooligans. For example, the UK Government specifically attributed the cause of the rioting to a conspiracy between English and Dutch hooligans. Instead, the observational and interview data spoke clearly of underlying group-level processes very similar to those observed during the poll tax riot. England fans understanding themselves as behaving legitimately – for example by gathering together, drinking and celebrating their identity – were systematically confronted by other groups, locals and police, in ways that England fans saw as illegitimate and indiscriminate attacks on the category as a whole. This pattern of intergroup interaction then, over time, fed an identity change among England fans such that large numbers came to see conflict, particularly against the police, as a legitimate form of collective self-defence. When these processes culminated in a baton charge by police against a large crowd of England fans the dynamics of power shifted, if only momentarily, and several England fans took the opportunity to participate in an anti-police riot (Stott & Reicher, 1998a).

This early ethnographic research therefore began to make clear that the dynamics of intergroup interaction were key factors underpinning both social identity change and thus the emergence of rioting. It was this realisation that formed the core development of the *Elaborated* Social Identity Model of crowd behaviour (ESIM) (Drury & Reicher, 2000; Reicher, 1996a; Stott & Drury, 2000). By way of confirmation, in 1998 England once again qualified for the World Cup finals, providing an opportunity to conduct further ethnographic fieldwork, this time in France. England were drawn to play their opening match of France '98 against Tunisia in the southern city of Marseilles. Hundreds of England fans arriving into the city on the days before the fixture found themselves confronted by unprovoked violent attacks from several large groups of local youths. In this context, England fans either found themselves, or others like them, facing a lack of protection from the police or otherwise attacked by them. Once again, our research identified a pattern where crowd participants became united psychologically through a social identity defined in terms of opposition to what were seen as illegitimate outgroup actions. It was evident that in this context of 'common fate' those prepared to confront those hostile outgroups, in other words 'hooligans', were empowered and rendered as prototypical ingroup members. Moreover, it was apparent that these dynamics were historical and ongoing and fostering a form of identity and agency among England fans that was feeding the potential for collective violence from one situation to another. Given that the authorities and local populations hosting England fans expected 'hooliganism', they were acting in ways that created a social context which further promoted the production of collective conflict as a kind of self-fulfilling prophecy (Stott, Hutchison, & Drury, 2001).

It was apparent from this body of work that if the authorities wanted to address the levels of crowd conflict evident among England supporters, they needed to change the way the fans were being policed. Further evidence of this contention came from our exploration of the collective behaviour of Scottish fans at the same tournament, who had by then become well known for their boisterous but non-violent 'carnivalesque' behaviour, despite a notorious history of 'hooliganism' within Scotland itself. What our research identified (Stott, Hutchison, & Drury, 2001) was that this normative change, in contrast with England fans, was little to do with the absence of 'hooligans' so much as it was a product of similar social identity and intergroup processes. With little expectation of violence, it was apparent that police and locals were much more welcoming to the Scots. Indeed, it was evident that their boisterous drunken antics were much the same collective behaviours as those that were being interpreted as 'hooliganism' when exhibited by England fans. In effect, the social context was one whereby Scotland fans were able to collectively express their identity without provoking hostility from locals or coercion from police. In turn, Scotland fans' corresponding experiences of intergroup legitimacy paralleled with displays of a strong 'self-regulation' culture, whereby, as a form of 'norm enforcement', ingroup fans understood to be posing a threat of initiating intergroup hostility were actively rebuked, sometimes violently, by other Scotland fans. Additionally, where Scotland fans were confronted by contexts of intergroup illegitimacy they too showed evidence of similar shifts toward seeing conflict as both appropriate and normative for their category as a whole.

From research to application

The journey from research to application has been far from linear and straightforward. Rather it has been an iterative process where knowledge and practice have evolved in combination. It was evident from our work on the 'poll tax riot' that police actions were, at least in part, driven by their adoption of classical theory in order to understand the dynamics of crowds and rationalise and inform their strategic and tactical responses to them. Through further research we identified that this perspective led police to see crowds as volatile and open to 'hijacking' by violent groups. This was associated with prioritising the control of crowds through the use of relatively indiscriminate force and an ignorance of the impacts of their own coercive actions on the dynamics of identity change and collective violence (Hoggett & Stott, 2010a, 2010b; Drury, Stott, & Farsides, 2003; Stott & Reicher, 1998b). By implication, our research also exposed the limited capability of the UK Government and police approaches toward the prevention of football 'hooliganism' at international football tournaments; which relies heavily upon the surveillance, categorisation and coercive control of 'hooligans'. As such, we began communicating with the Football Association and the national police leadership within the UK, asking to talk with them about our research. They wrote back informing us that there was nothing to be learnt from research as they were fully cognisant of the underlying issues and happy with their existing approach. Nonetheless, during the next European Championships, Euro '2000, England were drawn to play Germany in the Belgium city of Lens and pictures of rioting fans being liberally sprayed by police water cannon adorned the front pages of the English newspapers. Once again research identified the central role played by heavy-handed policing in these disturbances (Adang & Cuvelier, 2000; Stott, 2003).

What changed officials' minds was the level of political embarrassment arising from the mass deportations of England fans from Euro '2000. The then Labour Government set up a Working Group chaired by policing Minister Steve Bassam. The Working Group was organised by David Bohannon, an influential civil servant who at the time led the Home

Office Public Order Unit. As a result of my participation on the Working Group (itself a result of working relationships with the Football Supporters Federation developed in Marseilles during France '98), Bohannon became aware of our then newly published paper on the dynamics of disorder in Marseilles. As a result of his awareness of our research and his own personal experiences of Euro 2000, he too recognised the importance of influencing the policing of English football fans when they travelled abroad in order to address the underlying problems. As a result, we began a consultation that would see the Home Office fund a programme of ethnographic work to develop a research-based model of good practice for policing fans and to use this to try to influence policing at the forthcoming European Championships in Portugal, Euro 2004.

There were several ways in which this Home Office funding assisted in creating a relationship between research and impact. Perhaps most importantly, the funding came with no direct criteria for its use other than a general remit to foster research collaborations with international networks of police officers and academics. Given the flexibility of this funding, it was possible to be dynamic and proactive in the approach to data gathering and dissemination. When teams qualified through the competition and subsequent draws were made it was possible to rapidly book flights and accommodation, travel to host cities and observe the policing approach firsthand. As a result, we conducted 35 observations at fixtures across 9 different European nation states in the space of roughly 2 years. When these fixtures took place in Portugal, as several did, it was possible to build relationships with police in the host cities and feedback findings in a manner that engaged directly and immediately with their preparations for the forthcoming European Championships. During this time, the research inevitably became far less focused on academic publication than on conducting and producing work that would be of practical value to police practitioners. Nonetheless, from these observations it was possible to theorise principles (Reicher, Stott, Cronin, & Adang, 2004) and build a model of good policing practice (Stott & Pearson, 2007) that went on the underpin the policing of Euro 2004.

The research-based model revolved around two key concepts: 'dynamic risk assessment' and 'balanced tactical profile' (Stott & Pearson, 2007). These concepts called for a policing approach based on understanding the identities at work in a crowd and being oriented toward the importance of the legitimacy of intergroup relations. This required the police to focus on the facilitation of positive, rather than merely the control of negative, behaviours. At the same time the policing style should be 'low profile', not reliant on large displays of police capability to exercise force as a deterrence but, on friendly communication-based engagement with crowd participants by officers in standard uniform from the outset. The observations had noted that where this style of policing was in place it had the effect of helping to build perceptions of police legitimacy among fans and was associated with the maintenance of non-violent crowd norms. Given it was achievable to access several of the policing operations being observed we also determined that such engagement assisted with police assessments of the levels and source of any emergent threats and problems. In other words, the 'graded' or dialogue-led tactical approach meant that the police were better positioned to conduct ongoing dynamic risk assessment that meant they were able to respond more proportionally, or in a balanced manner, to the actual risk (i.e., shared situational understanding between police and fans as opposed to risk perceived by police alone) and solve minor difficulties before they escalated. This assisted in avoiding the disproportionate and undifferentiated police coercion that research had identified as being another key dynamic of riots.

Through the substantive and varied consultations with the Public Security Police (PSP) in Portugal, across the two years leading up to Euro 2004, the model we provided was seen as valuable because it helped the PSP develop and validate a use of force policy for the tournament. It is worth noting that all of this was achieved without a single associated academic publication, primarily because we simply didn't have the time or the need during this intensive period of impact-focused fieldwork to write up the research in academic form (see Stott & Pearson, 2007). It was far more important to disseminate this data and analysis directly to the police at suitable moments, openings that arose sporadically and opportunistically often during the fieldwork itself.

Given the impact of the research on policy for the tournament, I then applied for and was fortunate to be awarded ESRC funding[1] to undertake an empirical evaluation of the policing of Euro 2004. This large-scale mixed methods study produced further evidence to confirm the effectiveness of a social-identity–based approach to policing crowds in this context. In summary, the PSP successfully implemented the theory-led model in all areas under their jurisdiction, which included all of Portugal's major cities and seven of the tournament stadiums. Speaking to the success of the policing approach, in these areas there were no major incidents of collective conflict. This was associated with widely shared perceptions of police legitimacy and high levels of self-regulation among fans. Where collective conflict did emerge, it did so in areas controlled by Portugal's' second police force, the Guarda Nacional Republicana (GNR), who as a gendarmerie adopted a policing approach far more reliant on indiscriminate coercion and one not informed by or adopting our theory and evidence-based model (Stott et al., 2007, 2008).

Shortly after the tournament, the international networks of policing practitioners we had developed through our pre-tournament work were well positioned to feed the model of good practice into guidance of the European Union (EU Council, 2006, 2010). These EU structures of international police cooperation, established in the wake of the Heysel stadium disaster, play important roles in shaping policing approaches toward football fixtures with an international dimension in Europe. As a consequence, the ESIM-led, facilitation-oriented, graded policing similar to that adopted at Euro 2004 has been a feature of international guidance ever since. As such, at the subsequent European Championships held in 2008 and 2012, similar models were developed and implemented and very few incidents of collective disorder have taken place (Adang & Brown, 2008). In fact, the only major incident of collective disorder at this particular European tournament since 2004 took place in Marseilles during France 2016 involving England fans where there was very strong evidence that, contrary to guidance, the policing model was identical to that our research implicated as a causal dynamic during France '98.[2]

As a result of the ethnographic work, during and in the lead up to Euro 2004, we came into regular contact with the UK's national police portfolio holder for football, then Chief Constable of Staffordshire David Swift. As a consequence, he invited a presentation of what had been achieved in Portugal to be delivered at the 2004 annual conference for police football commanders in the UK, from which further research opportunities, funding and collaborations emerged, this time regarding the policing of football crowds in the English domestic leagues. A key objective for this next stage of the research and impact development was to understand the extent to which an ESIM-based analysis could help ascertain ways of reducing the levels of conflict in that domain. Through this collaboration we were able to undertake a series of observations and secure an ESRC CASE studentship that enhanced capacity to further develop theoretical understanding of the issues and dynamics involved (Hoggett & Stott, 2010a, b; Stott, Hoggett, & Pearson, 2012; Stott, Livingstone, & Hoggett, 2008).

The changes supported by research in this context were relatively small-scale and piecemeal and as such we began to understand some of the problems of and barriers to impact in this context, whereby there was an apparent reluctance to undertake reforms despite a clear evidence case that reform would be valuable (Hoggett & Stott, 2012). Then, in April 2009, a newspaper seller called Ian Tomlinson was making his way home as he was struck with a baton and pushed over by a police officer involved in the dispersal of a protest. As a result, Mr Tomlinson died shortly afterwards. Following a national newspaper campaign to expose the role of police use of force in the death, the Metropolitan Police Service (MPS) invited an inquiry by Her Majesty's Inspectorate of the Constabulary (HMIC) that itself grew into a full and comprehensive review of public-order policing in the UK. During this period, colleagues and I wrote an article for a leading police magazine discussing our research and the implications it had for policing. In particular, the article was critical of the fact that, despite the major progress that had been made in the science of crowd psychology, training for public order commanders in the UK was still teaching classical crowd theory as its underlying rationale. We argued that this conceptual framework had contributed to the situation surrounding the death of Mr Tomlinson because such knowledge was undermining police decision-making.

The article's publication in a police magazine was important because it demonstrates at least three things about the journey from research to impact in this domain. The first is that the connection between research and policy is sometimes driven by political crisis, not some neutral processes of curious enlightenment. Change is not always invited but often has to be driven. Here the door to police reform only opened because somebody died and, as a result, political pressure emerged. Second, researchers have to be ready to step through the doors if and when they open. The impact that subsequently emerged here was the result of an existing array of knowledge-based partnerships between academics, police and government that had been in place for some years and which had already produced peer-reviewed output and impact in the domain of football. Third, it was an article in a professional periodical and an unpublished report, not merely academic publication, that turned out to be pivotal in terms of generating research impact. Shortly afterwards, the HMIC subsequently commissioned me to write a report on the relationships between crowd psychology and policing. That report, never published in an academic journal,[3] contributed to the HMIC's report calling for substantial police reforms, published as *Adapting to Protest* (ATP). ATP devoted an entire chapter to crowd psychology, within which it accepted the core recommendations arising from our work on crowd policing and recommended that the ESIM should replace classical theory as the conceptual basis of public order policing in the UK. Moreover, it adopted most of the core recommendations that I made in the report regarding the need for reform to police training and increased capability for dialogue and communication (HMIC, 2009).

The impact and legacy of the research

ATP was a formal acknowledgement of the impact of our research on policy toward the policing of protest in the UK. However, there was still some considerable distance to travel in terms of translating this policy into policing practice. The first step on that journey was the translation of the recommendations made within ATP into statutory guidance for police. This required the rewriting of the Association of Chief Police Officers manual of Statutory Guidance for public order policing, then called *Keeping the Peace* (ACPO, 2010). At this time the UK's national policing Public Order Portfolio was held by the then Chief Constable of South Yorkshire Police who appointed a particularly progressive Temporary Chief Superintendent under his command to lead on the day-to-day delivery of the project. By coincidence that Temporary Chief Superintendent, Martin Scothern, had worked closely with me on the earlier project on the policing of football and was an advocate of our research and theory. This proved to be pivotal because it meant he was able to navigate the competing objectives of those involved in these committees and processes to steer key aspects of our, and ATP's, recommendations into the revised manual. Once that had been achieved, and the manual published, it gave licence to him to innovate. Moreover, he had also been appointed as the tactical Commander for a major policing operation surrounding the Liberal Democrats' Spring Conference, to be held in Sheffield City Hall in April 2011. Through our long-standing collaboration and in the wake of the new guidance we were now in a position to collaborate to design, develop and train the first unit of public order Police Liaison Officers (PLTs), create a strategic plan around their use and conduct research on their highly successful implementation (Gorringe, Stott, & Rosie, 2012; see also Waddington, 2012).

The second step on the journey toward extending the reach and scope of the impact occurred in the wake of the 2011 English riots, when in

September of that year Martin Scothern and I were invited to give a presentation on our innovations and research on PLTs to the Annual Conference of the Police Superintendents Association. We happened to be on the platform with the then Assistant Commissioner of the Metropolitan Police Service (MPS) responsible for public order policing in London, Lynne Owens. As a result, AC Owens invited a follow-up meeting to explore extending the approach to the MPS. At that meeting I made clear that given the resistance we were likely to encounter there was a need for her to appoint an organisational *champion* to drive the project forward. In handing over to her replacement as she moved on to become a Chief Constable of Sussex Police, the new Assistant Commissioner Mark Rowley was luckily also very supportive, and appointed Superintendent Colin Morgan from their Public Order Unit to lead the project within the MPS.

As a result, by 2012 new Police Liaison Teams had been developed in both MPS and Sussex force areas and we had been able to conduct further research around their implementation (Stott, Scothern, & Gorringe, 2013). The lead taken by these forces fed into a growing national approach via the College of Policing and by 2014 I was a Co-Investigator on an ESRC-funded Knowledge Exchange project led by Professor Adam Crawford in the School of Law at the University of Leeds. This interdisciplinary leap into Criminology was immensely rewarding in several ways, not least that I was able to assist in developing a research-based approach to policing through this ESRC project called the N8 Policing Research Partnership. With four strands to the project, I co-led the one on public order along with Dr Geoff Pearson from the University of Manchester. As a key part of this we held a national PLT conference where we hosted representatives from 27 UK police forces and estimated that, by that time, around 75% of UK forces had implemented PLTs and, at time of writing, they now form the default primary tactic for every major demonstration across the UK. Moreover, our more recent work on the spread of the 2011 riots has impacted further on a new version of the courses delivered by the College of Policing to all public order commanders in the UK.

Lessons learnt

What I hope this makes clear is that the route from research to application, what we now refer to as 'impact', in this field at least, is not straightforward. It is simply not a case that we as academics merely developed research and abstract knowledge that was then subsequently applied. While theory development was undoubtedly part of the process, it was also increasingly co-produced in partnership with the very practitioners we were seeking to influence. In other words, the practitioners were often themselves active participants within the ongoing knowledge production process, not just passive recipients of it. It was also the case that 'impact', in the highly politicised domain of public order policing, required navigating complex political processes that were often a consequence of circumstances well beyond our control. Indeed, such is the cruel nature of our work that others' misfortunes were ultimately our opportunities to drive a reform agenda over its next hurdle in the hope that we could make future adversity less likely.

Thus, one of the lessons learnt from our impact is to rethink what it was that we had been doing methodologically. It is apparent that the empirical approach that was emerging was akin to what is commonly referred to as Participant Action Research or PAR. PAR has a long-standing tradition, based on the seminal 'Action Research' of Kurt Lewin (1946) where the primary purpose of research is less about theory development than it is about driving progressive social change. The central aim throughout has essentially been to provide a platform seeking to assess and enhance operational police practice through engaging police officers and other stakeholders directly within the research process (Crawford, 2017; Meyer, 2000), with the primary goal influencing their operational practice (Elliot, 1991; McNiff & Whitehead, 2005; Winter & Munn-Giddings, 2001). This approach has never been politically neutral but designed deliberatively to enhance and empower democratic and human rights-based forms of policing. Thus, the methodology now adopts Koshy et al.'s (2010) definition of PAR as an approach for improving practice as part of the process of change. The primary method employed to gather data to inform this co-production has always been qualitative and ethnographic, combining observation and interview techniques with other forms of data where it has been possible to do so. These methods are now well-tested in the context of both football crowd behaviour (for an overview see Pearson, 2012; Stott & Pearson, 2007) and policing (Rowe, Turner, & Pearson, 2016).

From an impact perspective, PAR is a very useful vehicle for gathering data and simultaneously using that evidence to drive police reform. On the one hand it ensures that our data is much more fully informed because it enjoys the expertise of operational practitioners and has access to information that would otherwise be unavailable. On the other, given the police are involved in its production they are far more inclined toward seeing that knowledge as legitimate and better positioned to apply it more rapidly into their own practices. However, the epistemological approach does not sit comfortably within Psychology (indeed within academic life more generally), which tends to be dominated by positivists using quantification and experimental paradigms. Therefore, it has been very difficult – if not sometimes impossible – to publish in mainstream journals, whose editors would often judge such work as tangential to 'core' issues within the field. The specialist nature of the audience we seek to engage also means that it is important to publish in specialist policing journals, which by their very nature have relatively low academic impact metrics.[4] Indeed, as I have tried to make clear, the most influential articles and reports in terms of this story of impact have not been published in academic journals at all. Moreover, at a personal and professional level, it was never easy to travel to a football fixture in continental Europe, be required to embed oneself within the normative context of those events, which were sometimes quite conflictual, dangerous and often involved being in close proximity to criminal behaviour, then find yourself back in a university later that week (re)adjusting to the norms and sensitivities of the academic environment (Pearson, 2009).

The future of impact in this domain

The autobiographical narrative of this impact journey on the policing of crowds is self-evidently a historical one that has been taking place over several decades. Indeed, when it began, the concept of 'impact' did not really exist and only emerged in the academic lexicon as a result of formal research evaluation processes in the UK in 2014. Prior to that, academic performance was measured almost exclusively against academic publications and there was scant regard given to working in applied contexts. Yet, there can be no doubt that the impact agenda is now firmly embedded into the UK research landscape and that as such it is much easier for academics to legitimise a more 'applied' agenda. However, in the increasingly neoliberal world of academia academics are, in the UK at least, often left with the sense that 'impact' is only as good as the next REF impact case study, as your latest ebbs into insignificance. The question very quickly arose, where next?

Despite very high levels of resource invested in the policing of football events, incidents of disorder or violence continue to occur sporadically at all levels of the game and there are over 2,000 individuals arrested each year. Further, the police are also under pressure from the UK's largest fan organisation, the Football Supporters' Association, which has an ongoing campaign called 'Watching Football is Not a Crime', designed to 'monitor the police in their dealings with football fans and work with them to ensure that all fans are treated fairly and within the law.' In such a context it becomes increasingly important to look systematically at the nature of football policing to understand what could be done to improve effectiveness and efficacy. Yet at the same time, despite the fact that across the last ten years the policing of demonstrations in the UK has witnessed substantive change, the policing of football crowds in the UK has, to date, yet to undergo similar reform, despite being covered by the same statutory guidance (Stott, Pearson, & West, 2019). This is somewhat ironic given that, as we have shown here, much of the research used to underpin that guidance was developed in the context of policing football crowd events. Thus, the next step in the journey of 'additionality' in impact has been to refocus on the policing of football 'hooliganism'.

Our research work in this area has already been far reaching. Through long-standing collaborations, we had already been able to leverage our ideas into policing outside the UK. For example, there is now a nationally coordinated 'dialogue'-based policing approach to domestic football leagues in Denmark (Havelund et al., 2011) as well as on the railway network (Friis & Havelund, 2012) that are linked directly to our research. Correspondingly, since the approach in Denmark was implemented, the levels of confrontation, associated arrests and criminal damage on the railway network surrounding football fixtures in Denmark have been falling exponentially year on year. Moreover, in Sweden our social-identity–based crowd theory has also been used to underpin human-rights–based reforms to public-order policing since 2005 (Adang, 2012). Then, in April 2014, a fan of Djurgårdens IF, one of Stockholm's major football clubs, was killed as a result of violence surrounding their season's opening fixture in Helsingborg. This led to an opening to develop a new project called 'Enabling an Evidence Based Approach to the Policing of Football' or ENABLE. Funding from a charitable foundation in Stockholm called 'Gålöstiftelsen' allowed for a series of fieldwork observations of the safety and security operations surrounding 13 high-profile topflight football fixtures. These observations involved multiple stakeholders – including police, club safety and supporter liaison officers from the UK, Denmark and Sweden. The programme of work culminated in a report, a series of dissemination conferences in Stockholm and Gothenburg as well as two related academic publications that in turn have gradually impacted upon policing practices (Stott, Havelund, & Williams, 2019; Stott, Khan, Madsen, & Havelund, 2020). As this project has developed, in partnership with others, we have managed to attract funding, from the N8 Policing Research Partnership and the English Football League, to develop similar projects in the UK and in Switzerland. As a result, we are currently working with police and football authorities across England to implement reforms based on our research and will then undertake a programme of research to evaluate the impacts of these changes (Stott et al., 2019).

Conclusions

Both in the UK and in Sweden the ENABLE framework has allowed us to develop a programme of Participant Action Research that has facilitated opportunities for relatively rapid reform in police policy and practice. But it is clear that substantial organisational barriers often stand in the way of 'uptake'. It is also the case that there can be considerable scepticism, lack of understanding and sometimes even active resistance to 'knowledge-led' approaches within police organisations. Therefore, achieving impact in this domain requires an acute sensitivity to the political dynamics of the organisations that one is seeking to influence and to develop skills in working within these to drive reform. But one thing is clear, in developing a roadmap to impact we must remember that the success of the social-identity approach in helping to understand and then meaningfully address forms of crowd violence has come about through partnership. Throughout its development and application researchers, police officers and indeed fans and protestors have worked together to foster the co-production of knowledge – that at first helped them understand the contemporary policing challenges but then to also meaningfully and powerfully address them. To that end, we are now working on further theoretical development based upon an analysis of the spread of the 2011 English riots. This work is helping us to address the social-psychological dynamics of identity and empowerment through which the riots originated and then began to spread (Ball et al., 2019; Stott, Drury, & Reicher, 2017; Stott et al., 2018). What will flow from this work in terms of impact is unclear at this stage but hopefully through the lessons learnt and pathways to impact we have secured so far, we will be able to utilise this knowledge in ways that bring about beneficial change.

Notes

1 RES-000-23-617
2 https://thepsychologist.bps.org.uk/hooliganism-euro-2016-social-psychology-english-disease
3 www.scribd.com/doc/62156760/Crowd-Psychology-Public-Order-Policing-An-Overview-of-Scientific-Theory-and-Evidence
4 Despite claims otherwise, it is clear that journal impact metrics are still used as a core ‘measurement’ of the academic quality – and hence value – of the papers published therein.

References

Adang, O. (2012). Reforming the policing of public order in Sweden: Combining research and practice. *Policing and Society*, 7(3), 326–335.

Adang, O., & Brown, E. (2008). *Policing football in Europe: Experiences from peer review evaluations*. Apeldoorn, Netherlands: Police Academy of the Netherlands.

Adang, O., & Cuvelier, C. (2000). *Policing Euro 2000: International Police co-operation, information management and police deployment*. Apeldoorn, Netherlands: Police Academy of the Netherlands.

Association of Chief Police Officers. (2010). *Manual of guidance on keeping the peace*. Bramshill, UK: National Police Training.

Ball, R., Stott, C., Drury, J., Neville, F., Reicher, S., & Choudhury, S. (2019). Who controls the city?: A micro-historical case study of the spread of rioting across North London in August 2011. *City*, *23*(4–5), 483–504.

Barrows, S. (1981). *Visions of the crowd in late nineteenth century France*. London: Yale University Press.

Brown, R., & Pehrson, S. (2019). *Group processes: Dynamics within and between groups*. Hoboken, NJ: Wiley & Sons.

Carey, J. (1992). *The intellectuals and the masses: Pride and prejudice among the literary intelligentsia 1880–1939*. London: Faber and Faber.

Crawford, A. (2017). Research co-production and knowledge mobilisation in policing. In J. Knutsson & L. Thompson (Eds.), *Advances in evidence-based policing* (pp. 195–213). Abingdon, UK: Routledge.

Drury, J., & Reicher, S. (1999). The intergroup dynamics of collective empowerment: Substantiating the social identity model of crowd behavior. *Group Processes and Intergroup Relations*, *2*(4), 381–402.

Drury, J., & Reicher, S. D. (2000). Collective action and psychological change: The emergence of new social identities. *British Journal of Social Psychology*, *39*(4), 579–604.

Drury, J., Stott, C., Ball, R., Reicher, S., Neville, F., Bell, L., … Ryan, C. (2020). A social identity model of riot diffusion: From injustice to empowerment in the 2011 London riots. *European Journal of Social Psychology*. doi:10.1002/ejsp.2650.

Drury, J., Stott, C., & Farsides, T. (2003). The role of police perceptions and practices in the development of 'public disorder'. *Journal of Applied Social Psychology, 33*(7), 1480–1500.

Elliot, J. (1991). *Action research for educational change*. Buckingham, UK: Open University Press.

EU Council. (2006). Council Resolution of 4 December 2006 concerning an updated handbook with recommendations for international police cooperation and measures to prevent and control violence and disturbances in connection with football matches with an international dimension, in which at least one Member State is involved. *Official Journal of the European Union* C 322/1.

EU Council. (2010). Council Resolution of 3 June 2010 concerning an updated handbook with recommendation for international police cooperation and measures to prevent and control violence and disturbances in connection with football matches with an international dimension, in which at least one member state is involved. *Official Journal of the European Union*. C165/1.

Festinger, L., Pepitone, A., & Newcomb, T. (1952). Some consequences of de-individuation in a group. *Journal of Social Psychology, 47*(2), 382–389.

Friis, M., & Havelund, J. (2012). *DSB football guides – A Danish solution to an international problem?* Norderstedt, Germany: Good Hosting, Vol. 1.

Gorringe, H., Stott, C., & Rosie, M. (2012). Dialogue police, decision making, and the management of public order during protest crowd events: Dialogue policing, crowds, public order. *Journal of Investigative Psychology and Offender Profiling, 9*(2), 111–125.

Havelund, J., Ilum, J., Jensen, M. A., Nielsen, B. P., Rasmussen, K., & Stott, C. (2011). Event policing - Dialogue in the policing of mass events in Denmark. *CEPOL European Police Science and Research Bulletin, 3*(4), 3–7.

HMIC. (2009). *Adapting to protest*. London: Her Majesty's Chief Inspector of Constabulary.

Hoggett, J., & Stott, C. (2010a). Crowd psychology, public order police training and the policing of football crowds. *Policing: An International Journal of Police Strategies and Management, 33*(2), 218–235.

Hoggett, J., & Stott, C. (2010b). The role of crowd theory in determining the use of force in public order policing. *Policing and Society, 20*(2), 223–236.

Hoggett, J., & Stott, C. (2012). Post G20: The challenge of change, implementing evidence-based public order policing. *Journal of Investigative Psychology and Offender Profiling, 9*(2), 174–183.

Koshy, E., Koshy, V., & Waterman, H. (2010). *Action research in healthcare*. London: Sage.

Le Bon, G. (1895). *The crowd: A study of the popular mind*. London: Allen & Unwin.

Lewin, K. (1946). Action research and minority problems. *Journal of Social Issues, 2*(4), 34–46.

McClelland, J. S. (1970). *The French right: From De Maistre to Maurras*. London: Jonathan Cape.

McClelland, J. S. (1989). *The crowd and the mob: From Plato to Canetti*. London: Unwin Hyman.
McNiff, J., & Whitehead, J. (2005). *All you need to know about action research*. London: SAGE.
McPhail, C. (1991). *The myth of the madding crowd*. New York, NY: Aldine de Gruyter.
Meyer, J. (2000). Using qualitative methods in health related action research. *British Medical Journal, 320*(7228), 178–181.
Neville, F. G., & Reicher, S. D. (2018). Crowds, social identities, and the shaping of everyday social relations. In C. J. Hewer & E. Lyons (Eds.), *Political psychology: A social psychological approach* (pp. 231–252). Chichester, UK: Wiley-Blackwell.
Nye, R. (1975). *The origins of crowd psychology*. Beverly Hills, CA: SAGE.
Pearson, G. (2009). The researcher as hooligan: Where 'participant' observation means breaking the law. *International Journal of Social Research Methodology, 12*(3), 243–255.
Pearson, G. (2012). *An ethnography of football fans: Can, cops and carnivals*. Manchester, UK: Manchester University Press.
Postmes, T., & Spears, R. (1998). Deindividuation and anti-normative behavior: A meta-analysis. *Psychological Bulletin, 123*(3), 238–259.
Reddy, W. M. (1977). The textile trade and the language of the crowd at Rouen, 1752–1871. *Past and Present, 74*, 62–89.
Reicher, S. D. (1982). The determination of collective behaviour. In H. Tajfel (Ed.), *Social identity and intergroup relations* (pp. 41–84). Cambridge, UK: Cambridge University Press.
Reicher, S. D. (1984). The St Pauls riot: An explanation of the limits of crowd action in terms of a social identity model. *European Journal of Social Psychology, 14*(1), 1–21.
Reicher, S. D. (1987). Crowd behaviour as social action. In J. C. Turner, M. A. Hogg, P. J. Oakes, S. D. Reicher & M. S. Wetherell (Eds.), *Rediscovering the social group: A self-categorization theory* (pp. 171–202). Cambridge, MA: Basil Blackwell.
Reicher, S. D. (1996a). Social identity and social change: Rethinking the contexts of social psychology. In P. W. Robinson (Ed.), *Social groups and identities: Developing the legacy of Henri Tajfel* (pp. 317–336). Oxford, UK: Butterworth-Heinemann.
Reicher, S. D. (1996b). 'The Battle of Westminster': Developing the social identity model of crowd behavior in order to explain the initiation and development of collective conflict. *European Journal of Social Psychology, 26*(1), 115–134.
Reicher, S., Stott, C., Cronin, P., & Adang, O. (2004). An integrated approach to crowd psychology and public order policing. *Policing: An International Journal of Police Strategies and Management, 27*(4), 558–572.
Rowe, M., Turner, E., & Pearson, G. (2016). Learning and practicing police craft. *Journal of Organizational Ethnography, 5*(3), 276–286.
Rudé, G. (1964). *The crowd in history*. New York, NY: Wiley.

Sighele, S. (2018). *The criminal crowd and other writings on mass society* (N. Pireddu & A. Robbins, Trans.). Toronto, Canada: Toronto University Press.

Stott, C. (2003). Police expectations and the control of English soccer fans at 'Euro2000'. *Policing: An International Journal of Police Strategies and Management, 26*(4), 640–655.

Stott, C., Adang, O. M., Livingstone, A., & Schreiber, M. (2007). Variability in the collective behaviour of England fans at Euro2004: Public order policing, social identity, intergroup dynamics and social change. *European Journal of Social Psychology, 37*(1), 75–100.

Stott, C., Adang, O. M., Livingstone, A., & Schreiber, M. (2008). Tackling football hooliganism: A quantitative study of public order, policing and crowd psychology. *Psychology, Public Policy and Law, 14*(2), 115–141.

Stott, C., Ball, R., Drury, J., Neville, F., Reicher, S., Boardman, A., & Choudhury, S. (2018). The evolving normative dimensions of "riot": Toward an elaborated social identity explanation. *European Journal of Social Psychology*. doi:10.1002/ejsp.2376.

Stott, C., & Drury, J. (2000). Crowds, context and identity: Dynamic categorization processes in the "poll tax riot". *Human Relations, 53*(2), 247–273.

Stott, C., & Drury, J. (2017). Contemporary understanding of riots: Classical crowd psychology, ideology and the social identity approach. *Public Understanding of Science, 26*(1), 2–14.

Stott, C., Drury, J., & Reicher, S. D. (2017). On the role of a social identity analysis in articulating structure and collective action: The 2011 riots in Tottenham and Hackney. *British Journal of Criminology, 57*(4), 964–981.

Stott, C., Havelund, J., & Williams, N. (2019). Policing football crowds in Sweden. *Nordic Journal of Criminology, 20*(1), 35–53.

Stott, C., Hoggett, J., & Pearson, G. (2012). 'Keeping the peace': Social identity, procedural justice and the policing of football crowds. *British Journal of Criminology, 52*(2), 381–399.

Stott, C., Hutchison, P., & Drury, J. (2001). 'Hooligans' abroad? Inter-group dynamics, social identity and participation in collective 'disorder' at the 1998 World Cup Finals. *British Journal of Social Psychology, 40*(3), 359–384.

Stott, C., Khan, S., Madsen, E., & Havelund, J. (2020). The value of Supporter Liaison Officers (SLOs) in fan dialogue, conflict, governance and football crowd management in Sweden. *Soccer and Society, 21*(2), 196–208.

Stott, C., Livingstone, A., & Hoggett, J. (2008). Policing football crowds in England and Wales: A model of 'good practice'? *Policing and Society, 18*(3), 258–281.

Stott, C., & Pearson, G. (2007). *Football hooliganism, policing and the war on the English Disease*. London: Pennant Books.

Stott, C., Pearson, G., & West, O. (2019). Enabling an evidence-based approach to policing football in the UK. *Policing: A Journal of Policy and Practice*. doi:10.1093/police/pay102.

Stott, C., Radburn, M., & Savigar-Shaw, L. (2020). Crowd theory, communication and policing. Book chapter submitted for publication.

Stott, C., & Reicher, S. D. (1998a). How conflict escalates: The inter-group dynamics of collective football crowd 'violence'. *Sociology, 32*(2), 353–377.

Stott, C., & Reicher, S. D. (1998b). Crowd action as inter-group process: Introducing the police perspective. *European Journal of Social Psychology, 28*(4), 509–529.

Stott, C., Scothern, M., & Gorringe, H. (2013). Advances in liaison based public order policing in England: Human Rights and negotiating the management of protest? *Policing,* 7(2), 212–226.

Taine, H. (1876). *The origins of contemporary France: The Ancien Regime* (J. Durand, Trans.). New York, NY: John F. Trow & Son.

The Guardian. (2016, August 8). £1.3bn troubled families scheme has had 'no discernible impact'. *The Guardian.* Retrieved from https://www.theguardian.com/society/2016/aug/08/13bn-troubled-families-scheme-has-had-no-discernible-impact.

Thompson, E. P. (1971). The moral economy of the English crowd in the eighteenth century. *Past and Present, 50*(1), 76–136.

Tilly, C., Tilly, L., & Tilly, R. (1975). *The rebellious century 1830–1930.* London: J.M. Dent & Sons Ltd.

Turner, J. C., Hogg, M., Oakes, P., Reicher, S. D., & Wetherall, M. (1987). *Rediscovering the social group: A self-categorization theory.* Cambridge, MA: Basil Blackwell.

Turner, R. H., & Killian, L. M. (1957). *Collective behavior.* Englewood Cliffs. NJ: Prentice-Hall.

Waddington, D. (2012). A "kinder blue": Analysing the police management of the Sheffield anti-'Lib Dem' protest of March 2011. *Policing and Society: An International Journal of Research and Policy, 23*(1), 1–19.

Winter, R., & Munn-Giddings, C. (2001). *A handbook for action research in health and social care.* London: Routledge.

Zimbardo, P. G. (1970). The human choice: Individuation, reason and order versus de-individuation, impulse and chaos. In W. J. Arnold & D. Levine (Eds.), *Nebraska symposium on motivation 1969* (pp. 237–307). Lincoln, NE: University of Nebraska.

INDEX